DOING RESEARCH

IN

ORGANIZATIONS

LCU / SJC

DOING RESEARCH
IN
ORGANIZATIONS

Edited by
ALAN BRYMAN
Senior Lecturer Department of Social Sciences
Loughborough University of Technology

ROUTLEDGE
London and New York

First published in 1988 by
Routledge
11 New Fetter Lane, London EC4P 4EE

Published in the USA by
Routledge Inc.
in association with Methuen Inc.
29 West 35th Street, New York, NY 10001

Set in Sabon Roman
by Hope Services, Abingdon, Oxon
and printed in Great Britain
by Biddles Ltd
Guildford & Kings Lynn

Library of Congress Cataloging in Publication Data

British Library CIP Data also available
ISBN 0–415–00257–5 (c)
0–415–00258–3 (p)

CONTENTS

ACKNOWLEDGMENTS

All editors owe a debt to their contributors and I am no exception. I should like to thank all of them for their cooperation and preparedness to respond to points and queries I have raised. I also wish to thank: David Stonestreet (of Routledge) and Peter Lawrence for helping to get this project underway and for their continual encouragement; Mike Bresnen and Martin Bulmer for their comments on my Introduction; and Gwen Moon for her help with typing some portions of this book. Finally, I wish to thank my wife, Sue, for her help with preparing the book for publication, and both Sue and Sarah for putting up with a nervous editor in the household.

NOTES ON CONTRIBUTORS

Huw Beynon has been involved in writing and research on issues relating to work and industrial organization for the past twenty years. He is author or co-author of *Perceptions of Work, Working for Ford, Living with Capitalism, The Workers' Report on Vickers*, and *What Happened at Speke?* His two-volume history of the Durham coalfield (with Terry Austrin) will be published in 1988. In 1986 his edited collection *Digging Deeper: Issues in the Miners' Strike* won the publishing for people prize at the Socialist Book Fair in London. Huw Beynon has taught at the Universities of Bristol, Southern Illinois and Durham, and is currently Professor of Sociology at the University of Manchester.

David Boddy is a Senior Lecturer in Management Studies, Centre for Technical and Organizational Change, University of Glasgow. He worked for Hawker Siddeley Industries before joining Glasgow University. He works as an Associate Consultant of the Coverdale Organization. His publications include, as co-author, *Organizations in the Computer Age* (1983), *Managing New Technology* (1986), and *The Technical Change Audit: Action for Results* (1987). He has written numerous book chapters and articles on various aspects of management development and the introduction of new technology. His current research interests concern 'converging' technologies and implications for organization design and management.

Mike Bresnen graduated from the University of Nottingham with a degree in Industrial Economics in 1978, and from 1978 to 1981 was registered as a postgraduate in the same department. Since 1982 he has been a Research Officer in the Department of Social Sciences at Loughborough University and, since 1984, a Research Fellow. He was awarded his PhD in 1986. His research interests have centred upon various aspects of the organization and management of construction work, including matrix management, inter-organizational relations, labour recruitment, and leadership. He is co-author of a number of articles on recruitment, leadership and temporary organizations in construction.

Alan Bryman is a Senior Lecturer in the Department of Social Sciences at Loughborough University. He has previously held research posts in the Industrial Administration Research Unit at Aston University and in the Department of Theology at Birmingham University. His main research interests lie in the fields of organization studies, research methodology, the knowledge acquisition phase in the development of expert systems, and labour market studies. He is co-author of *Clergy, Ministers and Priests* (1977) and author of *Leadership and Organizations* (1986). He is a co-editor of *Rethinking the Life Cycle* and *Women and the Life Cycle* (both 1987), both of which derive from being a joint organizer of the 1986 British Sociological Association conference.

David A. Buchanan is a Senior Lecturer in Organizational Behaviour, Centre for Technical and Organizational Change, University of Glasgow. He worked in personnel management in local government, and lectured in personnel management at Napier College in Edinburgh before joining Glasgow University. He is author of *The Development of Job Design Theories and Techniques* (1979), and co-author of *Organizations in the Computer Age* (1983), *Organizational Behaviour* (1985), *Managing New Technology* (1986), and *The Technical Change Audit: Action for Results* (1987). He has also written several book chapters and articles on work design and the management of technical change. His current research interests concern 'converging' information and computing technologies and their implications for management, organizational design, and performance.

Martin Bulmer is a Senior Lecturer in Social Administration at the London School of Economics and Political Science. His main teaching and research interests are in the methodology of social research, the utilization of social science in public policy making, the sociology of informal social care, and the history of the social sciences. He has authored or edited fifteen books, most recently *The Social Basis of Community Care* (1987), *Neighbours: The Work of Philip Abrams* (1986), *Social Science and Social Policy* (1986), *Essays on the History of British Sociological Research* (ed.) (1985) and *Social Science Research and Government: Comparative Essays on Britain and the United States* (ed.) (1987).

Rosemary Crompton is a Senior Lecturer in the Department of Economic and Social Studies, University of East Anglia. She has researched and published in industrial sociology (*Workers' Attitudes and Technology* 1972; co-author), and class theory (*Economy and Class Structure*, 1978; co-author). Her research with Gareth Jones (*White Collar Proletariat*, 1984) provided the empirical basis for her contribution to this collection. She is currently researching in the area of women and the professions, and her most recent book, as co-editor, is *Gender and Stratification* (1986).

David Dunkerley is Professor of Organizational Sociology at Plymouth Polytechnic. He has previously taught and researched at the Universities of Cardiff, Leeds, Iowa, Warsaw and Griffith. In addition to having written numerous articles on industrial and occupational sociology, he has also published *The Study of Organizations* (1972), *The Foreman* (1975), *Occupations and Society* (1975), *Critical Issues in Organizations* (1977; co-editor), *Organization, Class and Control* (1980; co-author), and *The International Yearbook of Organization Studies* (1980 onwards; co-editor).

David Hickson holds a Research Chair in International Management and Organization at the University of Bradford Management Centre, England. He worked in administration before moving into research at UMIST. His principal research has been: at the University of Aston on organization structures; at the University of Alberta, Canada, on intra-organizational power; and at Bradford Management Centre on processes of strategic decision making. He has been extensively concerned with cross-national comparisons. He has published in numerous research journals and is joint author or editor of five books, most recently *Top Decisions* (1986). He is Editor-in-Chief of the journal *Organization Studies* and was a founder of EGOS (European Group for Organizational Studies). He holds an honorary doctorate from the University of Umea in Sweden, and was a Fellow of the Netherlands Institute for Advanced Study for the year 1982/83.

Gareth L. Jones is a Lecturer in Sociology at the University of East Anglia, and is currently seconded to the Department of Organizational Behaviour, London Business School. He is joint author of *White Collar Proletariat: Gender and Deskilling in Clerical Work* (1984). He is author of articles on managerial ideologies and careers. His current research is on the change and continuities in managerial work.

Peter Lawrence is a Senior Lecturer in the Department of Management Studies at Loughborough University. He was formerly a Senior Research Fellow at the University of Southampton and a Lecturer at the University of Strathclyde. He has held visiting posts at Constance, Berlin, Stockholm and Twente. He has written numerous books and most recently is author of *Management in Action* (1984) and *Invitation to Management* (1986), co-author of *Organizational Behaviour: Politics at Work* (1985) and *Management and Society in Sweden* (1986) and co-editor of *Introducing Management* (1985). His main research interests lie in comparative management and the nature of managerial work.

James McCalman is a Researcher, Centre for Technical and Organizational Change, University of Glasgow. He is currently completing a doctorate on the linkages between foreign-owned and Scottish electronics companies (Paisley College of Technology). He is editor of the Glasgow Business School Working Paper Series. His current research interests involve in-depth case studies and a senior management survey studying management objectives in the use of information technologies. He has published case study findings in the *Journal of the Law Society of Scotland*, as well as several working and conference papers.

Derek Pugh is Professor of Systems and Head of the Systems Discipline at the Open University, having previously been at the Universities of Edinburgh and Aston and at the London Graduate School of Business Studies. At Aston and London he led research groups involved with organizational behaviour studies in a range of organizations such as business, industry, commerce, local government and trade unions. His current research interests are in the comparative study of top management decision making in a cross-cultural context. In addition to the Aston books given in the references to his chapter, Professor Pugh has been the joint author of *Writers on Organisations* (third edition, 1983) and editor of *Organisation Theory: Selected Readings* (second edition, 1984). Professor Pugh has recently been elected a Fellow of the International Academy of Management.

Barry A. Turner is a Reader in the Sociology of Organizations at the University of Exeter. After training in engineering and in sociology, he pursued research into industrial organizations at Imperial College and at Loughborough University, before moving to Exeter. For the past decade he has been studying decision-making processes associated with large-scale accidents and disasters, including, most recently, structural collapses of buildings. He also specializes in the use of qualitative methods to study organizational culture, and he has written a number of articles on this topic. He is the author of *Exploring the Industrial Subculture* (1971), *Industrialism* (1975) and *Man-made Disasters* (1978).

INTRODUCTION:
'inside' accounts and social research in organizations

Alan Bryman

Background

There is a strong tradition of collections of 'inside' views of the process of social research which has grown from a trickle in the 1960s (e.g. Adams and Preiss, 1960; Hammond, 1964; Vidich *et al.*, 1964); Jongmans and Gutkind, 1967, through a gathering of momentum in the early 1970s (e.g. Freilich, 1970; Golde, 1970; Habenstein, 1970; Spindler, 1970; Douglas, 1972), to a veritable torrent by the late 1970s and thereafter (e.g. Shipman, 1976; Bell and Newby, 1977; Bell and Encel, 1978; Shaffir *et al.*, 1980; Messerschmidt, 1981; Roberts, 1981; Ruby, 1982; Bell and Roberts, 1984; Burgess, 1984b). In addition there has been a growth in other sources of first-person accounts. A number of collections of papers have contained inside accounts (e.g. Spindler, 1982; Bulmer, 1982a; Burgess, 1985); there have been a number of books, predominantly by social anthropologists, which focus on the fieldwork experience (e.g. Bowen, 1954; Powdermaker, 1966; Wax, 1971; Johnson, 1975); detailed appendices to books based on the fieldwork experience in the manner popularized by Whyte (1955) and later Gans (1962); and a number of journals like *Human Organization* and *Urban Life* have carried inside reports of the research process.

These 'inside' or 'first-person' accounts are deemed to be important because of their provision of a picture of the social research enterprise which reveals the quirkiness and messiness that social researchers experience. They permit insights into problems faced and solutions achieved, thereby offering tips to others. For teachers of Research Methods courses, like the present writer, these accounts are a veritable boon, because anyone who has ever conducted social research knows that the content of the textbooks on Methods bears only a partial relationship with research itself. The problem for the teacher of Methods is that of conveying to students the ways in which research involves much more than, and is very often different in texture from, that which is implied by the textbooks. According to some commentators, the Methods text is essentially a prescriptive cook-book (e.g. Bell and Encel, 1978; Burgess and Bulmer, 1981), but it is also the case that it is descriptive too in the sense that the overall tenor of the research process that it puts across bears a striking resemblance to the reconstructed logic which forms the backbone to the journal research article. The inside view of research activity allows the student and the intending researcher to see that it does not necessarily conform to the dictates and procedures associated with the textbook and the research paper.

Quite why there should have been such a growth in interest in inside accounts, especially since 1970, is difficult to explain. There is little doubt that Hammond's (1964) *Sociologists at Work* was regarded as a great success, which almost certainly prompted others to bring such collections together. Whyte's (1955) appendix to the second edition of *Street Corner Society* also did much to raise interest. The growing critique of positivism and the quest for alternative epistemological and methodological foundations for the social sciences were instrumental in raising the researcher's consciousness of his or her assumptions and the structure of research. This period coincided with Gouldner's (1971) call for a more 'reflexive' approach to sociology, which implied a self-questioning approach to beliefs, assumptions, and practices. None of these factors can be held responsible for the burgeoning of first-person accounts, but together they have had a part to play.

However, the inside account has not been without its critics. They are, as Dingwall (1980) has suggested, highly anecdotal, so that it is not easy to build up a general picture of what they show. It is for this reason that the insights about actual research practice have not been as fully integrated into Methods textbooks as they might be. Further, we do not know how far the accounts involve a reconstruction and rationalization, viz. they may not be quite the 'warts and all' portrayals that they appear to be. On the other hand, as has been argued above, they do provide an alternative and arguably more realistic account of research, and it is surely this which helps to explain their popularity in many quarters.

But why another collection of inside accounts? It occurred to me that in spite of a growing interest in broader methodological issues in organization studies, there had been few inside accounts for researchers in this field. Some of the contributors to Adams and Preiss (1960) and two of the best known chapters in the Hammond collection – Blau (1964) and Dalton (1964) – were written in relation to organization studies. Habenstein's (1970) book contains some examples of research relevant to students of organizations, as does the Shaffir *et al.* (1980) collection. By contrast, the British collections (e.g. Bell and Newby, 1977; Roberts, 1981; and Bell and Roberts, 1984) did not emphasize research into large formal organizations. Thus, while there are some first-person accounts in American collections, they are fairly thin on the ground in the British works. It occurred to me that British writers whose research was conducted in formal organizations might have interesting stories to tell which might throw up points of difference and similarity in relation to other research contexts. However, I also decided that a small innovation in the overall format of these collections was called for since the volumes I have referred to have come to reflect a fairly standard format. I decided to include a discussion of the other chapters in the book written by a methodologist relatively unconnected with the research domain that provides the book's focus. Although I am fairly conversant with methodological issues, virtually all of my research has been rooted in precisely the context that my contributors are writing about – the large formal organization. A contribution written by, so to speak, an outside methodologist might produce an interesting slant on the other chapters and would simultaneously allow a small departure from the by now standard pattern of such collections.

With these aims in mind, I wrote to a number of people, both known and unknown to me, to solicit their possible interest in writing a chapter for me. Only two refused, each due to their existing commitments. There is always a problem of knowing how far to specify the sorts of issues you want your contributors to cover. Habenstein's (1970) volume contains chapters which were written to a very precise set of specifications. Burgess (1984b) provided a very comprehensive list of topics which might be covered. Bell and Newby (1977) provided a shorter and less detailed list. Like Platt, who in an appendix to *The Realities of Social Research* (1976) reports her feelings about imposing precise templates on contributors to a British version of Hammond's (1964) volume which she had been asked to organize, I experienced a sensation of great trepidation about compiling such a framework and constraining my contributors by it. Consequently, I opted for a fairly loose specification along the lines of the Bell and Newby and the Burgess volumes, albeit with a bit less detail than the latter's lengthy inventory of possible topics. The following is the main text of my guidance to contributors.

The overall orientation of the book will be to provide 'inside' views of the research process. I am disinclined to specify precisely what I would like the contributions to cover. The following list of topics may provide some ideas about the sorts of issues that might be appropriate:

- background to choice of research topic
- nature of data collection techniques used
- philosophical and practical issues underlying the choice of research design and techniques – the role of theoretical considerations in the approach to the research
- the negotiation of access to organizations and to respondents/ informants
- fieldwork successes and problems
- role of values and ethical issues in the research
- the coordination of the research team
- the relationship between initial project objectives and the outcome
- 'tips' for other researchers
- reflections on the response to your work
- reflections on the differences (if any) between research on organizations and social scientific research in other areas

This list is merely presented in order to give contributors an idea of the sorts of issues and topics I am getting at when talking about an 'inside view'. I have a feeling that many contributors will want to refer to some of these issues in any case.

In the event, some contributors have covered most of these topics, others a sample of them, and still others have focused on just one or two of my suggested topics.

Outline of the chapters

Huw Beynon is well known for his detailed, highly readable accounts of the experience of work in industrial enterprises (e.g. Beynon, 1973; Nichols and Beynon, 1977), but as his contribution makes clear, such research can be highly fraught because of the political sensitivities involved. He documents the resistance by large industrial corporations and trade unions to social science research and also the adverse response to reports of such investigations when they are undertaken. Beynon is also concerned with the interpersonal difficulties involved in research in industrial enterprises, particularly when the researcher is asked about the information gleaned from a different 'side' in the organization. Resorting to the commitment to confidentiality as an explanation for non-disclosure may be misinterpreted and so jeopardize future relationships with the 'side' seeking information; to give in may provoke a loss of trust among those who see their confidences as having been broken. In addition to his focus on the politically charged context of research in industrial organizations, Beynon puts forward some interesting observations about the interconnections between factories and the wider communities in which they are located.

Michael Bresnen's chapter differs from the others in this volume in at least two significant respects. First, the organizational context in which he carried out his research is a temporary system (Miles, 1964; Bryman *et al.*, 1987), namely the construction project, in contrast to the more permanent milieux in which the other contributors have worked. Of course, 'permanent' organizations go into liquidation, are taken over, and so on, but the construction project is a temporary phenomenon at the outset. Second, his is the only research project discussed in this volume which derives from investigations conducted for a PhD thesis. Since postgraduate research has been and is an important source of our understanding of organizations, it seemed appropriate to have an instance of work deriving from this context in the present volume. In his research, Bresnen selected five case studies in order to explore the management of construction projects. He describes very frankly the various shifts that his research strategy underwent, as well as a detailed account of the research process in relation to one of his case studies. One of the main themes to come out of his contribution is the significance of change in the context of the life cycle of projects; how, for example, a longitudinal element in the research design is especially necessary in a context where change is compressed into a relatively short time span.

David Buchanan, David Boddy and James McCalman base their chapter on their experiences of conducting research into the effects of the introduction of new technology on work experiences and work organization. Their strategy was to carry out case studies in each of the firms they investigated. They focus in their chapter chiefly on the negotiation of access, the maintenance of good relationships, and effecting an exit. They have much to say about the problems of conducting fieldwork in commercial firms and seek to offer advice to anyone intending to conduct similar research. Their main theme is to adopt a flexible and opportunistic approach to the handling of access and subsequent relationships.

The prime focus of the chapter by Rosemary Crompton and Gareth Jones is the negotiation of access and the maintenance of relationships after entry. They offer advice in connection with these issues drawing on their case study research on white collar workers in three contexts – a clearing bank, a local authority and an insurance company. Their account of hostility and suspicion to such research is potentially daunting, especially since they were unable to secure access to a manufacturing firm because of such impediments. The authors also provide details of their fieldwork procedures, especially in connection with their attempts to address two theoretical areas – Braverman's (1974) 'deskilling' thesis and the operation of internal labour markets – both of which have attracted a great deal of empirical interest in recent years.

While historical methods have been used to good effect within organizational analysis (e.g. Chandler, 1962) and industrial sociology (e.g. Friedman, 1977), they have tended to be underemployed by investigators conducting research in organizations. David Dunkerley argues for a greater concern with the historical dimension among researchers of different hues, for example, irrespective of whether they conceive of organization studies as primarily concerned with the enhancement of organizational efficiency. He notes how the 'critical' approach to the study of organizations which took root in the 1970s and in which he was an active participant (e.g. Clegg and Dunkerley, 1980), did much to inject a greater recognition of historical processes. His chapter provides details of his research on the Royal Navy dockyard in Plymouth in which historical methods predominated, and also some of the problems he encountered with the use of historical documents are detailed. He recounts the transition of his research from the study of an occupational community to an organizational analysis. In addition, the role of oral history as one of the main aspects of the battery of techniques used in this investigation is described.

For many years, Peter Lawrence has conducted research on managers and their activities in different countries, including Britain, Germany, Sweden and the Netherlands. His chapter reflects on his immense experience of carrying out studies in this comparative context. He notes how there has been a shift from a tendency to think of management practices in fairly general, universalistic ways to a more particularistic approach in which there is a much fuller appreciation of cultural differences. Lawrence is primarily concerned in his contribution with the manner in which he seeks to characterize the management styles and practices of a particular country. He points to many pitfalls which await the unwary comparative researcher. He enthuses about the advantages of direct observation of managers, while recognizing the need to enjoin this method with interviews and background information. He argues that the enterprise of comparative management research should be conceived of as an open-ended strategy, a view which stands in stark contrast to the hypothesis-led account of the research process that pervades much thinking in the social sciences.

Barry Turner's chapter is not about a specific piece of research as such, but is concerned with the nature of research in organizations. His main focus is on the study of organizational culture (an area which at the time of writing is very much in vogue) and the relevance of qualitative methods to its elucidation. The account he offers of doing such research entails an attention to the minutiae of organizational life. Turner links this orientation to a discussion of grounded theory, a set of procedures developed by Glaser and Strauss (1967) for the dovetailing of theory and data in qualitative research. His approach is one which recognizes and extols the subjectivity of such research in contrast to the predominant quantitative research approach within organization studies. Turner also acknowledges the anxieties that qualitative research may generate, such as the sensation of being over-whelmed by 'data'. He offers some solutions which reduce such risks or facilitate their management.

The Aston Studies are one of the best-known research programmes in organization analysis and have been one of Britain's most (many would argue the most) significant contributions to the field. Indeed, in his interesting essay on assuming the editorship of the *Administrative Science Quarterly*, John Freeman (1986, p. 298) has referred to the Aston research as one of the three major mileposts in the field of organization studies (the others being the Hawthorne and the American Soldier studies). In his chapter, Derek Pugh outlines the background and institutional context of the research. His account of a research group with roughly a year at its disposal to decide and argue about what to study will have the appearance of science fiction in the context of the abstemious funding of social science research in the 1980s. Nonetheless this lavish situation was available to the initial members of the research team at the University of Aston in the early 1960s. Pugh details the aims of the research group, its approach to doing research in organizations, its research instruments, and also some of the chief findings. He speculates at some length about the reasons for the very considerable impact of the Aston Studies which in large part he attributes to the explicitness and precision of their approach to conceptualization and measurement. In addition, Pugh has some interesting observations about the research team process and what factors make for a successful team.

In chapter 9, David Hickson presents a tale of two research projects, both concerned with the examination of power in organizations. His chief focus is the way in which the level of resources available to a team of researchers conditions the climate in which the research takes place as well as its efficiency. As Hickson makes clear, this is not to say that research is necessarily better when resources are in greater abundance, but that the nature of the research process will be affected. His contrast is between the teams which he assembled at the University of Alberta and later at the University of Bradford, the former in a climate of munificence, the latter in an environment of accelerating attrition. Of course, students of organizations should not be surprised that resource constraints have a pronounced impact on organizational processes. The development of open systems notions since the 1960s has etched an awareness of such issues on the minds of researchers in this domain. But we are often poor at applying concepts to ourselves and our own experiences, and in this respect Hickson's chapter is a jolt to any inattention to the role of resources in the research process. David Hickson was also a member of the Aston Group (covered by Derek Pugh) so his experience of research teams in the field of organization studies is considerable.

As stated earlier in this introduction, Martin Bulmer has a quite different role from the other authors in that he is largely unconnected with the field of organization studies but is well versed in a whole range of methodological issues pertaining to the social sciences and has written widely on such themes. He was asked to consider some of the methodological points raised by the contributors to this book. His conclusion is that organizational research does not throw up a cluster of methodological issues which are unique to the field, but that it does sharply highlight points which are relevant to the social sciences as a whole.

We have, then, a wide variety of chapters in at least two senses. First, there is considerable variety in the kinds of topics upon which the contributors have focused. While some contributors range fairly widely on the research with which they have concerned themselves (e.g. Pugh, Buchanan *et al.*, Crompton and Jones), others have emphasized particular topics (e.g. Beynon, Hickson, Turner). Second, considerable variety in the kinds of research being discussed is in evidence, from an accent on large-scale quantitative research (Pugh, Hickson) to ethnographic field research (e.g. Turner, Bresnen, Buchanan *et al.*), as well as research that fuses quantitative and qualitative methods (Crompton and Jones). There is also a discussion of the use of historical materials (Dunkerley).

In the remainder of this chapter, I shall focus on two areas: some of the ways in which the chapters reveal a departure from the textbook account of the research process, and some of the preoccupations that the contributors display. These two themes are not mutually exclusive, as will become apparent from the discussions, but the distinction is useful as an organizing principle. In addressing these themes, personal accounts of the research process other than those contained within these covers will be drawn into the discussion, as well as a number of other sources.

'Inside' and textbook accounts of the research process

The Research Methods textbook has been the staple diet for generations of undergraduates and postgraduates in the social sciences as a result of their teachers' need to provide them with a systematic representation of the research process. However, there is considerable disillusionment with the account offered by such texts, even though the image of the research process which is typically offered resembles the implicit view which underpins research articles and monographs. An idealized, linear, goal-directed model tends to be provided which seems in the eyes of many practising researchers to capture the essential characteristics of the research process very poorly. A number of writers of inside accounts of research in the social sciences have drawn attention to the tendency for textbooks to provide a weak portrayal of the nature and complexity of the research process, both in this book (Bresnen, Buchanan *et al.*) and in other collections (e.g. Moore, 1977; Newby, 1977; Ball, 1984). Such a contrast is implicit in Kaplan's (1964) acute distinction between the 'reconstructed logic' of the research process and researchers' 'logics-in-use'. When this distinction is recognized, the study of methodology aims to 'help us to *understand*, in the broadest possible terms, not the products of scientific enquiry but the process itself' (Kaplan, 1964, p. 23, emphasis in original). Clearly, inside accounts, whatever their defects, have an important role to play within such a broader understanding of methodology.

Interestingly, when a contrast is drawn between textbook and inside accounts, it is instructive to deploy some of the notions which have considerable currency in organization studies. For example, Pettigrew (1985) has pointed to the research process as more easily fitting models which emphasize incrementalism and political processes, rather than as a logical, rational, goal-directed sequence of steps. Both Pettigrew and Martin (1981) have pointed to the possible relevance of the 'garbage can' model of organizations to the practice of research in social research (though Martin's chief focus is on psychological research). According to this model,

> an organization is a collection of choices looking for problems, issues and feelings looking for decision situations in which they might be aired, solutions looking for issues to which they might be the answer, and decision-makers looking for work. (Cohen *et al.*, 1972, p. 2)

The very fact that the application of such a model to research in the social sciences can be countenanced may be treated as evidence of the disillusionment with an explication of the research process in terms of a rational, goal-directed, linear activity.

In spite of the very considerable role that inside accounts have played in generating an awareness of the partial (some would say inaccurate) version of the nature of research produced by textbook writers, the insights of the former have not been systematically integrated into the latter to any marked degree. It might have been anticipated that more recent textbooks would have absorbed some of the insights which can be extracted from inside accounts. There is some evidence of their assimilation into some recent texts concerned with ethnographic field research (e.g. Hammersley and Atkinson, 1983; Burgess, 1984a) but this development does not seem to have occurred to the same degree in relation to more general texts or to those concerned largely with quantitative methods. There are some barriers to dovetailing these two contrasting styles of explicating the research process. Probably the main obstacle is the difficulty of cutting a path through the idiosyncrasies of the growing number of inside accounts so that general lessons and features might be gleaned. In fact, this difficulty is ostensibly no different from the problem of case study generalization (a focus of some of the discussion below). The solution to this problem is often deemed to be eased by the accumulation of case studies, as Bulmer suggests, and the same principle ought logically to pertain to inside accounts. It ought to be possible to extract some generalities from the plethora of inside accounts that already exist. This section seeks to draw attention to a small number of such general points.

1 Researchers make mistakes In the introduction to his collection of inside accounts of research in educational settings, Burgess (1984c, p. 1) has drawn attention to 'a wealth of academic gossip about the false starts and *faux pas* that are part of the everyday world of the social researcher'. The possibility of such disruptions to the idealized account of research practice is strikingly depicted in Watson's (1970) description of the discovery of the structure of DNA. Researchers make mistakes and change their minds. In fact, the lack of guidance to some of the realities of social research that the textbooks offer can be held partially responsible for these tendencies. However, the tidy delineations of the research process in reports of research findings heavily contribute to the relative absence of a general awareness of 'false starts and *faux pas*', since they provide a linear view of how the results were arrived at. Consequently, writers of inside accounts who had been brought up on a diet of textbooks and sanitized research reports sometimes report their feelings of something being wrong with *themselves* when things do not go according to plan (Newby, 1977; Bottomley, 1978). Such a view is most likely to assail the relative novice; at a later stage, researchers know they will make mistakes and that they will get little guidance from textbooks. It may be far more responsible to make prospective researchers aware of such facts in advance than to imbue them with self-doubt as their plans go awry. The 'false starts' theme is somewhat less in evidence in this collection than in Bell and Newby (1977), for example. Bresnen, however, refers to his bewilderment during his initial stages of fieldwork on a construction site and the growing recognition of the fragility of his questionnaire when confronted with the realities of his milieu. Also, Dunkerley writes very frankly about the growing recognition of the over-ambitiousness of the research programme to which he had committed himself and the consequent need to re-focus both the problems to be investigated and the methods of enquiry.

2 The influence of funding bodies and gatekeepers There is a tendency in many textbooks to present an image of research as though its origin and course are largely uninfluenced by external institutions. But much research is funded or commissioned by external bodies and, where research is conducted within organizations, gatekeepers have to allow the researcher access. Those who fund and those who provide access may seek to influence research very directly. First, the research problem being investigated may itself be influenced by outside forces. Researchers may be invited to do research on specific topics, as were Davis (1964) with his *Great Books and Small Groups* research and Smith *et al.* (1960) who were invited to conduct research into a farm market-news system by the US Department of

Agriculture. Alternatively, researchers may become interested in conducting a particular investigation because there is available research funding for a particular field. The Economic and Social Research Council's current (at the time of writing) penchant for inviting applications for research in specified areas is just such a process. Of course, researchers may believe that they will be able to extract some relevant material for their own purposes or to tack on a slant more reflective of their academic interests. Thus Smith *et al.* (1960) believed that the Department of Agriculture's brief tied in well with their interests in mass communications, although their attempts to instil this element into their research plans were in the end largely curtailed by the Department. Nonetheless, the main thrust for much research may derive from the availability of funding or approaches by sponsors. Equally, research which requires funding but which is not considered worthy may never get done in spite of its theoretical relevance. The image of research problems as deriving from a deductive model of the formulation of research problems fails to take sufficient account of the importance of funding for the subject matter of the social sciences (and probably in other fields too).

Second, funding may alter the way in which research is done. Broadhead and Rist (1976), drawing on a number of personal experiences, have argued that sponsors often seek to propel research into a more natural scientific framework than researchers may wish, a point which receives some support from Platt's (1976) interviews with British social researchers (see especially p. 28). Further, Smith *et al.* (1960) show how their plans for conducting research into the farm market-news system (which would have entailed a community study coupled with sociometric analysis) had to be scrapped and a social survey be conducted instead. Even then, these investigators faced considerable interference over the conduct of the survey itself.

Organizational gatekeepers are likely to influence the research process too. This can occur as a consequence of their insistence on researchers conducting studies from which the organization will benefit and because of restrictions they place on the activities of researchers. However, this topic is essentially concerned with the problem of access to organizations which is dealt with in greater detail below when addressing some of the preoccupations of the contributors to this volume.

3 Luck and serendipity in research I am struck by the frequency with which authors of inside accounts refer to chance factors in research. Dunkerley writes about his good fortune in discovering largely unknown commissions on the dockyards after the re-orientation of his research; Buchanan *et al.* refer to a lucky encounter in a pub which allowed them to carry out one of their early studies of the effects of new technology; and Bresnen writes about a number of occasions during his research when he just happened to be in the right place at the right time for picking up a number of important leads. It may be that such unpredictable factors primarily rear their heads in the context of unstructured ethnographic research which is particularly capable of undergoing a change of direction and also permits a more opportunistic approach to making contacts and following up new leads. Nonetheless, the possible role of such 'untidy' episodes in research is yet another missing component in the portrayal offered by textbooks.

4 *The role of resources* Of all the contributions to this volume, Hickson's chapter on the contrasting resource situations of the Alberta and Bradford teams in which he was involved draws attention most explicitly to the role of money in the research process. His account of the different styles of research that were possible in these two milieux is very striking. Pugh's description of the lavish funding (especially by current standards) of the Aston research prompts one to wonder whether the immense success of this series of studies is at least partly influenced by such relative opulence. Freeman (1986), in his *Administrative Science Quarterly* editorial essay, has argued that the 'quality of data on which organizational knowledge is based' (p. 298) has not grown at anything like the same pace as the expansion of the field of organization studies itself. He continues, 'We do not have the resources to conduct . . . large-scale research, so we have avoided the many theoretical and technical problems such high-quality research generates' (Freeman, 1986, p. 298). The fact that he excludes the Aston research from this accusation is instructive in the light of its favourable resource position.

In the traditional textbook, the possible role of resources tends to surface in relation to very specific issues, such as their impact on sample size or the relative cheapness of postal questionnaires in comparison with interviews. However, their influence is much more pervasive. As Hickson's and Pugh's chapters make apparent, they can affect the climate in which research is done. Further, as Freeman's passage cited above suggests, the presence and absence of resources may constitute a key determinant of what is and is not studied, not to mention how research is done. Similarly, Martin (1981), arguing from the perspective of her 'garbage can' model of the research process, notes that resources are often powerful determinants of both the choice of a theoretical problem and also the methods used to study it. Platt (1976) found that some of the social researchers she interviewed used a social survey because it was the only feasible alternative in the light of the available time and resources. She also found that a number of her interviewees had collected qualitative data which they had to discard because of a lack of time to conduct the protracted analysis that such material requires. Dunkerley's discussion shows how his early research plans had to be abandoned because of the lack of adequate resources for his project; as a consequence, as noted above, the focus and methods shifted. His chapter raises a further interesting point in connection with the impact of resources, namely that when an investigation is to entail unconventional methods or approaches (as with the use of historical materials in his case), it is somewhat more likely that the required resource position will not be fully appreciated, so that a re-orientation will be required. It may well be that a concern about sailing into uncharted waters in this way deters researchers in the social sciences from experimenting with unfamiliar methods.

Clearly, the influence of resources on social research is pervasive yet tends to be accorded scant attention in textbooks. When it is taken as important the reconstructed logic of the deductive model of the theory → hypothesis → methods → analysis → results kind falters.

5 *The research team* One of the main lessons learned from Bell's discussion of the Banbury re-study in Bell and Newby's (1977) and Platt's (1976) investigations is the fragility of research teams. They can easily deteriorate into hotbeds of discontent over the distribution of work, the decision-making process, the authority structure, and the apportionment of credit. Hickson's example of the row within the Alberta team caused by the decision by himself and Bob Hinings, the other team leader, to produce a reader on power in organizations, from which the other researchers had been excluded, is indicative of the strife that can be incurred. Pugh has some interesting observations on the problems caused by the fission of the later stages of the Aston programme into a number of sub-groups and the differential perceptions of ownership of research and its fruits that ensued. He also argues for the involvement of as many members of the research team as possible in the formulation of research problems and strategies.

The relevance of resources recurs in this context, for as Platt (1976) and Hickson make clear, the fact that research staff are nearly always employed on short-term contracts is a source of immense insecurity for those so affected. It means that not too long after their initial appointments, research staff have to start thinking about putting in for a further grant or looking for employment elsewhere – hardly an ideal climate in which to carry out systematic research. Consequently, as Hickson notes in the context of his Bradford research, theoretical and methodological considerations tend to become increasingly cramped. In view of the pervasiveness of team research in the social sciences, particularly projects using social survey techniques, it is surprising that students of research methods are so rarely made aware of the organizational context of such research and its implications for the research process as such.

6 *The ethical and political context of research* Students of research methods are fairly well attuned to a number of ethical issues from textbooks in this field: questions of the ethics of covert observation and deception in experiments and the need for informed consent are examples of the sorts of issues which are addressed. However, ethical issues are often somewhat more extensive and ambiguous than such treatments of the topic imply. Bresnen expresses his unease about eavesdropping and deploying everyday situations to his own ends. He writes about the need to be cunning in order to achieve certain objectives. Similarly, observers are often aware that the overt/covert divide is not as clear-cut as is sometimes implied since they may be known and unknown to different people within a particular context (see e.g. Atkinson, 1981, appendix). Further, a number of first-person accounts of feminist research have drawn attention to the ethical problems of applying the prescriptions of research methods textbooks to women subjects (e.g. Oakley, 1981; Finch, 1984).

Research in organizations can be seen as something of a political minefield. This should hardly be surprising to anyone familiar with the literature on union-management relationships or the politically charged framework of organizational life (e.g. Hickson *et al.*, 1971; Pfeffer, 1981).

Beynon's contribution covers such issues in particular detail, noting for example the problem of being caught between company executives and trade union officials. His experiences echo those of Nicholson (1976) who encountered the problem of establishing a relationship with trade unions when access to a firm in order to study industrial relations was achieved through a management route, since considerable suspicion was engendered (see also Gullahorn and Strauss, 1960). However, the internal political factions within organizations affect the research process in still other ways. Both Bresnen and Buchanan *et al.* refer to the problem of the researcher ensuring that he or she is not used by different groups within organizations as a source of information or as a resource to be deployed against other groups. In particular, the possibility of the researcher becoming a source of information about adversaries is mentioned a number of times in such inside accounts; obviously, the researcher has to refuse such overtures, possibly hiding behind a plea of needing to be detached and a commitment to confidentiality, but such refusal may impose its own strains on all concerned. Again, the implications of the political nature of milieux such as organizations tends not to be a prominent focus of research methods training yet it may prove to be a more intractable problem in many instances than the development of the research strategy and instruments as such.

7 *The contexts of discovery and confirmation* There is a widespread tendency to view survey and experimental research (i.e. quantitative research) as suited to the confirmation and rejection of theoretical propositions and hypotheses; by contrast, qualitative research is depicted as placing an emphasis on the discovery of the novel and unfamiliar, which its more unstructured approach to data gathering is deemed to facilitate (see e.g. Bryman, 1984). This sort of position is expressed in different ways by Bresnen, Lawrence, and Turner. It is not that there is an absence of theoretical penetration or the testing of hypotheses in qualitative research, but that such phases of the research process emerge out of contact with one's data, as Turner's exposition reveals. I do not wish to take issue with this second point about the commitment of ethnographic and qualitative research to discovery. However, it does seem that inside accounts of quantitative research emphasize the element of surprise in such endeavour. Hammond's (1964) collection contains some rather neglected inside accounts which reflect this view. Blau (1964) expressed his distaste for a contrast between hypothesis-testing and insight-supplying research, arguing that his 'quantitative analysis of specific variables often produced unexpected findings' (p. 20). Lipset (1964), writing about his study of the International Typographical Union, which combined qualitative case study methods with a survey, maintains that some of his findings which derived from the latter technique were very surprising and that many new insights emerged during the analysis of these data. Davis (1964), drawing on his aforementioned Great Books study, argues that survey research comprises an artistic element in that the investigator has to *select* which variables are to be included in an analysis. In his view, two study directors with the same data set would differ substantially in the emphases which they would supply to its analysis. In the present volume, Pugh's remark that he is disappointed

that the effect of organizational size on structure was so all-embracing can be read in a similar vein to the contributors to the Hammond collection. My basic point is that while the connection of quantitative/qualitative with confirmation/discovery, on which many students are weaned, may be a useful general statement, it should not be read as a hard and fast principle.

8 The personal equation Two of the contributors – Buchanan *et al.* and Turner – draw attention to the possibility that there may be a tendency in discussions of social research methods to neglect the role of personal factors in the facility with which investigators are able to make particular techniques of investigation work for them. Buchanan *et al.* write about the personality of the interviewer as an important determinant of the extent to which interviewing in organizational contexts may be successful. They contrast their view with the purely technical account of interviewing to which we are normally exposed. Turner refers to 'skills of knowing' which he perceives to be differentially distributed and about the poor capacity many researchers possess for dealing with the ambiguity and lack of structure associated with much qualitative research. He also notes that some researchers are particularly astute observers. Such views are similar in tenor and implication to the remark that 'to a certain extent good participation observers . . . are born and not made' (Berk and Adams, 1970, p. 108). Quite apart from the very considerable implications of views such as these for the training of prospective researchers, they suggest that the textbook image of methods being selected to deal with particular research problems may not give a very complete picture.

Some recurring themes

In the preceding section, I emphasized a number of points raised by the chapters regarding the divergence between textbook and inside accounts of research. In this section, a number of themes and preoccupations which recur in the volume are delineated, whereas in the previous section my main concern was to make some tentative steps towards a general contrast between textbook and inside accounts.

1 The access problem The problem of gaining entry to organizations and then getting on with people who work in them is mentioned by nearly all of the contributors. Some of the issues regarding access have prefigured above, for example in addressing the role of luck in the research process, and Bulmer also focuses on the problem of entry in his chapter. The recognition of the difficulty of securing access for researchers in organizations led to the publication of *The Access Casebook* (Brown *et al.*, 1976) and can also be discerned in Habenstein (1970). Blau (1964) also experienced access difficulties in his attempt to study two bureaucracies, noting the possible problem of self-selection because the two organizations which accepted him were younger than those which had refused him.

Pugh reports that the original Aston study had few problems of access – only two of the 46 firms which made up the sample refused to cooperate. Other contributors who discuss access do not report anything like this level of cooperation. Crompton and Jones point to widespread suspicion and resistance to their research on white collar workers. In fact, they were unable to gain access to a manufacturing organization. Beynon also graphically reports considerable opposition to research from firms and unions alike. Buchanan *et al.* report that access to many firms is becoming more difficult, in part because firms are being deluged by requests for such research (see also Brown *et al.*, 1976, p. 14 and Platt, 1976, p. 44); by contrast, for the firms in the Aston sample in the early 1960s, the experience of being research subjects was novel. The growing resistance to organizational research parallels the decline in response to surveys of the general population in a number of countries since the late 1960s (Goyder and Leiper, 1985).

Inside reports of research provide a number of tactics which have been developed in order to overcome these barriers to entry. Bresnen, Buchanan *et al.* and Crompton and Jones recommend an opportunistic approach in which contacts, friends and relatives are used to the full. In this context, it is interesting to note Hoffman's (1980) view, based on his research into elite groups in the USA, that he extracted richer, less superficial data when he had established contact through such channels. The ability to engender interest in one's project in someone who is a member of the organization, and who can then act as a sponsor, is mentioned as a useful asset by a number of authors. Atkinson (1981) believes that had it not been for the support of the Executive Dean of the Edinburgh University Medical Faculty his study of the first clinical year of medical education would not have got underway. The value of such intermediaries is also mentioned by Van Maanen and Kolb (1985), drawing on their experiences in negotiating access for ethnographic research on the police and on mediation and conciliation agencies in the USA respectively.

Second, a number of contributors mention the advisability of offering a report of one's findings in order to secure access. Such a strategy is in conformity with Argyris's (1960) view that research must be 'need-fulfilling' in order to entice admission. In *The Access Casebook*, the desirability of promising feedback was mentioned by a number of the contributors, including Wright, Heller, Cherns, and Eilon. Further, as Beynon shows, managements and unions are increasingly taking the initiative in proposing feedback as a precondition for entry. Most of these examples relate to access to specific firms for case study research, but the same principle applies to larger-scale sample studies: for example, in a study of over forty construction projects (see e.g. Bresnen *et al.*, 1985; Bryman *et al.*, 1987a), my colleagues and I always promised a report to the various participants in our investigations. It may seem simpler to become a 'consultant-researcher' (especially since the provision of a report comes close to such a position), but such a role has some attendant problems too. In his research on urban food cooperatives in San Francisco, Zimmer (1981) found that there was a tendency for leaders to want to broaden the range of areas on which he offered them advice, and that it was difficult to establish independence from the leadership. Feedback is not always a prerequisite, of course. It does not seem to play a particularly prominent part in getting into schools, for example, where the access problem seems to be generally less fraught than was the case for many of the contributors to the present volume (see the discussions of access to schools in Burgess, 1984b). The fact that Fuller's (1984) inability to promise much benefit to the school whose pupils she wanted to study did not prove an obstacle is an interesting example of the general point being made here.

Third, the level within the organization at which access needs to be sought preoccupies a number of contributors. Like a number of contributors to the Habenstein (1970) collection – such as Lawton, Mauksch, and Beck – the desirability of starting negotiations at or near the top is recognized, although Buchanan *et al.* express some interesting reservations about such a strategy. As observed in the previous section, where trade unions are likely to be encapsulated in some way within the investigation, sole entry through top management is likely to be a source of difficulty, as Beynon's chapter makes clear. Kahn and Mann's (1952) advocacy of 'dual entry' is clearly relevant here. However, even this tactic may be fraught: Gullahorn and Strauss (1960) report an incident whereby a company objected to the former writer approaching the union for permission to study clerical workers because it felt that the granting of such permission was the management's prerogative.

Fourth, as all of the contributors to this volume whose research was of the ethnographic kind recognize, the problem of access does not cease when entry has been established. Bresnen, Beynon, Buchanan *et al.*, and Crompton and Jones all refer to the problems of getting on with people once access has been achieved. One of the chief difficulties seems to be that, in spite of researchers' protestations to the contrary, they are often seen as instruments of management who are there to evaluate or spy on their subjects and will report their findings back to senior officials. This seems to be a fairly common view of the researcher (see also Gullahorn and Strauss, 1960; Blau, 1964), which entry via senior management may merely reinforce. The researcher may also find his or her activities restricted once entry is achieved. Serber (1981), having successfully negotiated access to a Californian agency responsible for the state regulation of the insurance industry, found his research activities severely restricted after a while because of senior officials' growing concern that he would learn too much about the agency's failure to behave strictly in accordance with its public mandate. As a result, Serber's methods were determined by the amount of access within the agency that he was allowed (which points to another way in which an inside account clashes with a conventional textbook view of how methods of investigation are selected). Similarly, Strauss (Gullahorn and Strauss, 1960) recounts how he contacted a top union official of a US trade union he was proposing to study and successfully negotiated entry. He did not realize that this official was intensely disliked by local union officers and consequently encountered difficulties in dealing with them. Further, as Bresnen observes, researchers also need to cultivate the cooperation of the members of the organizations with whom they associate in order to tip them off about important situations, the observation of which would benefit the research (see also Gullahorn and Strauss, 1960; Serber, 1981).

Access to organizations is clearly very troublesome to researchers. The level of difficulty is well summarized thus: 'gaining access to most organizational settings is not a matter to be taken lightly but one that involves some combination of strategic planning, hard work, and dumb luck' (Van Maanen and Kolb, 1985, p. 11).

2 *The quantitative/qualitative research divide* As noted above, the contributors to this volume can be depicted in terms of their differential commitments to quantitative and qualitative research strategies. While the field of organization studies has been heavily influenced by quantitative research, there is a growing recognition of the role of qualitative methods. Crompton and Jones provide a very interesting account of the desirability of in-depth views of organizations in order to comprehend job titles; Bresnen argues that qualitative methods are very helpful in trying to come to terms with unfamiliar settings; both Lawrence and Turner emphasize the advantages associated with the flexibility and the directness of qualitative methods. In different ways, Bresnen, Bulmer, Crompton and Jones, Lawrence, and Turner draw attention to the often cited distinction between quantitative and qualitative research, with the first three of these five contributions arguing fairly explicitly for a *rapprochement* between these two research strategies. What is interesting about their discussion of these issues is that they all discuss quantitative and qualitative research (as well as the integration of these two styles of enquiry) in terms of 'technical' issues (Bryman, 1984). Quantitative and qualitative research are considered in the context of their respective strengths in relation to specific problems to be addressed, like the best ways of studying what managers in different countries do, or how the analysis of internal labour markets requires in-depth study of jobs and their titles. By and large, the broader epistemological issues of positivism versus phenomenology in the social sciences, which have underpinned many renditions of the debate about quantitative and qualitative research (Bryman, 1984), are absent in spite of various attempts to inject them into the study of organizations.

3 *The problem of case study generalization* Pugh points to the widespread use of single case studies of organizations at the time that the preparations for the Aston research were getting underway, as well as to the difficulty of drawing *generalizations* from such research. A number of the contributors to this volume (especially Bresnen and Dunkerley) draw attention to the difficulty of knowing how far generalizations from single cases of organizations can be stretched. Interestingly, much research on fairly large samples of organizations does not escape the problem of generalization. Freeman is worth quoting again in this respect:

what we know or think we know about organizations is based on samples providing little external validity. Researchers sample organizations or subunits of organizations in opportunistic ways. When they do achieve a modicum of generalizability, the populations from which samples are selected often are themselves defined arbitrarily. . . . They rarely work with samples that are representative of even the restricted types of organizations they choose to study. This has often led them to develop bodies of theory that do not apply generally. (Freeman, 1986, pp. 298, 300)

He cites his own research into manufacturing firms and restaurants in California as indicative of this latter point! Schwab (1985, p. 173) also points to the widespread use of convenience rather than probability samples in much survey research on organizations.

As a number of the contributors to this volume observe, the problem of case study generalization is not as intractable as its traditional depiction implies. Bulmer, for example, points to the need to accumulate case studies in order to promote a degree of leverage on generalization. But equally, as Bresnen, Dunkerley, and Turner suggest, case studies are indeed capable of addressing generality if this is understood in theoretical rather than statistical terms. Turner has constant recourse to the notion of 'grounded theory' (Glaser and Strauss, 1967) which entails an alternative framework for generalization from that associated with statistical criteria. Bresnen and Dunkerley respectively refer to the work of Yin (1984) and Mitchell (1983), both of whom sharply criticize the view that case studies are not capable of being generalized. Each of these authors argues that a case should not be thought of in statistical terms, i.e. as a sample of one. The argument for the prospective generalization of case study findings lies in their generalization to theoretical and analytic concerns. Dunkerley quotes Mitchell (1983, p. 207) on the irrelevance of statistical inference to the extrapolation of case study findings and the more important consideration of 'the cogency of the theoretical reasoning'. Similarly, Yin argues that the *analogy to samples and universes is incorrect when dealing with case studies*. This is because survey research relies on *statistical* generalization whereas case studies . . . rely on *analytic* generalization' (Yin, 1984, p. 39, emphases in original). While one may want to quibble with the implication that analytic concerns may be of lesser significance to survey researchers than they are to case study investigators, the basic point is an important one. Case study researchers have often been very apologetic about the external validity of their findings, but there is a growing view that such diffidence may be unwarranted. Further, such perspectives need to be more systematically integrated into textbooks, whose authors invariably depict the case study as deficient in these respects.

Conclusion

Again, the purpose of the preceding section was to draw out what appear to the editor to be some recurring themes and preoccupations among the contributors. As with the section on the contrast between inside and textbook accounts, the choice and presentation of the points emphasized are open to disagreement, but then the editor remains committed to the view, partly as a consequence of well over a decade's experience of teaching research methods, that one of the strengths of volumes like these is that students, prospective and even practising researchers, and teachers can extract a plethora of different themes which will resonate in different ways and with different implications for them.

Some issues are not considered as fully as they might be by the contributors; indeed, these are often points which are accorded scant attention by other inside accounts. As Bulmer observes, the knotty problem of the levels in organizations at which research is pitched is not explored a great deal, except by the Aston researchers whose focus on the organization-group-individual contrast is one of the programme's conceptual strengths (see Pugh). There is also insufficient attention to the question of the effects of the researcher's presence on those whom he or she observes. There are passing references to the issue: for example, Lawrence seeks to dispel the view that the researcher's presence may have a reactive effect on his or her subjects, in his case managers. But there are other dimensions to the issue, particularly for ethnographic researchers. For example, what are the implications of the tendency for most people to associate social research with interviews and questionnaires for the experience of being the recipient of direct observation or detailed un- or semi-structured interviewing? In this context, it is worth recalling Clarke's (1975) remark that one of the critical problems which participant observers face is that their subjects do not know how to be studied. Atkinson (1981) notes that his subjects – medical students – were not unused to the idea of social research, but tended to associate such endeavour with questionnaires, as indeed was the case among the more senior medical staff who had to sanction his access. As Atkinson (1981, p. 124) observes, ethnographic research is readily seen as 'woolly' and 'subjective' in such a context. The use of various questionnaires and inventories is fairly widespread in organizations, so it would seem important to have some details of the responses of subjects to the experience of ethnographic research (though this is not in the least to suggest that the response will be adverse), as well as to its products which *are* frequently revealed to subjects (in the form of feedback or respondent validation; see Buchanan *et al.*). An associated point is that there is little discussion of the implications of the possibility that many of the concepts, theories and findings associated with organization studies are known to those people who are investigated. There may be a considerable number of people who work in industry, the public sector, and elsewhere who have some familiarity with many of the topics with which researchers in organizations are concerned. Such acquaintance with organizational research may derive from training courses and undergraduate and postgraduate degrees in which subjects like 'organizational behaviour', 'management of human resources', 'organizational design', and the like often figure quite strongly. The implications of such well-informed informants and subjects for doing research in organizations is in need of some attention.

Finally, I am convinced that more attention needs to be devoted to the problem of time in organizations, a topic to which Bresnen gives some attention. Researchers do not attach sufficient importance to questions of change in organizations and its significance. Freeman (1986, pp. 302–3) has drawn attention to our limited knowledge of 'the speed with which variables change and causal processes occur' over time. Cross-sectional surveys are obviously vulnerable to this criticism (see, for example, Starbuck's, 1981, pp. 169–72 criticisms of the Aston research), not least because of their tendency to aggregate growing and declining organizations and to provide snapshots of organizational processes. But case studies are not immune from this accusation: they often produce truncated videos of processes rather than providing a feel for change. Bresnen's discussion of the immense change in the climate and morale at one of his construction projects, when he revisited it, is fascinating if only because of our awareness that an account solely in terms of either his initial or his later sojourn would have been profoundly misleading. The significance of the timing of research is explored in the context of schools by Ball (1983). He argues that much short-stay field research in schools ignores the timing of entry. The school year may be thought of as a cycle, and Ball observes that much of what goes on in schools at the beginning and the end of this cycle is omitted because of the tendency to commence investigations after the start of the school year and to conclude them before the finish. He argues that the timing of much ethnographic research in schools has introduced a systematic bias into this field. The possibility of such distortions in the kinds of organizational milieux with which the contributors to this volume are concerned needs to be considered. Bresnen has made a start with his discussion of the construction project cycle, but further scrutiny of this point is warranted. In short, the significance of time and timing in organizational research is in need of more attention than it is currently receiving. Historical studies of the kind described by Dunkerley may prove important in this respect.

I remain convinced of the virtue of inside accounts of the research process as a means of highlighting lacunae such as these as well as the various problems which investigators have had to confront. I very much hope that others will see the same virtues in such tales of doing research in organizations.

1

REGULATING RESEARCH:
Politics and decision making in industrial organizations[1]

Huw Beynon

Research into industrial and trade union organizations can be an extremely sensitive process. Both sets of organizations are capable of excluding researchers and regulating the information which they provide. Equally, these organizations – but most notably the companies – have research facilities of their own geared up to the internal needs and interests of the organizations they serve. Additionally, of course, in factories, mines and offices, these organizations can be in overt conflict with each other: competing for the loyalty and commitment of the employees – the members. Research in these contexts therefore can be understood as a *political* process; it involves the researcher in mediating power relationships. Often researchers get squeezed by this process; not infrequently they are squeezed out. Too often they are unprepared for the kinds of research decisions they will need to make; for the facts of tactical and strategic compromise which, in many instances, are the hallmark of empirical research in industry. It is upon this *political* process that this chapter will concentrate.

A friend of mine, a professional photographer, recently obtained permission to enter the docks at Teesport to take photographs. He was particularly interested in the arrival of a Nissan transporter ship which was bringing in parts to be assembled at the company's new plant at Washington. As the ship docked and the packing cases disgorged he was surrounded by officials who told him that it 'wasn't allowed' for him to photograph Nissan products; that certain things just couldn't be photographed. He told me that he began to think of himself as a spy: 'and I was only taking photographs of a ship and a bloody packing case'. As the company attempts to play down publicity on the Tees, so too, at the plant, has its Personnel Director made clear that in spite of all the requests by academic researchers for entry into the plant to investigate its development, 'the answer is no – nobody is getting in.'

Nissan's investment in a new car plant in the North of England is a sensitive issue. As such, the developments in the company's organization, its industrial relations and its workplace processes are unlikely to be subjected to detailed independent research. Another company – a US one – which moved to the North East in the last decade operated with a similar approach. In 1975 a research student (Shirley Hammond – a US national herself) approached the personnel management of Black & Decker at its branch plant in Spennymoor.

I was hoping to be able to talk with workers at the plant site and forwarded my interview schedule for consideration upon the Personnel Manager's request. In December 1976, the Personnel Manager at Spennymoor, who was from the south of England, set the mood of our first meeting – one of extreme hostility towards me and my efforts to conduct interviews in the community about 'his' company. I had never experienced anything like this meeting before. It began as a grilling by the apparently hostile Personnel Manager who was constantly seeking my ulterior motives which simply did not exist. Statements and questions like: 'What we can't figure out is why did you pick on Black and Decker? It is a small company. [!] It would be more interesting to have chosen a larger company like IBM. They're American and even more progressive. Why did you pick Black and Decker? . . .

'We like to remain as anonymous as possible. We don't want too many comparisons made with our style of management. *We do have comparisons made for and against us.* There is a tendency to level up and across in benefits in the community as a whole. For example, if people see something better, they want it. There is a levelling up for the mutual benefit of everybody. . . .

'*We manage our company in the best interest of our company.* . . .

'I doubt very much whether my company will cooperate with you. It's up to the [higher] management level [at Maidenhead]. *It's not my decision.*' (Hammond, 1981, p. 54)

In Sweden, the Volvo Company took a rather more urbane, but certainly equally effective, approach to independent academic research. For many years the accounts provided of their revolutionary new plant at Kalmar came from their president Pehr G. Gyllenhammer. In one of his books he wrote of how

Volvo has received many requests from social scientists and research people to make studies of Kalmar. However, their research was not very helpful when we were designing the plant, so we have rejected most of these outside requests . . . we don't want to find out what we did yesterday. We want to know what to do tomorrow. (Gyllenhammer, 1977, p. 73)

In part, this reluctance to provide 'entry' derives from the fact that the organizations and the researchers have different goals. The reference by Gyllenhammer to the need for prescriptive research is relevant, as is his view that the social sciences should develop research strategies to fit this need. Equally important, perhaps, is the closed nature of the industrial enterprise – its own internal culture, methods of working and knowledge. Historically, the rich and powerful have encouraged hagiography, not critical investigation. And, unlike the poor and weak, they have been in a position to determine the way they are investigated and the manner of their public exposure. They have also, when confronted with critical research findings, been quick to use this power to neutralize the critical impact. If we stay with the motor industry for a moment, it is interesting to recall the response which *Working for Ford* (Beynon, 1973) produced from the Ford Motor Company. The company's main aim was to establish that the book contained 'facts' which were untrue, and to make clear that the book as a 'report' was irrelevant, based upon little research and founded upon unsubstantiated allegations. The company's Liverpool spokesman remarked that it was 'particularly unpleasant' to find in the book an account of a man lying dead on the factory floor for ten minutes while the line continued to run:

It really is quite monstrous to suggest that any supervisor should, in any way, jeopardise the health of an employee . . . we have no recollection of this particular incident. . . . But it does seem appalling that someone who is not named should be making a serious allegation of this kind, suggesting that the men are being exploited. (*Liverpool Echo*, 30 May 1973)

In respect to this response, a public debate ensued in which shop stewards from Halewood appeared on a Radio Merseyside programme, and Frank Banton identified himself as the steward involved in that particular incident. He named both the foreman and the worker involved and added the correction that the man had lain near the line for eight and not ten minutes; he had timed it with his stopwatch. The point here is not to quibble about facts (although in any publication it's important to be sure to get them right!) but to indicate a 'discrediting process' which large organizations can instigate against research which is not to its liking.

This pattern of control operates equally powerfully in the public and the private sector. The National Coal Board, for example, has since its formation in 1947 exerted a monopoly control over both coal production and much of the information that relates to the coal industry. This information and control over its accusability and interpretation has been an extremely powerful weapon in the company's armoury. Not infrequently it has been used to its advantage, often as a means of *discrediting* its critics and any basis for independent research. In 1983, for example, John Mills, Deputy Chairman of the NCB, addressed the annual general meeting of the industry's white collar union, COSA. He commented briefly on the report on the industry produced by the Work and Environmental Research Group at the University of Bradford. This report had predicted a rapid decline in employment linked to the use of new technology in the mines. Mr Mills's comments are revealing: 'I do not want to be rude to our friends in the academic world, but we do not need outsiders to tell us where the industry is going.' Whatever the intention, this clearly is a rude remark – less offensive, however, than the corporation can be if its activities are questioned in any detailed way on the basis of 'outside' research. An example of this was revealed in 1986 when the NCB was involved in a series of independent reviews of its decision to close particular collieries. In the review of the Horden colliery, for example, the trade union called as an expert witness Dr Eric Wade, a man originally trained in mining engineering and involved in socio-economic research into the consequences of colliery closures. He was questioned by Mr Northard, the operations manager of the NCB, who was at pains not to discuss the substantive issues but the experience and character of the witness. The transcript reads as follows:

Q. Are you qualified to manage a coalfield?
A. No.
Q. What practical management experience have you had in operating?
A. I have no experience in operating because after 1966, when I obtained my PhD, it was rather difficult then for the Coal Board and they did not want people who had doctorates in management, so they suggested I should go elsewhere.
Q. For your information we have numerous people with doctorates.
A. I know. But at the time, shall we say, it was a rather difficult period. Lots of pit closures, particularly in the North East in that period – should I say the demand for my skills in the North East area – which I wanted – was not there. I could have had a job with the Board in a research capacity.
Q. You were never really interested in management?
A. I would not say that.
Q. You would not take your management certificate. People who are interested in management would take the management certificate.
A. I would have had to take just that section on mining law. Since I did not remain in the mining industry after 1966, after completing my work at Fishburn Colliery, I went to Cambridge to do postgraduate studies in economics.

Q. You have referred to Mr Edwards and his problem of trying to sell coal at prices that we were able to produce at.

A. Yes.

Q. Have you any personal knowledge of selling coal to commercial buyers?

A. No.[2]

The discrediting method is one aspect of this process of corporate defence. Another, less public, one lies in the practice of retaining data as 'confidential', refusing access to certain people in groups, and a series of strategic activities aimed at denying the existence of data. Eric Wade, for example, found himself excluded from the NCB's library of geological data, and that the staff at regional headquarters were under instruction to give him no information of any kind whatsoever. Similarly, researchers at the University of Durham found that, in their attempt to document the likely impact of colliery closures upon Easington district for the local council, they were not to be given access to critical information on employment patterns. The Board's letter read:

> Thank you for your letter asking for details of manpower, coal shipments, investment and capital for years 1978–83 . . . due to the current dispute we do not have the staff resources to obtain the very considerable amount of information you required. I must also advise you that I could not anticipate a date when even some of the information could be made available.[3]

The nicest of brush-offs, and one reproduced in another form in response to another researcher. A critical issue in all discussions of coal capacity in the UK, and therefore the future of collieries, is the amount of time which the face-cutting machines are in operation during a shift. Andrew Cox from the University of Newcastle was keen to establish evidence on any changes in 'machine available time', and he was informed by the NCB's Head of Business Planning that, 'The collection of information of this kind as a routine has now been stopped.'[4]

It would be wrong, of course, to think that industrial enterprises are unique in this respect. Trade unions are no less sensitive to detailed research into their operations, and the sparse literature on trade union and labour organizations is, in part, a consequence of this. Where researchers have published accounts which fail to match the dominant reality within the union they run the risk of attack and ridicule.

At the moment Arthur Scargill fills every one of his speeches with attacks on 'academics' and their misinterpretations of the union's history and of its conduct of the 1984–5 dispute. It is notable that these attacks outweigh in ferocity the invective he directs against the Coal Board. In 1975 (after a short article on the car industry in *New Society*) I was severely reprimanded by Jack Jones, the then General Secretary of the Transport and General Workers Union:

> It is a pity that Huw Beynon's welcome description of conditions on motor car assembly lines ends in a burst of misinformation and old-fashioned union-bashing. Presumably, Beynon, like so many other academics, wants to be on the side of the workers, but with friends like him, workers do not need enemies – and we have enough of those too! . . . It is only through their trade unions that workers can tackle and are tackling the problems Beynon describes so dramatically. Beynon, and other lecturers with a similar outlook, should leave their ivory towers and study what is really happening in trade union activity.
>
> You do not help workers (without giving any evidence whatsoever) by writing off the very organisations that those workers, purposefully struggling for a more human life, have created and are successfully using for this purpose. (letter in *New Society*, 26 June, 1975)

The language used in this letter is similar in its construction (reference to academics/enemies/ivory tower/out of touch) to that used by industrial corporations. And it makes clear that for researchers into organizational behaviour 'entry' is but one aspect of a generalized problem.

Large organizations, therefore, have the power to restrict research into their activities. Given this, the conclusion may be that such research is impossible or, at best, fortuitous. This would not be valid, however. The examples chosen so far have been of corporations particularly sensitive to investigation, generally or at the moment of the research contact. Equally the research (in certain cases) was of a particular kind. There is truth in the general proposition 'large-scale industrial organizations are generally sensitive to independent academic research and to the publication of its findings'. Equally true is the fact that many trade union organizations and business corporations feel that their operations and internal practices are ill understood and recognized by the 'outside world'. The statements by Gyllenhammer and Jack Jones are again interesting in this comparison. The 'ivory tower' image is a powerful one, but linked to it is a view that academics interested in the world of industry ought to leave those exclusive towers and provide a form of research which is both forward-looking and useful. There is no doubt that, given the trends in modern society generally and in British universities in particular, this emphasis will increase. Equally it is clear that such a development (if there is to be positive, independent, 'forward-looking' research, not mere platitude) will not be conflict free, either in its practice or its production.

In the early 1970s I was involved in a study of a chemical plant in the South of England with three other researchers.[5] In the preliminary discussions of this research with the companies we visited, Theo Nichols and I stressed the importance of research which attempted to 'tell it like it is'. Without using this phrase, we emphasized with management and trade union officials the importance of detailed accounts of how workplaces function, the operation of jobs and the patterns of organization involved in the production of heavy chemicals, gasses and fertilizers. We also stressed that the company's name need not be used in any publication, and that we would organize our research in a way which caused minimal intrusion into the operation of the plants and offices. This approach found favour with one of the six companies we contacted, and we visited the site on a regular basis for two and a half years.

In the late 1960s I had obtained access into the Halewood plant of the Ford Motor Company by a less circuitous route. The company was (like Nissan today) newly established in the area, and one of its personnel managers had delivered a talk at a local conference on local industry, in which he talked of the problem of labour turnover on Merseyside. My research supervisor (Joe Banks) was in the audience and suggested in a question that perhaps the *type of work* was a contributory factor. Mr Paul Roots countered this suggestion with the offer of a site visit and (later) of research access.

In these different ways, therefore, two companies were prepared to cooperate with academics and to see in their work a potential for mutual understanding. In the conduct of the fieldwork, a number of problems developed in each case which (in different degrees) worked against this. In both instances, they related to the position of the trade union in the factory and the patterns of interaction between managers and union representatives. At Ford, of course, my visit to the Halewood plant coincided with a sustained period of change involving workers and plant management which culminated in the severest of conflicts and strike action. At ChemCo., too changes were involved of a similar kind, with departmental restructuring and the introduction and development of a productivity deal aimed at altering the ways in which work itself was organized. The conflicts and stresses created by such changes can place the researcher in a situation which is extremely difficult to handle. At Ford and ChemCo., agreement had been reached with the branch and district officials of the trade union (in both cases the TGWU) before the research commenced. Without such prior agreement it is most likely that cooperation would have been withdrawn during the research, and such a fate has affected a number of industrial research projects. But this is not to say that once prior agreement has been arrived at the rest is plain sailing. At Ford and ChemCo., being 'in between' the union and the company, and therefore 'in the know' from both sides, as it were, proved a problem. Normally, reference to the idea of 'confidentiality' was sufficient to deal with the casual request – 'What does he think?'; 'What did he tell you?' But occasionally the enquiries were more persistent. At Ford, for example, the fact that I attended shop steward meetings and branch meetings of the unions was seen by some members of the Personnel Department as a potentially fruitful source of information. At ChemCo., one plant manager – who had lost the support of his small workforce who were deliberately sabotaging his efforts to increase production and succeed within the company – impressed upon us that we should tell him what was going on, that he needed information from us, that a lot depended upon it. In both these situations it was clear that to accede to the request would have endangered the continuation of the research strategy. Equally, there was a risk that refusal could have a similar outcome. Furthermore, it was clear, especially in the latter case, that to 'help' in any meaningful way would have required a quite different relationship between the company and the research project. At worst it would have involved a form of management consultancy which we were not happy about (considering there to be sufficient practitioners of that craft in the United Kingdom); at best, a reorganization of the consultative and negotiating procedures in the plant allowing for an open discussion between the parties to the issues and the problems involved. Neither were likely options therefore and in this (and the other) case the only viable solution seemed to lie in temporarily 'leaving the field' – attending to other pressing business at the university until the crisis blew over. In both cases absence achieved its objective.

The difficulties and pressures of situations like these have often nudged researchers into simplifying the research problem, through processes which do not involve the complexities of negotiation and discussion. One such solution involves a degree of concealed participant observation. It is interesting, for example, that one of the classic accounts of management practice was produced on the basis of Dalton's (1959) experiences as a manager. Equally, the most powerful accounts of shop floor organization and experience have been produced by men and women who have posed as factory workers.

In Germany Gunter Wallraff (1977) worked anonymously in a number of different workplaces; Goran Palm (1977) did the same in Sweden, as did Robert Linhart (1981) at Citroen in France. In Hungary and Japan two poets (Miklos Haraszti, 1971; Satoshi Kamata, 1983) spent time earning money as factory workers. In the USA academics like Richard Pfeffer (1979) have written about their experiences as factory workers, as has Sally Westwood (1985) in the UK. These studies now form an important collection of material on the inner workings of the factory system, most significantly on the questions of direct work experience and interaction. Interestingly, they have often been subjected to quite intense criticism by employers who have questioned their scientific status. In Germany, the Employers' Association of the Federal Republic felt that Wallraff's 'methods of investigation . . . must be categorically condemned.'[6] In Sweden, Palm's critics were equally dismissive: 'the author's method of collecting, structuring and analysing his data does not conform with any scientific standards.'[7] In Hungary, Haraszti was criticized by the authorities and accused of having 'falsified the facts'.[8]

The criticism by employers of people who have gone 'under cover' is perhaps not surprising, and it does bring to the surface many of the ethical questions which are raised in relation to concealed participant observation. But the *extent* of the criticisms is a further indication of the ways in which industrial organizations are 'sealed off' from the outer world. People talk differently in their workplace (so much so that 'factory language' and 'pitmatic talk' are understood concepts), and many of them behave inside them in ways far different from their 'normal behaviour' outside. One woman, a new recruit to a factory in the North East of England, discussed this. Liking the company of the women, she was surprised and embarrassed by the way they carried on – the language they used and the jokes they told. As such it was with some trepidation that she agreed to meet them outside work for a meal in a restaurant at Christmas. She was surprised to find that, outside of the factory, they were 'just like me'.

These points can be used to emphasize the importance of participant observation as the only way of investigating certain internal organizational processes. As a technique, however, it has severe limitations (its focus tends to be with the small groups) and it does, as I have implied, need to be handled with considerable care. Companies and employers are not alone in resenting their 'private lives' being exposed to public surveillance. In this regard the late Don Roy (e.g. 1955, 1960), the skilled ethnographer whose 'inside' accounts of factory life still rank with the best, had a clear solution. In 1976 I talked with him about his approach. He *always* maintained the anonymity of the organization and the workplace which he studied. I asked him why. He alluded to the ethical problems of the technique and added that he would 'hate any of them to read what I had written'.

For my part, I had always seen sociological research as a means of building and extending a dialogue between the sociologist and the public. In this regard I have tended not to write through anonymity, preferring to name people and organizations whenever possible, and to cope with this by discussing the research and the 'research findings' fully with the people affected by it before publication. One style of research has developed in a positive way along just these lines, and as such it can be distinguished from concealed participant observation as a strategic solution to some of the problems presented by research into industrial organizations. This research strategy involves the researcher in an open and positive relationship with one of the groups or interests involved in the industrial enterprise. One established branch of this strategy is, of course, management consultancy. The alternative approach – sometimes termed 'action research' – attaches the researcher to a trade union, or shop steward committee.

If research into industrial organization is beset with problems of entry and legitimacy, the problems associated with the study of labour organizations are, if anything, greater. Researchers (through non-membership) are often denied access to meetings; where the organization feels beleaguered or under threat members may be reluctant (occasionally under instruction) to talk with researchers; equally, where sensitive issues are involved there is no guarantee that the researcher will be told the truth. As such, in these contexts, 'action research' has a number of attractions which are both strategic and emotional. It involves researchers in using the 'research role' as a central and positive aspect of their relationship with the groups in question. It achieves 'entry' and 'acceptance', therefore, through stress on the instrumental value of research to the organization. Such approaches have been widely used in relation to community groups and, more recently, local authorities. In fact, one of the part-time students at Teesside Polytechnic who heard this paper as a talk in 1986, suggested strongly that, in regions like the North East (with enormous problems of structural employment change), academic researchers should link positively with planning departments in local authorities (where he himself worked) and produce alternative sources of data and knowledge.

There are many attractions to a strategy like this one, and in the late 1970s I was involved (along with Hilary Wainwright) in a piece of 'action research' in relation to the combine shop steward committee at the Vickers Company (Beynon and Wainwright, 1978). In many respects the research was fruitful but it was not without its problems. Working with the shop steward combine committee gave us direct access to their meetings, their records and to their members. The interviewing programme covering all the shop stewards in the company was easily arranged, and the initial postal questionnaire (a notoriously unreliable research tool) was returned, completed by each of the committees within the agreed time scale. Equally, although our relationship to the committee was known, the company was not overtly hostile and we were able to obtain some help and information from its headquarters. However, we were refused access to most of the company's plants (something, incidentally, which infuriated the shop stewards – 'their researchers are allowed in, why not ours?'), and the national officials of the trade unions involved were less than sympathetic to our endeavours. The point here, I suppose, is that identification with one group eases problems of ambiguity in conflict situations, but it raises others. One of these is of access to the plant. The other (more fundamental perhaps) has to do with the nature of social scientific research, and the kinds of knowledge it produces. Supporters of action research have tended to assume that 'knowledge' is not value-free but strongly linked to values and interests, and that a strong correspondence (even an identity) will exist between the projects of the group and the researchers themselves. There are problems with this notion, however. A strong commitment to the 'value-saturated' view of truth can easily work against the very processes which are vital to 'scientific research' into social organization. Researchers who have worked with trade unions have often experienced the sense that union officials feel that they know the answer and simply require the evidence to support this. Often the argument and disagreement in this process are as painful as in any other forms of research activity – more so perhaps. Equally, there is a tendency for trade union organizations (concerned with organizing around a particular interest in largely economic terms) to require particular kinds of short-term data from researchers, and to be less interested in strategic, speculative or puzzling findings and interpretations. If sociological enquiry is, in some important respects, an enquiry into the unknown (the Star Trek syndrome), it requires a similar approach in its audience. In the research with the Vickers shop stewards, this problem was overcome, partly, through a process of discussion which was built up around regular research reports. The strategy hit problems, however, when we felt that comparative data, with other shop steward combine committees, would be helpful and that we would not be as easily 'on call'. What we learned from this experience is that the assumption of correspondence between the aims and assumptions of the researcher and the group is unlikely to be true at all times. Given this, it is important that in any research strategy of this kind there are (at least) procedures for dealing with non-correspondence. Too strong a sell on 'action' might well leave the researcher as a hostage to fortune in which power (entry – 'if you want to carry on coming to these meetings . . .') or more usually muddle ('I thought you were supposed to be working for us?') determines strategy.

There is a further approach to the problem of organizational research and this involves doing it 'from the outside'. Much good research has been completed which has examined industrial organizations on the basis of gaining limited access to the company's plants or to its records. Shirley Hammond (1981), for example, completed her study of Black & Decker through calling on people at their homes, thereby using the 'community' as the point of entry. In Italy, Hilary Partridge (1986) has completed a quite detailed study of the developments in the labour process at Fiat with the minimal cooperation of the automobile corporation. She again relied heavily upon home interviews and also the range of information and data collected by trade union organizations and local groups.

This reference to the 'community', 'household' and 'local groups' is important, for it points to a critical feature of organization studies, and reflects an important strategic dimension to organizational research. All organizations have boundaries; these are formal, spatial and legal. With companies, they come together neatly at the perimeter fence and the security gate. (Black & Decker's security guard informed one picketing AUEW member – in dispute over union recognition – that the USA began inside the fence.) But the people who work there pass through the gate each day. While at work they are often members of the relevant trade union, whose own organizational form is based upon a structure (the branch, lodge, district . . .) not contained within the barbed wire. Equally, the people live in houses which are (most often – certainly in the UK) separate from the legal control of the corporation. There will be different 'degrees of fit' between workplace and residence, as will the relationship between union and workplace vary. Nevertheless these boundaries and overlaps (to which the Manpower Services Commission and Local Authorities can be added) provide important developments and options for organizational research in industry.

Most normally this option has been seen to divide between 'organizational studies' and 'community studies'. Such a dichotomy, however, can be a restrictive one in as far as it prevents the organizational researcher from developing new patterns of analysis (relations between 'inside' and 'outside') and alternative research strategies. In the late 1970s and the 1980s, I worked closely with Terry Austrin on a research project which examined work and political organization on the Durham coalfield. The aim of the project was to investigate the decline of coalmining and its new, modern form, alongside the experience of new industry and the changed pattern of dominance within and between trade unions in the local labour movement. The focus of this research therefore was on organizational forms and the interrelation and overlap within and between them. While the coal mines and the branch plant factories were central points of the problem the prime focus was upon that nexus of organizations – the 'labour movement' – which overlaps with and extends beyond the workplace.

This research, therefore, raised a number of quite difficult problems which were solved in a variety of ways, some of which have a bearing on the issues raised in this chapter. On the coalfield there was a reasonably good fit between 'community' and 'workplace' and as such (in a number of instances) we were able to use the household as a point of contact. In terms of the companies it was clear that they had different worries and concerns. Some managers were happy to talk with us and to show us around the factory, and the NCB was quite happy for us to be shown around the pits. Few were able to allow us into their workplace on a regular basis although some were and we took advantage of these as 'case studies'. Some companies and trade unions were extremely wary, occasionally for diametrically opposite reasons. At one factory (where a shop steward was a member of the Socialist Workers Party and had been giving the personnel manager a hard time) we were 'grilled' for over half an hour on whether or not the research was 'political'. At another – where we had arranged to have a discussion meeting with the shop steward committee – we were questioned in a more precise way on the nature of our political sympathies. Durham is a solidly Labour area, and the university has a rather ambiguous relationship with it. What we were being asked – finally in a most direct manner – was 'are you Labour?' The required answer left no room for New Left niceties about 'no illusions' and the like. Issues like this were multiplied in relation to the two main trade unions of the study, the National Union of Mineworkers and the General and Municipal Workers Union, within both of which there existed different political groupings – collections of interests with histories of antagonism or conflict. It was after one particularly arduous day that Terry Austrin remarked that the research resembled 'negotiating a minefield'.

Such negotiations take a great deal of time and an even greater degree of patience, a quality which is rarely mentioned in textbooks. But they are necessary if sociological research is not simply to run down the established tracks of its past and of our society. In the Durham study, the focus on the interface *between* organizations served to provide new and interesting perspectives on both labour movements and the internal structures of the organizations themselves. It pointed to the variety of *sources* of data available to the researcher and also to how the research process can itself provide information. As one way of negotiating the minefield, we produced our preliminary research findings in the form of discussion papers. These were distributed within the area and helped to legitimize our position as 'serious', 'independent', yet 'sympathetic' researchers, as well as providing the basis for many important discussions and interviews. Equally our position at the organizational margins provided us with a number of safeguards. We were not 'sucked in' to a particular community or to a particular group view; and this, we came to realize, helped provide us with a useful check on 'the true facts'. Most significantly, perhaps, a position on the edges sensitized our research to the interrelationship between 'members' and 'non-members' of groups and organizations. Perhaps the most critical example of this related to the miners' union. As a result of our research strategy we developed a close relationship with a number of lodges and access to their records and minute books. On the basis of these records and interviews with ex-lodge officials we built up a detailed account of the history of these local union organizations. However, it was only as a result of our other contacts in the villages that we discovered that one of these lodges had been involved in a serious conflict in the early 1960s. The conflict related to the NCB's plans to modernize the houses (here, company housing still survives) and the lodge's opposition to it on the grounds that the NCB required the loss of one ton of 'free' coal in exchange. The miners were provided with showers at work and their sons (as males) were allowed to use them at weekends. But not the women and girls. It was this which divided the village, saw the pit picketed by the women and the lodge meetings barracked. Yet there was no record on the union's file.

In considering the way through this, it is critical for the research process to be understood not as a highly formalized piece of rote learning, but rather as a creative act, an act which links the sociologist to the organizations being studied. As an act it is difficult to get right, and certainly there will be no easy medals. But it is one which we should practise and work on, and in doing so we can perhaps relate in a firmer and clearer way to the views of Per Gyllenhammer and Jack Jones.

Notes

1 An earlier version of this chapter was given as a talk to the part-time MSc students at Teesside Polytechnic and I am grateful to them for their comments and discussion.
2 'Independent review body into the proposed closure of Hordern Colliery', *Transcript of Proceedings*, Day 2, pp. 41–2, January 1986.
3 Quoted in F. Pyke, R. Hudson and D. Sadler, 'Undermining Easington', *Report for Easington District Council*, 1984, p.v.
4 Letter, 27 February 1986.
5 See Nichols and Beynon (1977) and Nichols and Armstrong (1976).
6 Cited in the Introduction to Wallraff (1977).
7 Cited in the Foreword by Peter Doherty to Palm (1977).
8 Taken from an account of his trial in the appendix to Haraszti (1977).

2

INSIGHTS ON SITE:
Research into construction project organizations

Mike Bresnen

When doing research in organizations it is usually possible to assume at
least some basic stability and continuity in the nature of the organization
over time. The electronics firm that operates in a complex and rapidly
changing product market and technological environment, for instance, may
undergo considerable changes in its work and form of organization (e.g.
Burns and Stalker, 1966). However, unless it goes bust, it is likely to
continue to operate (and to have operated) in more or less its present mode
for some considerable time: its physical coherence and continuity are
represented in the building(s) which it occupies. When doing research in
project organizations a different assumption needs to be made: namely that
the organization is characterized by its instability and transience, since
projects have a more or less definite starting point, a limited time scale and a
finite end point. Project organizations in construction, which are the subject
of this paper, exhibit characteristics that arise from two inherent features of
the project task: first, that the actual process of construction has to occur at
the particular location where the structure (a building or road, say) is to be
used; second, that the work involved at that location is both cumulative and
finite. Of course, construction *firms* do have an identity and continuity of
existence over time. Not surprisingly, such basic disjunctures in the physical
location and continuity of the firm's project operations as a whole then
create particular complexities for the firm, in terms of routinizing work
processes, standardizing procedures, economically allocating resources
internally, and so on. However, if one takes the particular *project* as the unit
of analysis, which is perhaps the most appropriate means of studying the
construction process, then one needs to take account of the fact that
particular project organizations exhibit features that stem from these two
distinguishing characteristics. That is, they are to some extent site-based and
transient. An additional feature to note is that individual projects in
construction are the focus of activity for a multiplicity of organizations:
clients, consultants, main contractors and subcontractors (e.g. NEDO,
1978). The actual 'constellation' of organizations involved may vary
considerably from case to case. However, a useful generic label for this type

of context is the 'Temporary Multi Organization' as described by Cherns and Bryant (1984). The project organization as such lacks the basic coherence that can be assumed in other types of organizational setting, since it consists of the aggregated total of subgroupings from a number and variety of different organizations which perform complementary functions in the design and construction of the building project. The research described in this paper took as its focus of interest this particular type of (multi-) organizational context. As a consequence, a number of methodological themes emerged which have a particular importance for the study of similar types of organizational setting, and perhaps a wider relevance to the study of organizations in general.

The study

Between 1978 and 1981, I was registered for a PhD (funded by the SSRC) in the Department of Industrial Economics at the University of Nottingham. My research was concerned with investigating the patterns and processes of interaction involved in the organization and management of construction project work (Bresnen, 1986). As an undergraduate in the same department, I had been interested in the workings of complex forms of organization – specifically matrix organizations (e.g. Knight, 1976). As a postgraduate, I decided to focus attention upon the implications of complex structures in project-based forms of organization for internal processes of decision making, communication, coordination and control. I was particularly interested in the roles and relationships of (multi-) organizational subgroups that were involved jointly in managing project work, and in their relative influence in joint decision-making processes.

The choice of construction as the setting for the study was largely a pragmatic one. First, it appeared to offer a widespread and readily accessible setting for studying project-based forms of organization. This was in the light of the comparative absence of readily accessible equivalents to the Apollo moonshot programme, and similar 'high-technology' ventures that formed the backbone of the empirical literature on project and matrix management at the time (e.g. Sayles and Chandler, 1971). Second, despite being less of a high-technology setting, the comparatively 'turbulent' environmental factors that I was looking for were also present – in the nature of product market conditions within the industry (e.g. Fleming, 1980). Individual projects may be highly idiosyncratic, and the work involved complex and subject to change. Such features and their implications for project management had been looked at to some extent in earlier Tavistock studies of construction work (e.g. Higgin and Jessop, 1965; Crichton, 1966). Furthermore, such features had also been linked to the structural characteristics of individual construction firms (Stinchcombe, 1959).

As I delved deeper into the literature, I found that the choice of construction as a setting was proving to be increasingly more fortuitous. On the one hand, studies of project management 'systems' rarely seemed to refer to what is undoubtedly its most common form in practice. Instead the bulk of attention was directed towards large-scale, high-technology ventures such as Apollo. In relating some of the concepts to the more down-to-earth setting of construction, I would perhaps be able to draw some important and useful comparisons and contrasts. In mainstream organizational research, it seemed, too, that the construction sector, despite its significance, was massively underresearched. Instead, it seemed to be singled out rather more as a 'special case'. Woodward (1965), for instance, specifically excluded construction firms from her sample. Perhaps the methodological complexities I am about to describe may throw some light on what I thought then was a somewhat peculiar omission. In any case, it gave me the opportunity then to explore construction in the context of findings derived from more widely based organizational theory and research.

Research strategy

Taking the construction project (rather than the construction firm as a whole) as the unit of analysis, I was interested in charting the detailed processes of interaction involved in its management. The research strategy that was chosen was to focus attention on a small number of case studies and to explore these longitudinally. A case study approach was chosen because of the essentially exploratory nature of the research. The range and complexity of the factors that I had set myself to study, and their potential effects, put a premium upon a strategy that allowed an *holistic*, rather than selective, study of circumstances and events on each project. It was the full individuality of the cases that I was to select, rather than their typicality, which was to be the main guiding principle of the study. As such I was accepting the limitations of not being able to make any *statistical* generalizations to a larger population of cases. Instead, I was relying upon the ability to make *analytical* generalizations (Yin, 1984, p. 39). The intention, then, was to select a sufficient number of cases (in the event five) such that sufficient grounds were available for making useful comparisons and contrasts, and drawing analytical inferences. A longitudinal component was built into the research since change, and the organizational response to it, were key issues to be explored in the study; for instance, whether changing patterns of influence in the management of the project over its course were contingent upon changes in the nature of the task being undertaken; whether, more generally, more static or 'mechanistic' (Burns and Stalker, 1966) frameworks for interaction were consistent with the requirements of a complex and changing task.

Having noted these reasons, it should also be said that there was a complementary, but more pragmatic reason for pursuing this type of research strategy. It is that I was initially unfamiliar with the nature of the construction setting itself in practice. The use of a longitudinal case study approach allowed me a good deal of leeway in being able to respond to the situational characteristics that I was likely to encounter in practice. This was particularly so when it came to understanding some of the ins and outs of the technical and legal (i.e. contractual) aspects of work on a construction project. In retrospect it was perhaps this last factor – the peculiarity of construction and my response to it – which was to influence significantly the subsequent course of events throughout my research, and in particular the types of methods I employed. In a sense, having expressed an interest in exploring and understanding the circumstances of construction, I was to become increasingly a victim of those circumstances as the study progressed.

Methods

I set about the study with the aim of using questionnaires, interviews, documentary sources and direct observation as complementary techniques to obtain a database of information, observations, views and opinions about the circumstances and events that occurred in each case. As such, I relied heavily upon the use of qualitative research methods for data collection and analysis. In large measure this reflected the exploratory nature of the research, and my initial lack of familiarity with the setting. In other words, I felt it was important to gain as full as possible an understanding of the context of social interaction in the management of each construction project (cf. Van Maanen, 1979). I was particularly keen on allowing for the individualism of each case, both with respect to the very detailed 'factual' information I intended to gather about each project and its participants, and also with respect to the range and variety of responses I was likely to get concerning various individuals' and groups' perceptions and attitudes towards the project, and how they felt it had been organized and managed. Consequently, I was concerned with allowing respondents their own frames of reference for describing and interpreting circumstances and events on the project, since their attitudes and the logic underlying these attitudes were important factors to be taken into account. For these reasons I was disposed to adopt methods that would allow for investigating as fully as possible the characteristics of the situation that were perceived to have influenced the process of management on site as they were understood and articulated by the people concerned.

The questionnaire I used supplied the basis for collecting information concerning the project, the organizations involved, and the management procedures with respect to that project. Unlike the normal type of questionnaire used in field research, its role was to provide a checklist of information that was needed, rather than a series of questions to be asked of a specific respondent or set of respondents. Therefore I was to use a number of key informants to provide information for this basic databank, as well as to refer to documentary sources (company manuals, contract documents and so forth) to supplement the information and cross-check details. This questionnaire was to undergo many changes from the original version I used, as the complexity of the situation I was attempting to record unfolded in the early stages of fieldwork.

Most of the important material on how the project had been organized and managed was to be derived from interviews with the key figures who were involved. Initially I had hoped to provide a fully structured basis for the conduct of interviews and to this end had attempted to devise detailed interview schedules. However, as I became more involved in the fieldwork, it became increasingly clear that the particular information and accounts I was getting relied upon a much more 'responsive' method of interviewing. I gradually ditched all attempts to structure in detail the questions I wanted to ask, and instead relied increasingly on semi-structured interviews and unstructured 'conversations' with my informants. I developed an interview schedule that was little more than a list of topics to be addressed in the interview – virtually an *aide-mémoire* – and took this as my starting point for the interviews. It was also my starting point for asking questions in following up particular chains of events that occurred on each case.

All of the information I collected by these methods was recorded manually in the form of field notes and a diary. In addition to these methods, I also made use of direct observation, through attendance at meetings on and off site, and more generally in the often extensive periods of time available between interviews. Direct observation helped me to pick up particular 'leads' that were worth following up. However, perhaps equally if not more important was the ability it gave me to gain a 'feel for the situation'. As I describe the first case study in more detail below, perhaps the significance of direct observation will become clearer. What should also be generally clear from the above is that the methods I used 'evolved' very much in response to the type of situation I encountered. Specifically, I became reliant upon much less structured methods of data collection than I had originally anticipated would be used.

Contact

The next section gives a brief description of my experiences on the first case study construction project I explored. The pseudonym I have used for this case is the Riverside Advance Works project, or RAW for short. It was an important and illuminating case in my research, since it gave me the first full opportunity to familiarize myself properly with the construction process in detail, and the patterns of organization and management that occurred in practice. It also gave me, of course, the chance to test out the ideas and methods that had been mulled over in the previous six months. The case was to have important subsequent implications for the theoretical and methodological direction of my work. It marked the beginning of a shift in my research towards incorporating complex *inter*organizational patterns of management. Further, and partly due to the complexities posed by the shift to an interorganizational focus, it marked the beginnings of what was to be the increasingly heavy reliance upon qualitative methods which I mentioned above.

I obtained access to the RAW project through personal contacts who put me in touch with the main contractor's planning officer. He 'cleared' my request for access and put me in contact with the firm's agent on site. The fieldwork I did on this site was in two blocks of three and two weeks respectively. Both times I stayed in the locality, the first time in a nearby hotel, the second time in a caravan on site. The firm's trainee foreman was especially helpful in making a reservation at the hotel (where he and others were staying) on my behalf, and in giving me lifts to and from the site. On the second visit it was his caravan, already shared with one of the firm's engineers, that he let me stay in.

While the means of establishing access – through personal contacts, and getting clearance from the firm – was the route I used in gaining access to the other four cases in my study, the pattern of fieldwork was not. In subsequent cases, I operated on the basis of daily (or blocks of two or three days') visits to the site at more regular and spaced-out periods of time during the construction stage. These visits were often timed to coincide with (monthly) progress meetings which I was allowed to attend, and from which I could follow up particular issues that emerged, using the additional time I had on site to follow up more general issues with representatives from the main participating organizations. I tried to avoid 'busy days', and my questions finished at around 5 p.m. when I and everyone else went home. I still relied on a close, continuing relationship with those I was interviewing. However, this was by no means as intense as it was on the first case, where for five weeks in total I ate and slept the RAW project. This greater personal involvement in the social setting of the RAW project should be borne in mind when reading the following account. Moreover, the research was exploratory, and concerned as much with understanding exactly what was going on as with testing hypotheses and research instruments. In the event it proved highly pertinent to both. However, the main aim of the following is to give some insight into the *type* of organizational context in which I found myself, and its implications for the methods I employed.

A case study cameo

The RAW project was a £2 million, twenty-month contract for the building of an infrastructure system of roads, paths, small bridges and drainage for a new housing estate that was subsequently to be built on the site. The client was a large metropolitan authority, which had employed its own in-house engineers to design the layout. The contract was let, on a selective competitive tender basis, to Roadbuilders Ltd. For a main contractor they were a comparatively small firm (with a turnover of about £10 million), who operated mainly in the region, and who specialized in marine and civil engineering works for public sector clients. This was the first contract they had been awarded by that particular client.

Roadbuilders had decided to sublet most of the work on the job to specialist subcontractors, and were to employ directly on site at most only about twenty joiners, concrete workers and general labourers. The total subcontractor workforce would reach a peak of about fifty during the middle stage of the project. A full-time staff of thirteen were employed on site to supervise the work on behalf of the main contractor (see Figure 2.1).

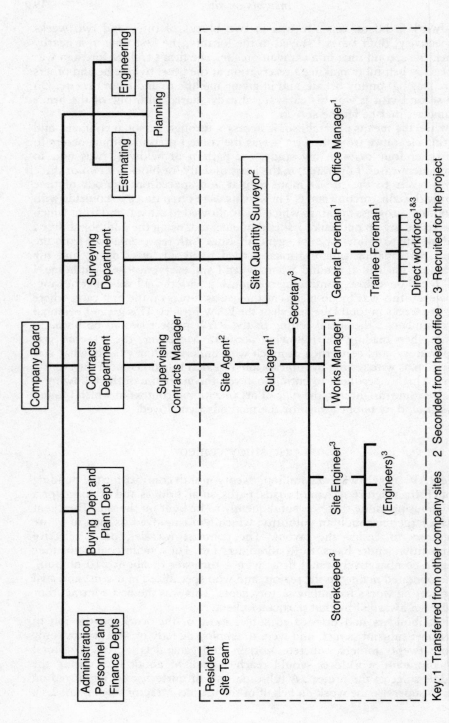

Key: 1 Transferred from other company sites   2 Seconded from head office   3 Recruited for the project

Figure 2.1 *Roadbuilders Ltd. Site management team and relationship to head office*

Most of these were involved on the project for its full duration; and most had been transferred from other company sites (although some had been recruited direct to the project, and some were seconded from the firm's head office). A resident site staff of nine also supervised the work on the client's behalf (see Figure 2.2). Again most were transferred, but some were also seconded from head office.

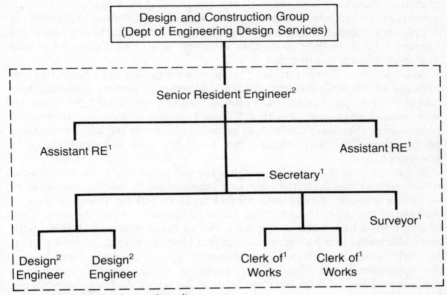

Key: 1 Transferred from other sites
     2 Seconded from head office

Figure 2.2 *The client's project management team on the RAW project, and relationship to head office*

My first block of fieldwork was between weeks 13 and 15 of the construction programme. The site had been fully set up, and the main work involved was in the laying of piled foundations and bulk earthmoving to level the site. The job was approximately a week ahead of schedule overall, and advance detailed plans were being drawn up for the more intense periods of activity that were to occur in the months ahead. My first week on site was something of a bewildering experience, in trying to fit together a picture of the situation from the few pieces of the jigsaw that I was managing to accumulate. Armed with the questionnaire that was to take quite a battering as a result of this first real taste of conditions in the field, I caught people for interview as and when they seemed to become available. I interviewed the surveyor on his role and the financial aspects of the job; the engineer likewise with respect to technical details; and so on. I ventured on to site – usually with the Sub-agent or Trainee Foreman as my guide – to get a clearer idea of the work involved, and the detailed technical aspects of the job. In between interviews and tours, and based in the Sub-agent's office, I ploughed through documentary sources (company manuals, contract documents, etc.) and sat in on the frequent discussions of details that involved (variously) the Site Agent, Sub-agent, Foreman, Engineer, Subcontractors' foremen and Assistant Resident Engineer (RE). As I became more aware of the important part played by the client's resident site team, I gained introductions and began to venture across the compound to conduct interviews and follow through particular issues and details. Although the people on site sometimes found it difficult to set aside time to respond to my questions, much to their credit they were very willing to discuss the project and their jobs on it when they could.

After the first week I think that they had grown accustomed to my presence as the site's resident 'student'. Whether or not my presence there had any effect upon the situation I find difficult to say. What I did ensure (as with subsequent cases) was that I caused no disruptions by interrupting people when they were too busy to see me. I also made the usual guarantees of confidentiality, and stressed my neutrality and independence as a researcher.

It was not until the second week that I began to get more of a 'feel' for the situation, and had collected sufficient information to make some sense of what was going on. By the same token I began to pick up 'undercurrents' in the type of responses I was getting: I was asking more or less the same types of questions I had asked at the start, but in being able to link them with particular issues that had occurred and that I had witnessed and followed up as 'leads', I began to glean slightly different types of answers. From behind the somewhat more bland descriptions of management practices and procedures I began to uncover the contentious edges. As I was based in the Sub-agent's office where many of the decisions seemed to be made, I became a witness to sporadic, slightly heated discussions about various issues – buying in plant or negotiating with subcontractors, for example. As I sought various people's views on these issues, tensions and contradictions began to emerge in the accounts.

Two particular events occurred during this first stage of fieldwork that stick in my mind as useful illustrations of how the situation began to unfold and how I responded to it. The first was a social gathering at the local pub after work towards the end of the second week. Most of the site management team were present with the notable exception of the Site Agent and, after about 8 p.m., the Sub-agent: both of these had fairly long journeys to commute home in the evenings. In their absence, and completely unprompted by me (although I was a willing listener), the conversation developed into an analysis of a 'gap' in attitudes that existed between senior and junior management staff on site; and also the 'attitude' of the firm, which many considered to be somewhat 'old-fashioned'. It was a 'letting-off of steam' after the week's work, that was helped along by the consumption of alcohol. The point here is not that it gave me the chance to collect 'reliable' data (not least due to my own altered perceptions through drink!), rather that it gave me useful leads that I could follow in developing my line of questioning on site. The reverse side of this coin, however, was that it sensitized me to the need to tread very carefully in pursuing my research. It also gave me the uneasy feeling of 'eavesdropping' and using the situation to my advantage – questions of ethics began to rear their ugly heads.

The second event occurred in the more sober light of day during the following week. It was a dispute that arose between the main contractor's and the client's staff on site. It centred upon the fact that the main contractor had assumed they had been given approval for changes to the details of one subcontractor's work package following informal discussions between the Sub-agent and Assistant RE. The Senior RE had learnt of this and had threatened that in future he would make sure all such dealings went through the appropriate channels; the Site Agent reacted by using the counter threat that in future they would let their respective head offices deal with these issues. To both of them, in subsequent interviews, the argument appeared to be an important point of principle. To the Sub-agent and Assistant RE, who were also interviewed, it was something of a 'storm in a teacup'. I myself interpreted this particular event as having some consider- able analytical significance. Regardless of the rights and wrongs of each party's case, it was evidence of a clear difference in assumptions about how the project was to be run. Additionally, it was symptomatic of what many on site felt was becoming a personal contest between the Senior RE and the Site Agent for control of what happened on site.

The point here is that, had I not been there in the office when the Assistant RE first came in to complain to the Sub-agent about the steps he had taken, I might not have been fully able to 'tap' these important underlying issues. I had been told of the tension that existed between the two senior managers, and which was manifested at the weekly site meetings, in what the Sub- agent described as often heated exchanges (I was not given access to attend these meetings). But it was only by happening to be there at the right place and at the right time that I managed to pick up an example of this tension. I was to be left with having to make sure that I did not overestimate or over- dramatize the significance of this particular dispute. However, in the meantime, it did give me a specific issue I could refer to in following up the leads that I was pursuing.

By the time that I revisited the site in the second block of fieldwork – in weeks 30 to 31 of the construction period – the situation had changed considerably and dramatically in a number of ways. The work was now in full swing, but the main contractor was facing considerable problems on site: the programme had fallen about a month behind schedule overall, mainly (everyone agreed) due to considerable delays associated with one particular subcontract; also Roadbuilders were losing money on the job from a number of other delays and problems on specific aspects of the work. The 'organization' on site had changed too: for a start, the subcontractors involved in the earlier stages had finished their work, and been replaced by a new set. Within the site management team, a new Works Manager had been brought on to the site, and there had also been some turnover amongst the junior engineers and clerical staff. Additionally, the problems faced by the main contractor had provoked more frequent visits by head office staff – the planning officer who reprogrammed the job, and also the company's office engineer and surveyor to advise on technical and financial matters respectively. The client's site team was much the same as before except that one of the design engineers had left.

On top of the problems faced on site, it became clear too that Roadbuilders as a whole were encountering difficulties. According to the Sub-agent, the company was experiencing a cash-flow crisis: it was not helped by performance on this project, although it was attributed mainly to difficulties being experienced on another of the firm's large projects. The full scale of the crisis only unfolded towards the end of the second week that I was there, when it emerged that the Quantity Surveyor who had been seconded to the site from head office had been sacked and replaced; and that this was one result of a 'shake-up' amongst senior financial management.

Whether as cause or consequence of these changes, relationships amongst members of the contractor's site management team had changed substantially too, and the 'morale' on site could only be described as being low. The relatively buoyant working and social atmosphere I had earlier encountered had given way to one in which virtually everyone complained of a lack of communication and coordination at work between team members, and of dissatisfaction at the change in the 'climate' on site. Occasional and largely half-hearted 'niggles' between production and engineering staff I had noticed on my first visit had developed into major bones of contention: one manager, for instance, described their weekly coordination meetings as being rather more like post-mortems. The 'gap' that had been noted between senior and junior management staff now appeared to have developed into something of a chasm: the new Works Manager, who was the most outspoken on the conditions he saw on site, complained of senior management having virtually 'divorced themselves' from the work. Working relationships with members of the client's site management team had ceased to be an issue, except insofar as having to 'cope' with what was seen by many to be their more organized approach created additional pressures for Roadbuilders in their contractual relationship.

For my own part, these conditions meant that I had to be even more careful not to cause any disruption or 'aggravation'. While people had got accustomed to my being around, and were more than willing to talk to me about the problems that were being faced, it meant that a good many of the comments made were in the form of analyses of the situation for which 'someone was to blame'. It is much too grand of me to claim that in that situation I wore the hat of 'counsellor' in the passive sense of listening and empathizing. However, I did do rather a lot of sympathetic listening to catalogues of problems, and suggested reasons for them and possible solutions.

Another point is that I too could easily have slipped into the reverse role of key informant: at one point the site engineer half-jokingly pointed out that it was lucky I was there since I could keep the Sub-agent informed of what had happened during the previous week. On another occasion over lunch he asked me some basic facts and figures about the head office organization, since he was thinking of leaving the firm and setting up his own business. Although he had only joined the firm immediately prior to this contract, I found the fact that he did not have this information somewhat surprising and perhaps symptomatic of the quality of communications in the firm at the time.

During this last visit I was less reliant upon the chance events that had characterized my first visit, since the issues were much more salient and explicit – it was very difficult not to notice what was going on. I pursued the same tactics of following specific leads and opportunistically seeking interviews and comments where I could. One of these leads led to an interview with the Assistant RE, shortly before I left the site. He gave his own interpretation of the problems being experienced on that site, and finished by predicting that Roadbuilders would probably be bankrupt by the following Christmas. His prophecy was nearly correct: the firm was put into voluntary liquidation some eight to nine months before the project's completion, and so its involvement on the RAW project came to an end. I had hoped to be able to revisit the site at a later stage in its development. However, this turn of events made it impossible. It had been a depressing outcome, as well as being a somewhat complicated start to my career as a researcher.

Themes

As I mentioned earlier, the RAW project was somewhat untypical of the five case studies in the pattern of fieldwork I undertook, and because it was the first exploratory study. However, the methodological themes that should have emerged from this account were common to the four other cases. Some of these themes will be more obvious than others. The more obvious ones, which will be briefly discussed first, concern the methods used in the field, and are pertinent to the in-depth study of organizations in general. The less obvious themes, and those which take centre stage in this chapter, concern the type of setting I encountered, with its implications for the study of project organizations in particular, and perhaps wider ramifications for the study of organizations in general.

The first more obvious point to make is that the process of obtaining access to the site was very much a pragmatic one. Because I was not trying to draw any statistical generalizations from my data, the parameters for selection of the cases were very broad, and the need for systematic sampling of any description was obviated. Indeed the final sample of five cases were very different types of project in many respects: the only features that they had in common were that they were all fairly large-scale new construction projects on formerly vacant sites in England. The availability of personal contacts, and the ease of negotiating access and obtaining the agreement of all the main parties concerned, therefore formed the main criteria for case selection. However, the cases did differ to some extent in *which* organization was the initial point of contact: in the RAW and two other cases, an initial introduction to the project and its participants was gained through the main contracting firm; in the two remaining cases it was through the client's design team. Given the fact that the type of information and accounts I obtained were often phrased – like in the RAW project – in terms of the responsibility or 'blame' of other parties for current problems, it put a strong onus upon me to ensure that it was understood that I was a neutral and independent observer, and that this stance was maintained. Generally, I believe that I was successful in getting this across, although it did involve constant and strenuous efforts on my part. Furthermore, what can also perhaps be gleaned from the above case description is that the need to get across my neutrality and independence was by no means lessened when it came to exploring intraorganizational issues.

The second theme that should emerge concerns the element of method-ological pragmatism in the field: the importance of opportunism, and not a little luck in happening to be there at the right time at the right place. Many issues that are important in the study of organizations and their management (for example conflict) occur only sporadically and in relation to specific events. In order to get a fuller understanding of the *dynamics* of the process (rather than, say, rely upon respondents to classify a situation as more or less conflict-free), it is helpful to be able to witness these events in 'real time'. As such you become very much dependent upon chance events and encoun-ters in the field. The element of opportunism comes in being able to follow up the leads that emerge, in order to get a more complete understanding and reach a coherent explanation of these events – whether or not the accounts you obtain coincide or conflict. This requires a more reactive (rather than preplanned) approach to what are essentially *emergent* and developing conditions in the field. The choice of informants to interview becomes dependent upon individuals' roles in relation to specific issues and events. Also, in the interviews themselves, the particular line of questioning becomes influenced by the nature of the responses given to particular questions. In turn the answers that you derive may prompt new lines of enquiry, and the circle of interdependence continues. With this approach there are attendant, more practical problems, that centre upon controlling the course of unstructured interviews and the range of topics addressed, without losing potentially valuable information. Simply taking notes becomes a difficult enough exercise; however, you are also involved to some extent in *analysing* the data as you go along. This type of approach puts a considerable onus upon the judgments you make in the field. It also tends to mean that the pattern of interviewing varies considerably: in my study the 'interviews' I conducted varied in length from ten minutes to three hours; they also ranged in type from semi-structured interviews to informal chats. Also, some people were interviewed more frequently than others, depending upon whether or not they emerged as key figures in the issues and events I was exploring.

A more general point is that the problem you are left with then is in being able to assert the full *reliability* of the methods used. According to Yin (1984, chapter 2), achieving reliability depends upon ensuring that the operations involved in the study could be repeated with the same results. However, to the extent that a more reactive approach is used, then being able to assert full reliability becomes an impossibility since the operations involved depend upon the particular circumstances and events that occur within that case study. A more reactive and unstructured type of approach is a double-edged sword: on the one hand, it yields valuable information and insights in a way in which a more preplanned and structured approach does not; on the other, you lose the benefits of a more or less exactly comparable database that you would otherwise have obtained using the latter approach.

A third theme concerns the role of the respondent as key informant. Such a role is important in organizational research, since often it is impractical to interview everyone concerning a specific issue (say, for instance, the degree of specialization within the firm). I found that even in a comparatively 'small' organization such as the RAW case, I nevertheless had to rely upon an extensive number of key informants to gain information about specific aspects of the work (for example stock control and accounting procedures). When it came to a hint of anything that could remotely be described as 'attitudinal data' I also found that, even in an organization this small, the meanings, salience and interpretation of circumstances and events varied markedly between those I was interviewing. Given practical limitations, you need to strike a balance: by assessing the relative merits of getting a deep and coherent insight into a certain issue from a key informant as 'representative' of one group (e.g. department or organization), against getting a multiplicity of views from various members of the same group. The tactics I pursued in the field tended to follow more closely the latter line. However, I used both tactics, depending upon the issue in hand and how I interpreted the respective validity of alternative approaches. Again, a lot depended upon the judgment I exercised on the ground.

A fourth theme to emerge is the importance of the social relationships that develop between researcher and researched. Like other communities (cf. Newby, 1977), the organizational community is a social network in which operate a myriad of psychological, social and political undercurrents. In entering this network to study the organization in depth, you become personally involved through the contacts that you make within it. It is not an easy task then to strike the balance that is needed between close, direct involvement on the one hand, and mentally distancing yourself from the situation on the other. Moreover not coming fully clean with your respondents (to avoid breaking confidentialities), eavesdropping (to gather leads), and generally being instrumental in 'using' the situation for your own ends create additional stresses which are not as salient if they occur in the false social setting of the laboratory. The point that is often missed about research in the real-life social setting of an organization is that many of the methods that are useful for obtaining reliable and valid case data rely upon some degree of cunning, deviousness, opportunism and persistence on the part of the researcher. Wearing the hat of 'student researcher' may help to resolve the dissonance this may engender; however, essentially it is to some extent part of an act.

Finally, although I did not directly address this theme, some mention needs to be made of the analysis of the data that I ended up with. Certainly I found this to be the most difficult part of the whole process. Partly this was due to the simply overwhelming mass of descriptive detail, anecdotes, general observations, and diverse views and opinions. Simply ordering and classifying this information proved an horrendous task: richness of detail may be the *raison d'être* of such an approach; however, it is also the *bête noire* when it comes to collating and 'coding' the information. If these tasks were difficult, the process of analysis was even more so. Apart from a basic databank of descriptive information about each case, I had gathered a multitude of stated views and opinions that offered causal explanations, general theories and holistic interpretations of events on each case – from various perspectives, in relation to specific as well as general events, and (often) at different points in time. The issues raised in these 'clusters' of data were to form the analytical 'core' of my inter-case analysis. Disentangling them in order to come to some coherent and analytically valid interpretation of circumstances and events across each case – while allowing for conflicting perspectives – meant that in fact I began the analysis of my dataset as a whole with an analysis of circumstances and events on each case. An awful lot of time was spent in: disaggregating factors and effects that had been identified in lengthy accounts; preserving the sense of their meaning to those who had described them and the contexts in which they had been given; cross-checking accounts for sources of (non-)corroboration; and developing counter-explanations based on different accounts. The process was a laborious and complex one to say the least. However, it was necessary in order to allow me to assert the validity of the case data I had collected.

The variable organization

The perhaps less obvious themes that emerge from the earlier account raise possibly the most important methodological constraints and contingencies facing those interested in studying the phenomenon of project-based forms of organization. It is simply the fact that the type of setting is not only *temporary*, but also subject to considerable *change* as circumstances develop through the various stages of the total project cycle. In a number of important ways this marks out the study of project organizations from research in more stable, routine and permanent types of setting which could be generally described as relatively more 'ongoing' in nature. This distinction has a number of important, and sometimes quite subtle, methodological implications.

The first problem is in being able to cope with the variable boundaries of the focal organizational group over time. The RAW case, as I pointed out, was one in which the organization changed somewhat in the four months between the two blocks of fieldwork. Changes to the internal organization of the site management team occurred, notably the secondment of the Works Manager, but also in the numbers of tradesmen and labourers that were employed directly by the firm as the work increased in its intensity. Moreover the course of events prompted the more direct involvement of head office-based staff, who had hitherto acted rather more at arm's length distance from the site. With these changes to the organization, it was not only the case that the pattern of key informants and key figures was likely to change, but also that perspectives on the organization itself were bound to differ – simply because the organization was different. What was also significant in this respect was the turnover in the subcontractors employed between stages of the work. Not only was it the case that different types of task were undertaken at various points in time, but also that different groups of individuals were performing them. In the study as a whole I found that the number and range of subcontractors, and their episodic and temporary involvement, created considerable problems in being able to explore fully and systematically the issues I wanted to examine. In one case, for example, a total of about forty subcontractors were involved over an eighteen-month period, at varying stages and for varying lengths of time: at any one point in time there were likely to be between ten and twelve subcontractors on site. In the event, I interviewed representatives from at least two subcontracting firms from each site. The various perspectives that they held, and the variable baselines against which they set their perspectives (i.e. the work they were doing), added an extra dimension to the process of analysis. The general point to be made here is that at different points in time, corresponding to different stages in the construction process, a different organizational (and multi-organizational) grouping existed.

The second point to make is that, at the start of the job, the organization was to all intents and purposes *new*. The site management team was comprised of a group of individuals who had been, variously, transferred from other sites, seconded from head office, or even recruited by the company specifically to work on that project. Some had worked together before, but not all, and the group as a whole was one that had not previously existed in its own right. The point here is that working and social relationships within the team developed as the job progressed on site. (The same of course applies to relationships with subcontractors and members of the client's team, in the wider project organization.) The observations I made in the early stages of the RAW project were all about early adjustments that were being made in the pattern of working and social relationships. The 'gap' in attitudes that occurred between members of the team had at that time been perceived and expressed, but had not yet developed into the 'chasm' that was to characterize relationships amongst the team later on. The direction that those developments took – towards the emergence of a less, rather than more, cohesive group – was influenced by the train of events on that project. However, the basis for this development was in the fact that members of the team were initially to some extent unfamiliar with one another and with others' different ways of working. Many people I have since spoken to about construction management have made it clear that this 'leaning curve' effect is an important factor. The general point here is that such a situation contrasts with the comparatively stable group settings found in other types of organizational context. It forces one to take into account the developmental dynamics of the organizational group over time, and the fact that basic features of working and interpersonal relationships may differ markedly between stages of the project's, and therefore of the group's, development.

A third and closely related point is that attitudes and perspectives change as the situation develops, and as the frame of reference for judging the situation broadens out. On the RAW case, for example, it is not difficult to predict that, had I administered a set of attitude scales to measure job satisfaction on both occasions, the answers given would have differed considerably. Static performance measures too would have given a poor indication of what was happening had not efforts been made to chart the changes that occurred over the comparatively brief period of time in which events took a dramatic turn for the worse. The problem with a developing and fast-changing situation such as that found on a construction project is in being able to capture such changes through allowances made in the methodology that is employed.

My own research used a longitudinal strategy to help explore change, and because of this and the nature of the study, there was no great need to standardize points of entry in time for each case to ensure an exact basis for comparability between them. Also there were practical difficulties in being able to gain access to sites at comparable stages of development, and to follow through to completion projects whose duration well outlasted the time period available for fieldwork. The periods of fieldwork in relation to each of the five case study project cycles are illustrated in Figure 2.3. As can be seen from the diagram, the points of entry varied, as did the periods of time spent visiting each case. This type of variation gives rise to two important methodological implications – particularly when comparisons are made between the three projects that were followed through to completion, and the two that were not. First, retrospective rather than 'real-time' commentary and accounts formed an important part of the database – with all its attendant potential problems of selective recall, *post hoc* rationalization, and respondents simply forgetting details. Although retrospective commentary was particularly important on the two projects where I began the fieldwork at a comparatively late stage, it was also important on the other projects, since in no case had I been present during their very early stages. The importance of this issue for studies of project management is simply that understanding the present often depends crucially upon taking into account the immediate past. Such an historical perspective may be important in the study of other types of organizational setting. But the time scale for comparisons is probably less likely to be as short (possibly a matter of weeks) as that which is relevant to the study of events in the organization and management of a project.

Second, perspectives change. In the projects I studied at late stages in the project cycle and through to their completion, a more 'global' frame of reference was used to describe circumstances and events on those projects: the frame of reference was the entire project, rather than a particular (albeit lengthy) stage of its development. The difference was particularly noticeable when it came to views and opinions concerning performance: the difference was between situations in which performance outcomes had been, or were in the process of being, realized, and those in which actual performance was

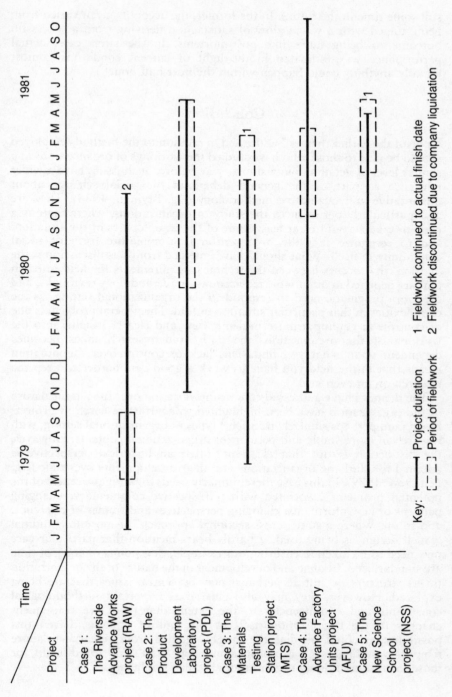

Figure 2.3 *Project durations and periods of fieldwork*

Key:
- ——— Project duration
- [- - -] Period of fieldwork
- 1 Fieldwork continued to actual finish date
- 2 Fieldwork discontinued due to company liquidation

Time / 1979 / 1980 / 1981
(J F M A M J J A S O N D)

Project:

Case 1: The Riverside Advance Works project (RAW)

Case 2: The Product Development Laboratory project (PDL)

Case 3: The Materials Testing Station project (MTS)

Case 4: The Advance Factory Units project (AFU)

Case 5: The New Science School project (NSS)

still some time in the future. In the former, the accounts given varied from being tinged with a warm glow of satisfaction deriving from a successful outcome to being more like post-mortems. In the latter case, actual performance was estimated in the light of current conditions: almost literally anything could happen within the next half hour!

Conclusion

None of the earlier themes I addressed in relation to the methods employed should be new to those who have studied the workings of organizations at a similar level of detail and in a similar way before. Such issues have a wider relevance as part of the general debate in the social sciences about quantitative and qualitative methodology (e.g. Bryman, 1984). They are also particularly pertinent to the study of organizations, where there is a need to take account of at least some of the complexities of the situation, and to recognize that the organization is a miniature form of social community in itself. What should have emerged from this discussion is the 'tension' that occurs between the technical requirements for field research that are depicted in often sanitized accounts in methodology textbooks, and the more pragmatic need to respond to the organizational setting, as the complexities in that particular situation unfold. The general problem is one of control: in gaining a more in-depth view and clearer insights into the working of the organization, the path your research takes becomes dependent upon what you find. This lack of control over the situation means that in the field you have to work a good deal harder to keep the research on an even keel.

The themes I have addressed concerning variation over time in the nature of the organization have been highlighted to contrast research in project-based (and perhaps similarly transient) types of organizational setting, with research in more stable and permanent organizational contexts. However, the distinction is not that clear-cut: often an historical perspective is adopted for studying organizations and their developments over time (e.g. Pettigrew, 1979). In this case there similarly needs to be an awareness of the potential problems associated with retrospective commentary, changing patterns of key informants, changing perspectives and frames of reference, and so on. Where a static, cross-sectional approach (or more longitudinal 'panel' design) is being used, it hardly bears mention that particular care may need to be taken in ensuring, for example, that points of entry in time are standardized. Change and development in the nature of the organization (in its structure or culture perhaps) may be central issues that are being explored. However, they may also emerge as important methodological constraints and contingencies to the extent that there are consequent changes to the organization itself as the unit of analysis. Given this possibility, it could be that the insights gained from research in more temporary settings such as construction may offer food for thought for those interested in doing organizational research in general.

3

GETTING IN, GETTING ON, GETTING OUT, AND GETTING BACK

David Buchanan, David Boddy and James McCalman

The art of the possible

The aim of this chapter is to offer the student new to research practical advice on the conduct of fieldwork in organizations. This advice draws on our experience of case study fieldwork in a range of organizations since 1980.[1] The aims of this research have been to develop our understanding of the nature and sources of the organizational changes that accompany contemporary technical change, and to examine how these patterns of change affect the roles and relationships of technology users and managers. We have explored personal perceptions of and reactions to change through interviews and observation, and have attempted to identify longer-term patterns of change through analysis of company documents of different kinds. It is to this type of research setting that the following discussion is primarily addressed.

We will examine in particular issues concerned with negotiating research access to organizations, establishing effective relationships with respondents, withdrawing from those relationships, and returning to an organization to follow up aspects of previous findings. These are issues which we have found central to the effectiveness of our work, and which can present the researcher new to this area with apparently insurmountable difficulties. They are issues which are not adequately covered in conventional texts which concentrate on epistemological, theoretical and procedural issues and often ignore the practical matter of conducting research of this kind. Scott (1965) offers a comprehensive guide to the more conventional issues; Burgess (1984a) also covers these topics, and supports the argument of this chapter by advocating flexibility and multiple strategies in fieldwork.

The main argument of this chapter is that the researcher should adopt an *opportunistic* approach to fieldwork in organizations. Fieldwork is permeated with the conflict between what is theoretically desirable on the one hand and what is practically possible on the other. It is desirable to ensure representativeness in the sample, uniformity of interview procedures, adequate data collection across the range of topics to be explored, and so on. But the members of organizations block access to information, constrain the time allowed for interviews, lose your questionnaires, go on holiday, and join other organizations in the middle of your unfinished study. In the conflict between the desirable and the possible, the possible always wins. So whatever carefully constructed views the researcher has of the nature of social science research, of the process of theory development, of data collection methods, or of the status of different types of data, those views are constantly compromised by the practical realities, opportunities and constraints presented by organizational research.

This argument is based on the view that doing research is a different kind of enterprise from thinking and writing about research. It is now widely accepted that research accounts in academic journals depart considerably from the research practices of their authors. They offer instead a 'reconstructed logic' (Silverman, 1985, p. 4) which brings the illusion of order to what is usually a messy and untidy process. We do not wish to propose that theoretical and epistemological concerns are not relevant. On the contrary, the debates surrounding these issues are central to our understanding of the nature of social science and the value of its findings. What we wish to stress is that a preoccupation with these concerns is *disabling*; the researcher who strives to tie up loose theoretical ends and firmly tighten the nuts and bolts of the methodology is more likely never to begin research.

One of our first studies in the 'new technology' area (Buchanan and Boddy, 1982b) illustrates this opportunistic approach. In 1980, we had several management students working on projects, for their master's degrees, examining the organizational changes that accompanied the use of new computing technologies. We decided to pursue these issues ourselves and started to look for suitable research sites.

One day early that year, over lunch in a real ale bar in Glasgow, a friend made a casual enquiry about our research. On discovering our interest, he suggested that we study his own company, which was based in an office block on the other side of the street, and which was developing a large (by 1980 standards) word-processing system. We then discussed what the company might be prepared to let us do, and the research design was settled over a mixed grill and two pints of beer.

The following week, after a couple of telephone calls and an exchange of letters, we met the manager responsible for the new system to explain what we wanted to do. In that meeting, it became clear that we should interview the head of the new word-processing section. The manager discovered that the section head was free, and our first interview with him started there and then. The following Tuesday, we went back to the manager to make arrangements to interview the typists who used the system. We were anticipating problems and delays with this, but the manager suggested that as the computer system was going to be shut down on Wednesday for maintenance, we could come back tomorrow at lunchtime and interview our first batch of video typists. He also asked if we would like to see the minutes of the working party which had decided how to install the system, and he produced from his drawer figures charting the performance of the company's typists since 1975. With this level of cooperation the research was completed very quickly.

The published account of this study implies that the research questions were based on a prior assessment of the literature and that the research design and methods were selected as most appropriate in this context. We did have some knowledge of the existing literature in this area, and we had a rough outline of the issues that we felt should be covered. But we had no time to conduct a systematic literature review. We felt that the qualitative case approach was appropriate, but had no opportunity to explore other approaches. We had no time to design and pilot interview schedules, which were hastily sketched out the morning before we started.

The practice of field research is the art of the possible. It is necessary to exploit the opportunities offered in the circumstances. If, when setting up a study, you ask to speak to someone who you have learned is likely to be a key informant, and your contact discovers that this informant can give you half an hour of his time immediately, you cannot reply, 'sorry, but I need a month to review the literature and pilot my questionnaire.' One strategy for dealing with the 'instant interview' is to explain your interest and ask your informant what questions he or she thinks you should ask. Or you can 'design' your interview schedule while your respondent gets you a coffee, and worry later about the epistemological issues which this may raise.

This particular study gave us fresh ideas and insights into the field. We would argue strongly that the opportunistic approach was appropriate and did not invalidate the findings. We would argue further that many published research accounts conceal similar stories of luck and bluff.

The frame of reference necessary for deciding on a research topic and writing up the results is quite different from the frame appropriate when working in the field. It is necessary to know in advance what the theoretical issues and problems are likely to be, especially if a tutor or an examiner or a journal referee is likely to quiz you about them afterwards. It is also necessary to interpret data and qualify conclusions in the light of how the data were obtained. Theoretical, philosophical and epistemological concerns are important, but they have to be clearly bracketed for the purposes of practical field research.

This opportunistic approach is supported by wider trends. Research access has become more difficult to obtain, for at least two reasons. First, further education has widely recognized the value of project work across a range of courses and many organizations have been deluged with requests for research access. We have been denied access in some cases only because someone else got there first. Second, as the economic climate has become harsher, in the private and public sectors, managers increasingly feel that they and their staffs have little time to devote to non-productive academic research activities. These trends encourage the organizational researcher to become more innovative, devious and opportunistic in the search for sites and data.

Getting in

Negotiating access to organizations for the purposes of research is a game of chance, not of skill. This section offers advice on how the odds which are normally stacked against the researcher can be improved in his or her favour. This is, however, also a game with few rules and an opportunistic approach is again recommended. We would like to offer five specific pieces of advice on negotiating access. First, allow for this to take time. Second, use friends and relatives wherever possible. Third, use non-threatening language when explaining the nature and purpose of your study. Fourth, deal positively with respondents' reservations with respect to time and confidentiality. Fifth, offer a report of your findings.

In our word-processing study, we secured access within a week. That is not typical. Gallie (1978) reported that he spent nine months getting permission to do case study research in a British oil-refining company. Our first approach to a computer manufacturing company was in May 1983 and we were finally granted access in July 1985. The researcher is dependent on the goodwill of organizational 'gatekeepers'. This dependency creates risks that are beyond the control of the researcher and which are difficult to predict or avoid.

Goodwill is fragile. We successfully negotiated access in 1981 to a local whisky blending and bottling company to study their applications of computerized process controls. We negotiated our way through the appropriate management hierarchy, and we then secured the agreement of trade union representatives. Local management, however, as a matter of routine notified the company's main board in London of our study, and they stopped it, against the wishes and advice of our local contacts.

The research timetable must therefore take into account the possibility that access will not be automatic and instant, but may take weeks and months of meetings and correspondence to achieve. The researcher must also be prepared for disappointment where the time and effort in making and following through an approach to an organization are wasted.

There is no conventional or standard way in which to approach an organization to ask for research access. We have been most successful where we have had a friend, relative or student working in the organization. That person can either arrange access themselves, depending on their position, or they can speak for and introduce you to someone else in the organization who can do this. We have been less successful with 'cold calls', either through the post or over the telephone. We would also argue that it is not necessary, and in many cases not desirable, to 'go in at the top'. Chief executives can be difficult to contact, impossible to meet, and often delegate 'academic liaison' decisions. Our contact with one company arose from a job advertisement, through which we discovered that they were introducing computerization, because they wanted to recruit a systems engineer, and which gave the name of the engineering manager responsible.

It is tempting to write or speak to managers with requests to carry out research in their organizations, by conducting interviews, the results of which you hope eventually to publish. The language of this approach is threatening and dull and we have found that a shift in wording can be more effective. We now tell potential respondents that we want to learn from their experience by talking to them and that we will write an account of our work, which they will see. The contents of a research proposal are also usually dull and threatening. When asked to state research aims in writing, we do so on one page only, ensuring that while accurate and clear it reveals as little detail as possible.

The terms 'research' and 'interview' have strong negative connotations, as to the public at large they imply surveys and questionnaires. Most people outside social science, and that includes most managers, have a stereotyped notion of the survey which involves time-consuming sequences of questions which combine the obscure and boring with the intimate and threatening. The media regularly reinforce this stereotype. Interviews may be associated with television practice where interviewees are regularly and systematically exposed and humiliated, or the term may imply a cold and impersonal procedure which discourages volunteers.

The term 'publish' also carries potentially threatening and negative connotations. To many people, this implies that commercial secrets and personal revelations will be revealed in the *Guardian* within the week. It is not widely appreciated that the lead time for publication in an academic journal can be between one and two years, and that the same applies to books. The language of 'research', 'interview' and 'publish' should therefore be avoided when negotiating research access.

Most people are flattered by reasonable requests to talk about themselves, and to pass on their experience, where they know it will be used in an academic context, to help with a project or on educational courses. The opportunity to reflect on one's working life systematically and to extract valuable lessons for others can be an extremely satisfying, but rarely experienced, process.

We thus use 'learn from your experience', 'conversation', and 'write an account', in place of 'research by interview leading to publication'. We usually ask for an opportunity to present our research request to interested organization managers. These presentations cover five main issues: our university base, our research aims, the ways in which we intend to collect the information we need (through conversation, observation and available documents) and the output which we hope to produce, including a report for the organization, teaching materials for us on our courses, and possibly academic papers. We also attempt to clarify the role in which we will be acting. To get cooperation from all levels in an organization, and not just from management gatekeepers, it is important to be seen as a neutral outside observer and not as a consultant or management agent.

The two most common reservations which can block research access concern time and confidentiality. Access will not be granted where it is felt that normal operations are likely to be disrupted, and where commercially sensitive material is likely to be disclosed. Gatekeepers in organizations often have views on these matters quite different from the expectations of researchers. The researcher thus has to respond positively to such fears, reservations and questions.

We have tried to develop strategies which anticipate and overcome these reservations. First, we make a point of trying to raise such objections before they are presented to us, and to indicate that we have successfully dealt with them in previous studies without difficulty. There are several ways of dealing with the complaint that work will be disrupted. Conversations (that is, interviews) can be held during lunch periods, or in the evenings, with the permission of those involved. We have also been asked to interview employees in pairs to save time, a procedure which has obvious dangers but which with care can generate a debate between respondents who qualify and elaborate each other's responses. Some individuals can speak to a researcher while working; we have used such non-participant observation and interviewing on several occasions, particularly in factories.

There are also several ways of dealing with the complaint that sensitive information will be disclosed, and again we try to raise and deal with this issue before it is presented to us. The first points that we make are that, to protect our reputation and goodwill, a report of our study will come first to the organization, at which stage we ask respondents to indicate sensitive information. The rationale for this is that if we are seen to be publicizing commercial secrets, we will have problems with future research access to other organizations.

Some methodological purists may complain that this procedure gives respondents censorship rights over research findings. This is correct, but is not particularly important, for the following reasons. First, we have normally found respondents more concerned with the accuracy of our accounts than with their sensitivity. One manager, for example, read our account, agreed that it was accurate, and commented that we had, 'said some fucking rotten things about this company', before consenting to the use of the company name in publications. Second, we have often found that constraints are relaxed as the study proceeds, as respondents learn more about how their information is going to be used, and as a closer relationship of mutual trust and understanding is established. In other words, the concern with confidentiality can reflect respondents' lack of knowledge of the research process and usually dissipates in the course of the study.

When negotiating access it is helpful to offer a tangible product in return for cooperation. Typically, this is a report of the findings in a form useful to the recipients (not a draft of your forthcoming conference paper). Given the opportunity, many gatekeepers can offer useful advice on the content of such an end of study report, advice which can usefully guide the research work and its overall aims. We will return below to the nature and content of such feedback reports.

Getting on

The nature of the relationship between researchers and researched is a topic that has attracted a lot of commentary and analysis. Here we will focus on two aspects of that relationship which are not often explored but which we have found important. The first of these concerns the highly personal relationship established with respondents. The second concerns the nature and use of feedback.

Once research access to an organization has been negotiated successfully, it then becomes necessary constantly to renegotiate access to the lives and experiences of the individual members of that organization. 'Getting on' with respondents is fundamental to the quantity and quality of data collected. The permission of senior management, a letter of introduction, and academic affiliation, do not themselves achieve sustained levels of cooperation. Respondents must be satisfied in two respects. First, they must understand the aim of the study and feel that they can contribute to it. Second, they must feel that the researcher is trustworthy, and has a genuine desire to listen to what they have to say.

The success of this renegotiated access depends on the *personality* of the researcher. The standard advice to the interviewer covers basic skills and procedures, such as adopting styles of appearance and speech appropriate to the setting, and responding in a non-evaluative and non-partisan manner to requests for comment and advice. There are numerous sources dealing with research interview types, or the conduct of a participation observation study. The social and interpersonal skills involved have been examined in depth and these can be learned with practice.

We use the term personality here to mean the individual's characteristic ways of thinking, feeling and behaving. However, the researcher, as an individual with needs, interests and preferences, is usually missing from conventional, 'technical' accounts of the interview. The personality and preferences of the researcher are typically overlooked, but are central to the progress of fieldwork. The interpersonal skills required in research interviewing can be taught or acquired through experience. But these skills must be deployed in the context of the researcher's genuine desire to learn about the lives of respondents. They are of limited value where they are used mechanically, as a guide to the sequence of steps to be worked through, or to different types of questions and modes of speech.

One personality prerequisite for dealing with the demands of organizational research is therefore a sincere curiosity about the lives and experiences of others. It is difficult to conduct this type of research successfully without such a disposition. The skilled, but mechanical, approach is likely to ignore the many apparently trivial remarks and passing comments in the interview which if pursued could lead to further insights and improved understanding. The researcher has to be attentive and ready to put the interview guide aside when such occasions arise. You cannot sustain this degree of attention unless you *enjoy* this kind of work.

A second personality prerequisite concerns the deployment of interpersonal skills that establish the close relationship with respondents necessary to elicit personal, and potentially sensitive and embarrassing, information. If the research interview is to last for half an hour, this intimate relationship must be struck rapidly, and the researcher must have the skill and motivation to achieve this.

This argument does not negate the importance of social skills. But the researcher who is not *comfortable* in this type of setting, whose dispositions and preferences lie elsewhere, would be better advised to use other research approaches. The survey questionnaire can be a comforting mechanism which puts considerable physical and psychological distance between researchers and their respondents.

The organizational researcher has to ask personal questions of strangers, and seek opinions and descriptions of feelings and experiences that many people have not even considered discussing with close friends and relatives, and on occasion have not systematically explored for themselves. Members of organizations speak from positions of comparative power, influence and vulnerability, and the researcher may seek information that could potentially compromise those positions. Respondents often demand answers that would require researchers to take sides in disputes, or to reveal information gathered in confidence.

Interviewing skills thus have to be supported by considerable interpersonal sensitivity. The researcher has to do more than follow rules and procedures. Stephenson and Greer (1981) argue that researchers must be alert to the problem of ignoring data because of the 'ordinariness' of the contexts and conversations in which it arises. As well as remaining alert to the stream of data which presents itself, it is necessary to communicate enthusiasm both for the subject being studied and for what the respondent may have to say about it. It is often useful to attempt to establish common ground with an interviewee, through casual conversation about mutual friends and interests, and to achieve this in a natural and not in a contrived manner. From his experience of organizational research in America in the 1940s, Blum (1952, p. 38) argued for self-disclosure:

At the preliminary stages of the fieldwork, interviews were administered in the usual fashion. But in the attempt to create a permissive atmosphere I found myself becoming involved in a conversation during which I told the interviewee several things out of my own life. This departure from the regular interview procedure led to a notable change in atmosphere and a greater facility in obtaining information.

Blum calls his interviews 'interview-conversations'; similarly, Burgess (1984a) speaks of 'interviews as conversations'. This approach should not be regarded as an irregular departure from 'the usual fashion'.

We usually ask each organization to nominate a 'link' person through whom our arrangements to meet interviewees, and collect appropriate documents, can be made. The link need not be a senior manager, but a person who can monitor and report on our progress to the gatekeepers who allowed us access. The link becomes a useful administrative mechanism, but is also a valuable source of information. Does such a close relationship with respondents compromise the objectivity of the data? Blum (1952, p. 37) also argued that the researcher 'requires a high degree of consciousness' and that:

Besides insight into personal relationships, the researcher must know something about the position of the people in the community and in the factory, the role they play, and the reactions of other people to them. Only a careful evaluation of information in the light of these factors can indicate their real meaning and significance as research data.

There are at least three responses to those who argue that close relationships with respondents corrupt the data they disclose. First, rich information is a product of close relationships of mutual trust and respect, as numerous anthropological studies have shown. In our experience, where the relationship between the researcher and the researched is for any reason weak, the data that are grudgingly disclosed are limited. Second, attempts to use or mislead a researcher are usually transparent, and information offered in this spirit can be checked with other sources, if not discounted. Third, attempts to protect or distort information can be used as data, as indicating areas of particular sensitivity which require explanation. If the relationship between researcher and respondent is close, these problematic aspects can in some cases be raised as issues for further questioning and elaboration, although this requires judgment and tact.

One particularly difficult issue, which fortunately we have met rarely, is a manager's insistence on joining the researcher for an interview with another person. This compromises the role of the researcher and any claims to confidentiality of data. On one occasion, when we wanted to discuss our report with a group of employees, their supervisor came and sat at the back of the room, because he wanted 'to listen to what they have to say'. We asked him to leave, but he insisted that he would 'not get in the way' and that we should carry on and ignore him. We repeated the request for him to leave, which he again politely rejected. We finally asked his manager, who happened to be our 'link', to remove this intruder, who never spoke to us again. Embarrassing, but necessary.

In a study of a hospital laboratory, a chief scientific officer – the link – would not leave the researcher alone to interview secretaries who worked with the new computerized records system. He claimed that the secretaries had asked him to be present, but this clearly coloured their responses to questions about their opinions of the new technology: 'great system, fine, no problems'. This kind of interference demolishes the permissive atmosphere which the researcher has to create, but can be difficult to avoid, as in this second case.

Where possible, we tape record interviews, and refusals are rare. A request to record a conversation should present no difficulty where the purpose of the study is appreciated, and where respondents know that their conversations will be used in confidence and cited anonymously. Tape recorders are now reliable, 'accepted technology'. Note taking during interviews is adequate, but for our purposes does not capture the richness of the verbatim account which can be used to support and enliven reports and publications (see Mintzberg, 1979). We return a transcript of each interview to the respondent for comment. This is a highly effective procedure, for a number of reasons, but it creates problems concerning transcription and censorship.

The tape recorder appears to be the ideal interviewer's tool. Very few academics are proficient in shorthand, and very few can reconstruct conversations verbatim entirely from memory. These problems are solved by recording. In our experience, however, the tape has to be transcribed by the interviewer. We have been able to use highly competent secretaries to transcribe tapes for us. But this has proved to be highly unsatisfactory, for them and for us, for four reasons.

First, this procedure ties up vast quantities of secretarial time in a task that to someone not intimately involved in the research is indescribably boring. The opportunities for error through inability to sustain attention to the task are thus high. Second, if the sound quality is poor, someone who was not present at the interview has great difficulty in following the conversation. The interviewer, on the other hand, can reconstruct most gaps from memory. Third, the person transcribing the tape also has to be familiar with acronyms and company jargon. It has on many occasions taken us longer to correct the errors due to carelessness, poor sound and company-specific language on a transcribed tape than it would have taken us to transcribe the tape ourselves. The best way to transcribe a tape uses the technology of a dictation transcription machine and word processing. It is also possible to save time by transcribing only those portions of a conversation of particular interest – and only the interviewer can make these decisions. Whatever method is used, the ease of taping during the interview is offset by the time required to get the conversation accurately off the tape and on to paper in some form.

The fourth reason why tapes are best transcribed by the interviewer, particularly where they are to be fed back to respondents, concerns the need to 'clean up' or 'sanitize' the conversation. Our respondents know that their transcripts will be used, anonymously, to construct an account of an aspect of the organization's recent experience of technical change. It is also widely known that when people speak, they do not construct grammatical sentences that flow without repetition. Ordinary speech comprises false starts, pauses, rephrasings, and numerous odd grunts and exclamations that convey only the fact that thought is taking place before the next main utterance.

We have faced complaints from respondents who asked that these 'errors' be taken out of their accounts before being used in our reports. The two components of the typical response to the 'full' transcript is that respondents do not want their utterances to be presented in this incompetent way, and that it is the interviewer's responsibility to present the account in an 'acceptable' manner. We do not need the full clutter of a transcript designed for conversation analysis. We need an account that accurately represents and effectively communicates the statements of the interviewee. Sanitization involves minor alterations to assist that representation and communication, and does not in our view corrupt the data. The judgment involved in deciding which items in a transcript to clean up has to be that of the interviewer. The extent to which sanitization is 'common' practice may be discerned by examining the interview quotations in research reports, such as Beynon (1973), Nichols and Armstrong (1976), and Nichols and Beynon (1977).

We feed our sanitized interview transcripts, taped or based on notes, back to respondents partly as a check on the accuracy of the information, and partly as a means of sustaining our relationships with respondents, some of whom find this procedure novel and exciting. But does this feedback process influence the behaviour of respondents and contaminate the study? Discussions of these issues (e.g. Bloor, 1983) normally assume that the feedback is the 'sociological' account, written for an academic readership, perhaps for a professional journal, and using appropriate conceptual and theoretical terminology. We provide 'descriptive' feedback only, with a request to check its accuracy. If this feedback did influence behaviour in some way, the nature of that influence should be treated as further research data.

Feedback introduces censorship, which in our experience is minimal and unimportant. One example involved a report back to an organization which included this verbatim passage from a recorded interview:

He is the only person in the country that can understand his own software. But because he was in a position at the time when he was working for us to cajole people into buying and using his software, now that he has left he has got us by the short and curlies, as it were.

The person who said this agreed to this wording without comment. But a more senior manager in the organization felt that his managers should not be known to be people who speak in this manner and an alternative wording was dictated over the telephone, concerning the fact that 'now that he has left, the company is dependent on his goodwill when we need help'. This level of censorship is, we feel, both typical and insignificant. Of far more importance is the number of cases where the account which we have constructed contains errors of fact, omission and interpretation, and where the feedback process has enabled us to correct these. Whatever one's view of the status of purely descriptive or narrative accounts of facets of the social and organizational world, these are useful to respondents and are useful to the researcher as a basis for further development and exploration. We will look at these issues in the following section which deals with the nature of the report of a study prepared for an organization.

Relationships with respondents in organizations must therefore foster Blum's 'permissive atmosphere'. An opportunistic approach which identifies and uses particularly cooperative informants, and which uses self-disclosure and interview feedback where appropriate, is consistent with this atmosphere, as long as the researcher is sensitive to the potential bias in single-source information and the need to cross-check. There are numerous ways in which the researcher can exploit the neutral, 'outsider' role of 'professional stranger' in an organization (Agar, 1980) to obtain information about its members, their relationships, and their behaviour.

Getting out

The best strategy for withdrawal from an organizational research site is to agree, and to keep, to a deadline for the data collection. The amount of information that can be gathered concerning an organization and its members is potentially infinite. It can therefore be difficult for the researcher to decide finally to leave the organization, to gather no more information, and to begin the process of analysing and documenting what data have been collected. This can be an awkward psychological leap, as there is always the possibility, usually a strong probability, that vital information has been overlooked.

The process of withdrawal must however be *managed* to maintain the option of returning for further research, or for future researchers if not in the interests of the project in hand. Action that could close the site for further research must be avoided, such as failing to meet commitments in the form of a report of the study, or publishing information without the permission or knowledge of the organization.

We have normally spoken to the link in each organization to let them know that we have completed this stage of our work and that we are returning to our offices to write a report for them. It can be useful to confirm this in writing, and to set a deadline for submission of the report. One aspect of research that we have not raised explicitly is that researchers crossing the boundaries of organizations, on the way in and out, deal normally with middle and senior managers, who have standards and expectations of appropriate behaviour that are less relaxed than those prevailing in many academic institutions. Researchers who disappear without explanation may not meet those expectations. A short letter explaining the researcher's intentions and thanking staff for their cooperation is appreciated.

Research work typically has few deadlines, which is one explanation of why research output is typically late. The process of agreeing deadlines with organization managers fills this gap and helps to ensure that the work does indeed get done.

The nature and content of the report of the findings for the organization are critical to sustaining the research relationship. Our practice has incorporated two simple guidelines. First, we make a point of asking what kind of report the organization would like us to present, and prepare it separately from the account for our own use. In one company, a senior manager asked us to give him our report along with a short management report that identified five specific points for the further consideration of his management team. In another, we were granted access on condition that we documented the history of the plant and changes in work organization over the previous ten years. In neither case was the request inconsistent with our own intentions, and in both cases the research access was maintained by fulfilling these requests. The nature of the feedback requested can itself give further insights into current management preoccupations and interests.

Second, the report that we present to the organization is a descriptive, narrative account which follows the case study format on which the research is based. This is not an 'academic' document; it is not concerned with theoretical and conceptual issues, it contains no references to the literature, and it contains no criticism or evaluation unless this is contained in the conversations with respondents and is related to the purpose of the study. We regard this as a 'base document' which we ask respondents to check for factual and interpretive accuracy. This base document, once revised in the light of the feedback we receive, becomes a source of teaching materials and publications, but is not itself used for these purposes.

As argued in the previous section, this feedback process allows the information to be checked, and helps to sustain the relationship between the researcher and key staff in the organization researched. The changes we have been asked to make to documents have been slight, and have mainly concerned our errors of fact and interpretation. We have not been subjected to attempts to censor findings, although we could perhaps have been lucky in this respect. Our informants have been more concerned with the accuracy of our accounts, 'warts and all'.

We indicated at the outset that this chapter would deal with practical matters and not with theoretical issues. It is, however, appropriate here to explore briefly the status of the narrative acounts which we feed back to organizations and which form the basis of published papers. These reports, unlike individual interview transcripts, are not entirely in the words of respondents, although they are interspersed and supported with verbatim quotations. These reports, unlike scholarly papers, are not directed at theoretical issues, and arguments are not overtly expressed in sociological or psychological concepts. As accounts that lie between sociological analysis on the one hand and conversation on the other, their status is problematic. But as we have indicated, given the practical realities of producing such accounts, this dichotomy between analysis and conversation is not on inspection as clear-cut as it might appear.

The researcher must accept that such accounts are imperfect (they contain gaps and misunderstandings), frozen in time (respondents change their views), and negotiated (respondents suggest, and insist on, changes to fact, emphasis and interpretation). But in our opportunistic view, these flawed accounts are valuable because they are *useful* both to the researcher and to the respondent. Their use depends on the extent to which they are seen to be adequate, appropriate, *competent* accounts of the organization from the point of view of respondents. It is this perceived adequacy, appropriateness and competence that enables the researcher to proceed, given the caveat that claims and conclusions are always presented in the context of the limitations and imperfections of the data.

Getting back

Getting back to continue research is not necessarily simple and automatic. It is a matter for renegotiation, and once again this process has to be managed effectively. The first entry negotiation forms a 'contract' which may be perceived by organization gatekeepers to be broken by the researcher who assumes that access has been granted permanently, and not on a time-bounded basis for a specific purpose. (We are currently facing the possibility that our 'contract' with an organization, for access to pursue our research in return for a report on related themes of interest to management, will be broken by them.)

Re-entry has to be renegotiated, unless this was part of the initial arrangement, or unless the researcher is invited to continue the work for some reason. In one of our projects, we were committed to longitudinal studies of organizational experience of technical change over three years. So the possibility of further access to update our first accounts was raised in our initial negotiations. In each case, however, we were careful not to try to commit the organization over the three years of our research. We quickly found that this protracted involvement inhibited cooperation. Instead, we indicated that, if the first phase of the study went well from our point of view, we would ask managers to review our work, and seek permission to continue the research, especially if it had been of some value to them.

It may be tactful to allow time to pass before asking for further research access. Our contacts have typically been spaced at least six months apart, but the appropriate interval depends on the circumstances and the judgment of the researcher. Organizations likely to be, or likely to feel, 'over-researched', for reasons mentioned earlier, may be easier to get back into if left alone for a suitable period.

The main problem with elapsed time is of course staff loss. In one case, every manager interviewed in the first stage of our study had left by the time we returned to carry out the follow-up – with the single exception of our link. In another case our link, a fairly senior manager, left just as we were about to negotiate access for the second phase, but he was replaced by the manager through whom our contact with the organization was first established, and who was interested in our work. So in these cases we were extremely fortunate.

Our opportunistic approach uses various devious strategies for sustaining contacts in organizations which might provide useful future research sites. Friendships are sustained beyond the research work and outside the organization. (This must not be taken to imply a wholly instrumental attitude to friends and friendships on our part!) Managers can be invited to contribute to our university teaching work, as seminar leaders, guest lecturers, and conference speakers. These invitations are usually welcomed, and we generally ask managers to speak on themes and topics related to our research work. Managers are also informed of and invited to join other courses and programmes run by the university, not necessarily by our research team. It is useful to do whatever in the circumstances it appears appropriate to do, to maintain relationships with respondents. As in one of our cases, it may be over two years before these strategies prove fruitful.

The darker side of research

We have argued in this chapter for an opportunistic approach to fieldwork in organizations. This argument is based on the view that the researcher in the organization has to shift into a working context that demands modes of thought and action different from those which apply in the study or in the library.

But before this is taken to imply a 'free for all' or 'anything goes' approach to data collection, in which you get what evidence you can any way you can, let us qualify this argument and put it in context. The ultimate goal of the research enterprise is to gather empirical evidence on which theories concerning aspects of behaviour in organizations can be based. This goal determines broad methodological guidelines and ethical constraints for the conduct of research. These guidelines and constraints determine the, albeit loose, boundaries of competent and acceptable research. Activities that lie outside these boundaries have to be regarded as some other kind of enterprise, such as management consultancy. The claim for research as the art of the possible and the plea for opportunism do not therefore rule out the need for controlled, systematic, morally justifiable methods and scientific rigour.

We have in this chapter deliberately constructed a one-sided view of the research process, using our experiences in illustration, in a conscious attempt to cast light on the side of research that is often found only in the shadow of apparently more significant theoretical and methodological concerns. Some of the issues that we have raised are quite out of place in conventional research methods texts, and what is now required is a broader recognition and appreciation of these 'darker' realities of field research work.[2]

Notes

1 The current research on which this chapter draws is supported in part by the Economic and Social Research Council. Publications from this work include Buchanan and Boddy (1982a), and Boddy and Buchanan (1986).
2 Readers wishing to follow this argument in more depth may find useful the collection of papers in the special edition of the *Journal of Management Studies*, July 1983, and the discussion in Chapters 3 and 12 of Shipman (1981). Watson's well-known work, published in 1968, may be regarded as an illustration of opportunism in action in a natural science setting.

4

RESEARCHING WHITE COLLAR ORGANIZATIONS:
Why sociologists should not stop doing case studies

Rosemary Crompton and Gareth Jones

Social researchers of all varieties, but especially those committed to first-hand observation of one sort or another, face similar methodological and organizational problems concerned with the successful negotiation of access and its subsequent management. In this paper we will begin by offering some commonsensical advice on the access problem as it occurred prior to and during our research on white collar work and workers. We will then consider the problems and possibilities of carrying out fieldwork inside large white collar bureaucracies. Finally, we will attempt to relate our practical experience of extensive fieldwork to more abstract methodological and theoretical considerations. (Our research was funded by the then Social Science Research Council.)

Access

Those interested in the study of work and its organization face the problem of access in acute form. Whilst Whyte (1943) and Polsky (1971) faced difficulties in negotiating their entry to the social world of the 'corner boys' and 'the hustlers', they could at least begin their research without formal permission. We had to endure long and often unsuccessful vetting by mostly suspicious managements before we could even commence fieldwork. The problem is worse for those who carry the label 'sociologist'. Increasingly, the ill-grounded tirade from some sections of government and the media against sociology and its practitioners has made negotiating access to work organizations even harder. Some have retreated into more 'acceptable' niches – management scientist, organizational analyst. We stuck (perhaps obstinately) to 'sociologist'. These difficulties of gaining access may help to explain why in-depth empirical studies of complex organizations are still something of a rarity. Given these difficulties, are there any useful rules of thumb which may make its successful negotiation more likely?

Prior to our research on white collar workers (Crompton and Jones, 1984) we made approaches to a number of large organizations. Ideally, we were looking for one or two case studies in the finance sector, one in the public sector (probably a local authority) and one in manufacturing. We wanted to examine the clerical work in detail in a variety of settings but were especially interested in financial organizations because they had experienced both rapid expansion of employment and a high level of technological change, relevant to our interest in the changing content of clerical work. We were successful in gaining access to a large clearing bank (referred to as Southbank), a local authority (Cohall) and an insurance company (Lifeco). Despite repeated efforts we could not gain access to a manufacturing organization, which created serious difficulties when comparing our sample of clerks with both the national population and the previous major empirical study of white collar work (Stewart, Prandy and Blackburn, 1980).

What lessons can be learned from our successes and from our failures? First, it is important to make early contact with managers who are senior enough to allow access. There is nothing more galling than to spend several months in negotiation and subsequent preparation for fieldwork, only to have access denied at the last minute by a level of management you have never even met. However, it is just as important that detailed discussions are held with more junior levels as well, and the relevant unions and staff associations where they exist. Not only will unions have the power to deny access in some organizations but they may also, if they can be convinced of the utility of your project, provide crucial information which you are unlikely to obtain from 'official' sources. In all our case studies union officials and/or activists were extremely important in smoothing our way and in providing information. Sociological investigations inside organizations are very dependent on obtaining different sources of information. If any kind of critical perspective is to be developed it is essential that you do not become restricted to managerial viewpoints. This is not simply an assertion that 'objective' academic study requires you to take into account different or conflicting views of the organization but rather that you cannot begin to develop insights into the way the organization functions until you have grasped that it is viewed differently by different interest groups. Hopefully, as enquiry continues you may be able to identify the generative mechanisms of these varying perspectives. This strategy does not require that you adopt some fictitious position of value neutrality. On the contrary, if the critical intentions of sociology are to be pursued it is crucial that you observe and enquire with all of your consciousness, not with an important bit of it artificially shut off. In organizational sociology as everywhere else we may repeat C.W. Mills's remark, 'I have tried to be objective, I do not claim to be detached.'

Even if you approach the correct level of management and the relevant employee organizations you are not guaranteed success. You should utilize (or cultivate) any informal contacts within the organization that may help to promote your credibility with those who will decide the access question. (All this may sound cynical but we found on several occasions that some previous acquaintance with influential insiders proved very valuable.) Above all, prepare yourselves well for presentations to management and unions. With practice we could produce a fairly persuasive one- or two-hour presentation and field most of the awkward questions. At this stage it is essential to be honest; you should ask for all the access you think you will really need; do not try to slip in extra access later. This is not simply a moral homily but rather practical advice. Limited access may not be worth having and you can spend much time collecting data which turns out to be less than useful because you were not allowed access to some crucial area.

There is also a sense in which you require more than simple access alone; you require some kind of commitment to the project from management, employee associations and the respondents themselves. Grudging or forced access will lower your response rate and produce unwilling interviewees and elaborate interview 'performances' designed to hide as much as they reveal. It is for these reasons that you need to offer something in exchange for access. At one level this can take the form of a report which is related to an issue of organizational concern. In our experience, it is important that this is made available to management, unions and staff associations. Of course, there may be areas of sociological research which require more of a degree of subterfuge (to use a euphemism). If full access is not given to research reports, one party or other will certainly feel that the research has obtained sensitive information which should be available to all. To be honest, our reports tended towards the anodyne, containing as much 'factual' information as possible, and little discussion. Nevertheless they did offer the organizations some return.

For the respondents, you need to offer something rather different. In particular, you offer a listening ear. However this will not be achieved without clear and absolutely reliable guarantees concerning confidentiality. Various interest groups within organizations may press you on this but in our experience you improve the quality of your own data and help to enable future research if you stick resolutely to complete confidentiality. Once individuals are assured of your independence they seem, almost always, to welcome an opportunity to discuss their work, their aspirations and their discontents. Unpromising interviewing rooms can almost take on the atmosphere of the confessional! Given the continuing importance of individuals' workplace life in their overall social experiences, it is gratifying that they are prepared to spend quite a lot of time discussing it with relative strangers.

Problems of fieldwork

Let us assume that the previous commonsensical advice helps you to negotiate access and to establish the necessary rapport with your respondents. How should the research be conducted once you are in? Of course, there is no one answer to this question. The methods you choose and the research tools you develop will be related to your particular interests. Nevertheless, there may be enough commonality about researching inside organizations to support some general principles. In our case we decided to use a combination of methods involving relatively unstructured exploratory interviews, a structured self-completion questionnaire administered to a relatively large number and semi-structured interviews with a smaller number of respondents (for details see Crompton and Jones, 1984, p. 6). Our choice was guided by our particular concerns, the existing state of research in the field, previous experience, the helpful advice of colleagues working on similar problems, and time and cost constraints. No doubt most researchers work through a similar list before arriving at their choice of methods. Our point here is not to rehearse that process but to consider the opportunities which offer themselves once inside work organizations, and to convey the excitement of trying to observe and understand organizational processes.

Current organization theory makes much of the concept of organizational culture, the shared norms, values and symbols which seem specific to an organization as part of the research. Those who employ participant no. 2). Access to this area cannot be gained through the use of research methods employed at a distance, no matter how well designed the research implements are. You have to regard *all* the time you spend inside the organization as a part of the research. Those who employ participant observation techniques will already recognize this but it is important to stress that it holds just as strongly for those using more formal techniques. Organizational culture will demonstrate itself in all kinds of ways and places. For example, the organization may allow or encourage the personalization of offices. Or does it have strict, hierarchically significant official furnishings which act as signs for the status-conscious? Are there ways of dressing which suggest your aspirations in the organization? Is it all right to loosen your tie in warm weather or is this a sign of marginality? How can the tension between the genders be successfully managed? How are patriarchal relations reproduced in the minutiae of organizational life? All of these questions (and of course many others) will require that you are observing constantly. You may not make immediate sense of an observation but it is important that you record it.

We found it very useful (though exhausting) to talk through our notes with each other at the end of a day's fieldwork. This has the function of 'fixing' observations and also gives the opportunity to explore possible explanations. There is also an advantage in having mixed-gender research teams. Often more information can be gathered by having researchers who can gain informal access to 'man-' or 'womantalk'. For example, men may talk informally to another man about women who have been promoted in a way that they would not to a woman, or women may talk more freely to another woman about sexual harassment.

As we suggested at the beginning of this chapter, the point of these remarks concerning access and method is to connect fieldwork practice with the generation of sociological explanations. We would like to illustrate this connection between method and theory by working through two themes of our research: first, the attempt to classify varieties of clerical work, and second, understanding internal labour markets. Before we do this, however, we need to say something about the relationship between quantitative and qualitative research.

Issues in methodology

Much debate in sociology has concerned itself with the relative strengths and weaknesses of qualitative and quantitative methodology. The debate has often been acrimonious and generated rather more heat than light. Its origins are philosophical but its catalyst was the apparent success some social sciences like economics and psychology achieved through the use of methods developed in the natural sciences, in particular the use of certain measurement techniques. The opponents of the application of positivistic methods in sociology accused social positivism of reifying the social and becoming obsessed with measurement which turned out to be spurious. The social world, they argued, was the fragile construction of actors and had no reality *sui generis* which could be the domain of measurement. The proper subjects of sociology were the processes of constructing and maintaining the social world. These processes could only be revealed by close first-hand observation, such as that employed in participant observation. The debate (if that term can be used) even had its political analogue. The social positivists, employing quantitative methods, were accused of social engineering, of stressing determinism over free will, constraint over intention, and necessity over contingency. In heady late 1960s versions of this brew they even appeared as servants of the ruling elites. Phenomenological sociology, using qualitative methods, stressed the importance of human agency, the fragility of social structures and their reproduction in the minutiae of everyday life. Although the debate is no longer as acrimonious as hitherto (Goldthorpe, 1973) the cessation of hostilities seems to have been achieved by an agreement to differ rather than any consensus or a final solution. In contrast we would like to say, quite simply, that in organizational research it is not a mutually exclusive decision between quantitative and qualitative methodology. In reality it is very difficult to study organizations without using both sorts of methods. In any event quantitative data always rests on qualitative distinctions. We are, therefore, sceptical of research which purports to represent organizational realities but which uses market research techniques. Organizations cannot be studied at a distance. Conversely, 'organizational studies' which did not describe the structure of positions, rules and hierarchies, etc. would also be suspect, however sensitive and insightful the observers' account in other respects.

Of course, different methods are appropriate for different problems. For example, we have argued that the mechanisms of the internal labour market have organizational specificities (Crompton and Jones, 1984, chapters 3 and 4) which can best be researched using qualitative methods. The often confusing world of organizational titles can be penetrated, and the extent of real mobility more accurately assessed. However, if you wish to present evidence about the operation of internal labour markets you will have to collect some quantitative data. For example, you will need to know the average number of jobs moves made before becoming a bank manager, or the aggregate effects of post-entry qualifications on promotion. Such questions require quantitative methods. The issue turns on the appropriateness of methods, not with taking sides in the debate between qualitative and quantitative methodologies.

As we suggested, we see a connection between the way our research was conducted and the treatment of two important areas of theoretical debate. The first concerns the nature of clerical work. In its most modern form the question relates to Braverman (1974) and the 'deskilling' thesis. Braverman's work attempts to demonstrate that the historical development of capitalism imposes certain conditions on the nature of work. In particular, there is a progressive separation of conception from execution such that all labour processes under capitalism are systematically deskilled. That is, workers are robbed of control of their own actions through the use of discretion based on skill. Much of Braverman's own evidence relates to manual work but he also argues that the same process of deskilling has occurred to clerical work, being extremely critical of those 'bourgeois' social scientists (such as Lockwood, 1958) who persist in reproducing the myth of the skilled clerk. We were interested in exploring the Braverman thesis as it applied to clerical work. Of course, this is not simple; the deskilling thesis is essentially an historical one and we were taking a snapshot view of clerical work. This problem can be approached in a number of ways. First, we can use historical accounts of clerical work and there are some useful sources (Crompton and Jones, 1984, pp. 16–29). Second, we used previous sociological studies and in particular Lockwood's classic study (Lockwood, 1958). Most important of all, however, was to collect accurate data about what clerks were doing now and, where appropriate, to ask them how their work had changed. The methods that we used to tackle this question are intimately related to the conclusions we came to. Let us describe the process.

Our first practical research task, after access had been negotiated, was to focus in on the particular departments we would look at in depth. We did this with at least the intention of comparing departments using different kinds of technology, since an important vehicle for deskilling in Braverman's view is technical change. Some departments had used computerized systems for some time, others were undergoing change and some were still relatively untouched by computer-based technology. Next we interviewed managers in these departments asking them to outline the work of their departments and to describe the functions of those who worked in them. These managerial interviews proved to be quite important, not because we took them as infallible but because they sensitized us to important issues in the work flow and enabled us to ask informed questions (and especially probes) when we subsequently interviewed clerks. Finally, we interviewed 262 clerical workers. Even this is not straightforward. We had already realized that the internal gradings of the organizations did not represent unproblematic maps of the labour process. They were themselves a reflection of organizational and industrial history, trade union activity and management strategy which varied from organization to organization despite an underlying continuity in the tasks which were being performed. We had to try and move beyond them to examine the clerical and administrative organizational labels which applied to particular occupations. Such a process would be impossible without prior organizational knowledge. For example, if you simply asked organizations to distribute questionnaires amongst clerical workers it would be impossible to contextualize the information received. The organizational 'labels' reported would have to be accepted as unproblematic accounts.

About two-thirds of the interviews were conducted by us (and we made sure that we worked in all three organizations). After collecting some face-sheet data we asked our respondents to describe their work. These descriptions were recorded verbatim and we probed respondents on the basis of our previous managerial interviews. As experienced fieldworkers we felt that this was producing 'good' data. Many, many interviews later we had compiled significant amounts of this 'good' data. We had detailed descriptions of the work carried by jobs of different kinds of clerical workers. We now faced a difficulty common to many social researchers. How can we use this data by aggregating it in some way? In practical terms this turned into a question of 'to code or not to code'? We argued about this for many hours. Part of the problem was that we felt dissatisfied with the alternatives to coding. For example, the selective use of quotations to illustrate points – a kind of ethnographic salt and pepper – seemed less than satisfactory. Even though this technique is very useful in bringing life and understanding to a text we felt it needed to be used in conjunction with a method which represented all the data. In particular, if we were to test the Braverman thesis we had to provide some measurement of the skill incorporated in clerical work, and therefore aggregate the work descriptions. (Our debates were made more agonizing by our shared commitment to first-hand data gathering. One of the aspects of this is that you can take into account the *contexts* in which people reported certain features of their work. Having taken considerable trouble to collect this contextual information you are loathe to seemingly ditch it at the aggregation stage.) Our discussions, however, had a rather more satisfactory outcome than this gloomy picture may suggest. We did decide to code (detailed description in Crompton and Jones, 1984, pp. 60–2 and p. 252) and to break the work description down into types of task which we then scored initially as either present or absent and then on a three-point scale based on the extent of control exercised by the worker. The precise technical formula which we used is not our concern here; rather we want to make the point that because we had insisted on carrying out much of the fieldwork ourselves, focusing on the contexts in which the data was collected, we felt confident of handling the coding exercise. At a procedural level we should say that we did the coding itself together. This enabled us to check up on each other and to discuss difficult cases. (If we were making up '*ad hoc*' coding rules then at least we could ensure we had the same ones!)

We are not trying to claim that we were able to produce some entirely objective system of classification. The concept of skill, of course, is itself subject to theoretical dispute. Much of the critical response to Braverman's work turned on his use of the term. Therefore, the code embodied our own theoretical dispositions. For example, we took the view that the notion of skill was intimately connected to the question of control and our classification reflects this. However, handling the data in this way did enable us to address some of the empirical questions generated by Braverman's work. We were able to demonstrate that for our sample contemporary clerical work utilizes relatively little skill in Braverman's terms and that the level of skill varied with the level of computerization. In one sense at least, then, we could confirm the Braverman hypothesis (Crompton and Jones, 1984, chapter 2). That is not to say that we could, on the basis of the work description data and our own observation, conclusively resolve the debate concerning the nature of clerical work or that concerned with the automation of non-manual work. Our sample was neither large enough nor representative enough. Further, the examination of a dynamic model like Braverman's requires longitudinal data which we did not have. However, we could show that by examining the impact of computerization both between organizations and between departments within the same organization there was a clear connection with levels of skill held by clerical workers. We could also show that by comparing our data with, for example, Lockwood's (1958) account of clerical work, there had been a diminution of the skill of the clerical worker.

Our attempts to demonstrate the historical change were hindered by the scarcity of data on the nature of clerical work. With the notable exception of Lockwood we could find little that was based on a close examination of the work itself.[1] Certainly there were many a priori discussions of the situation of clerical workers, often, like Braverman, debating their alleged proletarianization, but these rarely contained anything more than fragmentary evidence. There are, it seems, methodological reasons for this. There is a long tradition in the sociology of work, deriving mainly but not exclusively from Marx, that there are significant connections between the nature of an individual's work, their life chances, and their class position. It is in precisely this tradition that Braverman's work is located and which has itself generated the 'labour process' position. We believe that this is indeed a rich area of enquiry. However, it is ultimately dependent on close and careful examination of work itself. While a set of theoretical propositions has been generated, the general paradigm rests upon empirical observation. In the main, the study of work in advanced capitalist societies means the study of work in organizational settings. We would argue therefore that advances in sociology of work should feed off detailed organizational studies, and that the sociology of organizations should not be separated from the wider sociological discussion of the impact of work on class and life chances. Equally, the development of social stratification theory, especially if it derives from the tradition described above, depends on empirical work in organizational settings. To repeat an argument we have already developed (Crompton and Jones, 1984, pp. 34–41), if the objective of 'stratification' classifications such as OPCS categories and those of the Hope-Goldthorpe scales are to 'bring together, within the classes distinguished, combinations of occupations and employment statuses whose incumbents would typically share in broadly similar market and work situations' (Goldthorpe and Payne, 1986, p. 3), then detailed case study evidence is the only reliable source of information – particularly relating to 'work situation'.[2] Certainly a considerable proportion of such work needs to be based on first-hand observation and enquiry directed by theory. In the study of clerical work the ratio of a priori reasoning to empirical enquiry was, to put it mildly, too high.

Fairly substantial theoretical schemes concerning the relations between work and class have been constructed on a relatively slight empirical base. However, our empirical research did indicate support for the overall thrust of Braverman's thesis, but it also generated certain reservations. Braverman claims that the operation of deskilling in the non-manual labour process produces 'proletarians'. We argue that the class effects of deskilling are mediated by two intimately related filters: first, the impact of gender on the structuring of clerical work, and second, the impact of gender on the operation of the internal labour markets. It is to this latter factor that we now turn to illustrate the links between theory development and method.

Before we do this we need to rehearse some of the arguments which have been mounted against Braverman and which we tried to take into account when we began our research. The first objection relates to Braverman's implicit account of capitalist strategies for exercising control over the labour process. For him, control is achieved through the separation of conception and execution and the concentration of conception in the hands of managers who act as agents of the capitalist. Deskilling, therefore, takes place in order to increase direct control over the worker. Several critics have argued that this is only one of the strategies available to the capitalist. Friedman (1977) suggests that, given the enormous potential for disruption and resistance by labour, deskilling and increasing direct control in this way can actually produce negative consequences.

One of the most developed critiques is that of the radical labour-market theorists. They argue that control may be achieved by fragmentation of the labour force through the control of the labour market (Gordon *et al.*, 1982). Rather than the labour market directly representing the various 'qualities' of those offering their labour for sale, it is structured by employers, who offer differential employment status and rewards, to divide the labour force thereby weakening concerted attempts at resistance. One particular version of this approach is of special relevance to clerical employees. Edwards (1979) argues that three forms of control can be identified in capitalist enterprises. First, 'simple control', in which the worker is directly and personally controlled by the capitalist. This form is characteristic of early forms of capitalist development or where small firms persist in competitive markets. Second, 'technical control', which is achieved through the organization of the labour process or the principles of scientific management. This amounts to control through deskilling. Third, 'bureaucratic control', which is achieved by 'embedding control in the social structure of the social relations of the workplace' (Edwards, 1979, p. 21). In practice the organization structure is turned into a finely graded hierarchy of positions. The employee is tied into the structure by the prospect of moving up this ladder of positions. Such a strategy produces control through having an organizationally committed workforce. Compliance is secured by predictable movement through an organizationally specific internal labour market. This last strategy is clearly characteristic of many large white collar bureaucracies, such as the ones we studied, and this phenomenon of mobility from clerical work is crucial to the other major critiques of Braverman and other 'proletarianization' theorists.

Goldthorpe, for example, on the basis of the Nuffield Social Mobility Study, argues that notwithstanding any changes in the content of clerical work, proletarianization must still be rejected because of the high rates of intergenerational mobility from routine clerical positions into both higher level non-manual occupations and manual work (Goldthorpe, 1980). Mobility out of clerical work plays an equally important part in the work of Stewart *et al.* (1980). They argue that the thesis of clerical proletarianization rests on a fundamental misconception about the class structure; that is, it continues to translate occupations into class positions in an entirely unproblematic fashion. Instead, we should distinguish between 'jobs', that is, structures of work tasks, and 'incumbents' who fill jobs. It should not be assumed that all incumbents of similar jobs have a shared class position because individuals move between jobs over time in different ways. Thus the class characteristic of any particular job is partly determined by the characteristics of the incumbent. In the case of clerical occupations they do not represent a uniform stratification position because 'the meaning of clerical work will not be the same for all engaged in it' (Stewart *et al.*, 1980, p. 112). In particular, most young men will leave clerical work, mostly promoted into higher-level non-manual occupations, while women and older men are unlikely to move out along these paths. Here again, then, high levels of male promotion from clerical work are crucial to the rejection of proletarianization. This is all the more so since Goldthorpe explicitly claims, and Stewart *et al.* imply, that promotions out of clerical work into administrative and managerial positions constitute a class move. It became clear that if we were to examine these ideas adequately in our research we would need to focus on promotion and the operation of the internal labour market. We claim that to understand these processes you need to adopt an organizational case study approach.

All the organizations we studied operated internal labour markets which defined the limits of promotion and the characteristics which were required to obtain it. It is worth exploring the differences between them in order to demonstrate that they need to be studied from close quarters.

Southbank represents a classic example of a relatively closed internal labour market with a clearly labelled hierarchical structure. Most recruitment is of school leavers (though a much smaller number of graduates are also recruited). All entrants have reasonable academic qualifications and after a year recruits are encouraged to take the examinations of the Institute of Bankers. (However, our interview material suggests that young men are rather more encouraged than young women.) After about a year all recruits are placed in a 'tier', which is an explicit marker of the employer's career expectations of the individual. For people who have 'careers' in the bank the major clearers still operate a no-poaching agreement though the picture for 'jobbers' – that is, staff who have been identified as having few career prospects – is rather different and banks do recruit each other's staff at the lower grades. This is especially common amongst women returning to the labour market after child rearing. For all those who wish to achieve promotion geographical mobility is essential. Career staff combine hierarchical and geographical moves. The necessity of mobility is explicit to all aspiring to a career in the bank. The characteristics required for promotion in the bank are therefore made quite clear. Success lies in pursuing an organizational career (Brown, 1982), acquiring post-entry qualifications and exhibiting a willingness to be geographically mobile.

Lifeco organizes its internal hierarchies rather differently. First, it had moved its headquarters from London to the Eastern Region. Not all employees had made this move and there had been, therefore, significant recruitment of young people. This relocation has had a massive effect on the operation of the internal labour market. Nevertheless, historically, Lifeco has rewarded long service with promotion. Therefore, like Southbank, it seems to encourage the pursuit of organizational careers. However, because there is not a 'no-poaching' agreement in the insurance industry individuals may, if they wish, pursue careers which involve mobility between organizations – in Brown's (1982) terms, occupational rather than organizational careers. The question of post-entry qualification was also handled differently. In Southbank, it is made quite clear that IOB qualifications are crucial to promotion. In Lifeco, a great deal was left to the discretion of department managers to encourage and facilitate the acquisition of post-entry qualifications. More generally, there was a greater emphasis on subtle indicators of your fit with the culture of the organization. Special merit attached to being active in the Sports and Social Club, particularly if you could play certain sports well. (The sports in question, cricket and football, largely excluded women.) On one occasion, we heard a departmental manager say that he had 'a decent left-armer' joining the department. Initially we thought that this might be some arcane insurance jargon; in truth it concerned cricket. In Lifeco, then, there was a more diffuse notion of fit with the organization and while historically organizational strategies for career advancement were appropriate there existed the possibility of pursuing an occupational one.

Cohall combines some of the features of both Lifeco and Southbank. It recruits at all ages, like Lifeco, but it places considerable importance on post-entry qualifications, like Southbank. It has in many respects a more complex internal labour market because it carries a much wider variety of activities. There are, in consequence, several routes to promotion. Certainly some promotion can be obtained through long service. However, this tends to be quite limited, reaching only to lower-level managerial positions. Analysis of the job histories of senior managers showed that a high proportion had moved between employers, often within the public sector. These individuals were pursuing an occupational career strategy, bolstered by acquiring post-entry qualifications. The choice of such qualifications was much wider than at either Southbank or Lifeco and one element of success was to choose the qualification with the highest promotion potential.

These differences between organizations in terms of the structuring of promotion are only available via the case study method. If high rates of male promotion are considered crucial to the rejection of the thesis of clerical proletarianization, then it is important to examine organizational differences. Strategies appropriate in one organization may not work in another. Nevertheless, it has to be conceded that at the aggregate level we did discover high rates of male mobility, very much in line with that claimed by other studies. However, as the research progressed we came to question the significance of much of this 'promotion'.

Both Goldthorpe and Stewart *et al.* have argued that movement out of clerking into managerial and administrative work constitutes significant social mobility. Indeed for Goldthorpe it is *explicitly* a class move (Goldthorpe, 1980, pp. 40–2). As our empirical enquiries developed we became increasingly unclear about the boundaries between 'clerical', 'administrative' and 'managerial' work. Certainly we learned not to take organizational definitions and job titles as authoritative guides to the nature of the work. For example, in Cohall the distinction between clerical and administrative work was 'officially' represented by 'clerical' and 'AP' grades but the real differences in work were often small; sometimes the grading might depend on the characteristics of the occupant. In Southbank, in contrast, the manager's clerk, still on a clerical grade, carried out a much wider range of more skilled tasks than others on clerical grades inside the bank. In Lifeco, team leaders in promoted positions did much the same work as those they led. They acted much more as well-experienced clerks who could help others with more difficult cases. The same arguments apply to the managerial classification. Amongst those with managerial titles could be found authoritative, unambiguous managers with clear functional control of hiring, firing and the disposition of organizational resources, as well as those who carried out tasks much more similar to those in clerical occupations. In our view, occupational titles may even be manipulated in order to create the appearance of mobility when the nature of the work changes very little. Certainly, our earlier theoretical arguments expressing doubts as to whether such promotion constituted a class move (in Day *et al.*, 1982) were empirically confirmed.[3] However, such observations can only arise from thorough acquaintance with the precise details of the division of labour in particular settings. They could not be made if one took the organization's view of its own hierarchy. You need to move beyond this if you are concerned with the real organization of the labour process. If we are right then we need to re-evaluate the significance of male promotion as an important argument against clerical proletarianization. The dynamics of the world of work, especially during a period of rapid technical change, are not neatly encapsulated by occupational titles. Rather, careful first-hand observation of work in its organizational setting is crucial.

Conclusion

In this paper we have tried to suggest that concern with close observation with work in its organizational setting pays theoretical dividends. In the case of the sociological study of clerical work two important questions are illuminated by the organizational case study method. First, the extent of clerical deskilling – a key test of the Braverman thesis – requires detailed examination of the work in *context*. Without our first-hand observations we could not have coded our work description data and it is only on the basis of work such as this that the extent of deskilling can be evaluated. Second, the operation of internal labour markets in large white collar organizations – a subject of importance both to the thesis of clerical proletarianization and the more general area of social mobility – is better understood in organizational context. The differences between internal labour markets can be examined as well as casting doubts on the significance and extent of promotion. We would go further and suggest that in the development of theory in crucial areas of social science like social stratification there has been an inadequate connection between theory building and empirical justification. There needs to be a closer relationship between the careful observation of work in its organizational context and the development of theory both in the sociology of work and of stratification. Commitment to such organizational research will require the combination of qualitative and quantitative methods if it is to feed theory development.

Notes

1 Although the nature of *work* was crucial to Lockwood's argument, he did not, in fact, collect original research material describing the work itself.
2 Goldthorpe himself would seem to accept this argument. See, for example, Goldthorpe and Payne (1986, p. 21) which makes reference to the 'monographic sources' (unspecified) used in constructing a revised class schema. He seems reluctant, however, to accept the logical implications of the argument. That is, if the monographic sources out of which the schema is constructed suggest that a similar title may be used to describe a very different series of 'work situations', then some caution should be exercised in interpreting subsequent empirical findings, that is, it may be mistaken to treat the *schema itself* as if it were a totally reliable research instrument. See Hindess (1973) and Prandy (1986) for further elaboration of this point.
3 Goldthorpe and Payne (1986) have recently suggested that our empirical findings do not support our argument on the grounds that 'If such degrading or "dilution" had gone on over recent decades within the service class of our analyses, one would have expected this to show up in some deterioration of the mobility chances of men originating in this class, relative to those of men of other origins. But . . . there is no indication of this whatever' (p. 20). This completely misses the rather

simple point we wish to make. We argue that the 'service class' content of
an increasing proportion of managerial *jobs* is more apparent than real.
This argument can only be explored empirically by examining the *jobs*,
rather than the movement of people in and out of them. It is the *nature* of
the hierarchy that we dispute, rather than the relative mobility chances of
men located on its 'continuum'. At this point the debate may be criticized
as being potentially sterile, that is, only a matter of where the cutting
points on the hierarchy occur. There is, however, rather more than this
involved. If Goldthorpe wishes to persist with his assertion that the 'real'
service class is actually expanding, then he must surely accept the
'upgrading' thesis – as indeed, he appears, in part, to do (Goldthorpe and
Payne, 1986). We would argue, in contrast, that the 'upgrading' thesis
gives a rather misleading account of work in contemporary societies, and
is an unreliable basis from which to develop predictive/interpretive
arguments.

5

HISTORICAL METHODS AND ORGANIZATION ANALYSIS:
The case of a naval dockyard

David Dunkerley

Introduction

Many social science disciplines and sub-disciplines have employed an historical perspective with considerable success. Yet within organization analysis the emphasis has largely been upon describing and analysing contemporary phenomena, with scant regard being paid to how present characteristics may have emerged from past happenings. This chapter seeks to achieve a number of aims under the general objective of exploring the possibility of using historical method in the analysis of organizations.

Starting from a general discussion about history and the social sciences, the chapter moves on to account for the fact that in the past decade a shift of paradigm has occurred in the study of organizations. This shift has necessarily involved the need to examine critically, not only the theoretical position of organization analysis, but also its empirical base and the kinds of methods traditionally employed. The somewhat ahistorical nature of much organization analysis is seen as a failing and as an area that requires attention by theorists and empiricists alike.

The author was himself involved in the debate over the orientation of organization analysis and was one of those to criticize the lack of historical attention in the literature. It is, however, one thing to take a critical stance yet quite another to attempt to remedy perceived deficiencies. The bulk of the chapter therefore gives an account of a study undertaken of a large state organization where the methodological emphasis was upon using historical methods. These are described. The difficulties in undertaking the research are also addressed. It will be seen, however, that a number of interesting and worthwhile aspects of the organization were investigated that are capable of translation into more general analysis.

Historical analysis and organization analysis

A fine line has always been capable of being drawn between history and many of the social science disciplines such as sociology, social anthropology, political science and economics. Indeed, it could be argued that in the sense that, say, the sociologist is unable to undertake his/her analysis without an historical dimension so, too, the historian is dependent upon a sociological understanding to complete the task. The boundary between such disciplines is necessarily somewhat artificial. Although the coming together of the disciplines has perhaps accelerated in recent decades, the link has always been there. Take sociology as an example. The 'Founding Fathers' of the discipline – Comte, Marx, Weber, Durkheim – based their analyses of society and social phenomena upon an historical construct. The concern of early sociology with seeking an explanation and understanding of the transition to industrial society could only be achieved with an historical insight. The complex changes of the nineteenth century were recognized as phenomena that had historical roots and which themselves would be historical artefacts in due course. The emphasis, then, was on process rather than on the here-and-now. It would be easy to suggest that such a posture was inevitable because of the speed and direction of social change in the nineteenth century. To ignore such change and process would imply professional neglect. By the same token, whilst the form of society, *per se*, may not have changed so rapidly after the late nineteenth century, it would be a case of neglect to ignore the historical dimension of society and social phenomena in the twentieth century.

This is not to suggest that social scientists have been guilty of such neglect. They have not. The dimension of process has often been recognized as a vital link between action and structure – the latter being incomprehensible without an appraisal of the former. But what is meant by this? Is it sufficient for the social scientist simply to provide a description of what has gone before? Clearly, this is not the case. All that would be provided would be a descriptive background which might well be interesting but would probably not be illuminating with regard to providing explanation or prediction. Nevertheless, even an historically descriptive account is preferable to no historical aspect at all. There is perhaps a tendency among social scientists to adopt less of an historical position the more they move away from the macro level of analysis. This, of course, is easily understood. If one is concerned to analyse broad societal change then historical analysis must be employed; at the more micro level of attempting to understand a social phenomenon such as juvenile crime or a political phenomenon such as voting behaviour at the sub-national level, the temptation is to concentrate upon the present without reference to the past. If reference does occur then it would tend to be descriptive and provide little more than an interesting background to the present.

This is not the place to enter into a debate over the definitions of and relationships between concepts such as process, structure and action. What is our concern is the methodological problem of analysing the concepts in the real world – specifically, the world of organizations. In his exploration of historical sociology, Abrams (1982) emphasizes that it is 'events' that provide us with the necessary tool for undertaking such analysis. He writes,

events do seem to provide the distinctive matter in terms of which
historians construct their reality. The field is almost always specified as a
course of events . . . it is clear that the idea of a course is arrived at only by
way of the idea of events. (Abrams, 1982, p. 190)

So it is that events enable us to structure social action with regard to time.
An event, in other words, arises from the past, structures the present and
affects the future. An event is something that is observable and measurable,
it has empirical meaning. There are two aspects to this. An event is capable
both of analysis in its own right and of understanding process. Events are
not abstractions but concrete phenomena. This concreteness enables us to
demystify the abstract nature of concepts such as action, structure and
process.

This discussion on the general links between history and the social
sciences is relevant when we come to examine the position of organizational
analysis. There is some question as to where to place the latter in the
cafeteria of academic enterprises. Much depends upon the intentions of the
researcher as to whether the generic term 'business and management
studies' or that of 'social sciences' is the umbrella under which analysis takes
place. The former is more concerned with practical issues that could make
an organization more effective and efficient; the latter with understanding
the functioning of organizations regardless of whether such understanding
may lead to greater efficiency. It is the contention here that both approaches
can benefit from an historical dimension and insight. Indeed, without such
an approach the analysis is necessarily incomplete.

Things have not always been so. The so-called critical approach to
organizational analysis that emerged in the mid-1970s in the UK and USA
identified a fundamental weakness in the analysis of organizations, namely
that researchers on organizations had tended to adopt an ahistorical
methodology both empirically and theoretically. It is precisely when
researchers wish to introduce a more theoretically sensitive analysis – that
is, to move away from the empirical mode characteristic of much of
organizational analysis in the 1950s and 1960s – that an historical
approach is required.

The present author and his colleague Stewart Clegg embarked on a major
attempt to re-orientate the theoretical basis of organizational analysis in
two publications – *Critical Issues in Organizations* (Clegg and Dunkerley,
1977) and *Organization, Class and Control* (Clegg and Dunkerley, 1980).
How successful we were in this venture is for others to judge. What we did
was to advocate the adoption of a 'political economy' perspective in the
analysis of organizations. Such a perspective involves, *inter alia*, examining
forms of control: control as introduced by dominant groups over
subordinate groups; control taking differing modes according to historical
setting. Thus it was that the analysis, in being more theoretical than many
previous writings on organizations, *ipso facto* became more historical in
nature. By problematizing the concept of organization, by recognizing that
'organization' cannot be a taken-for-granted phenomenon, by questioning

the empirical reality of organization, this move towards greater historical understanding became more and more necessary:

> We must construct an explicit and theoretical model of our object of analysis which is related to the historical development of our concrete empirical object of organizations. In doing this we may find that if we wish to say anything other than the most general things about empirically visible aspects of its structure (e.g. size, centralization, etc.) our faith in the category of '*the* organization' may have been premature. (Clegg and Dunkerley, 1980, p. 502)

In this way we argued that organization structure is a reflection and expression of particular modes of rationality. Such modes can only be identified through an understanding of historical processes. Our definition of organization in terms of sedimented structures that are historically and temporally located enables the analysis to account for the changing forms of control over the labour force. The analysis, in fact, identifies a shift in such forms of control from essentially coercive to manipulative.

This chapter is not the place to expand on the theoretical issues identified by the alternative approaches to organizational analysis that have emerged since the mid-1970s. The original accounts together with revisions and critical comments are easily available. What we are more concerned with here is identifying the extent to which the theoretical propositions are capable of translation into empirical reality – whether, in fact, the normative dictats can be applied in practice. It is, in other words, one thing to expound a methodological position from the relative comfort and safety of a library; it is quite another to put the methodological position to the test.

The Naval Dockyard Study

The study reported here to illustrate the use of historical methods in organizational research started life with somewhat different aims and objectives from those it finished with. Originally, the aim of the investigation was to chart the rise and decline of a distinctive working-class community in the Devonport area of the city of Plymouth. This area had been the home of the Royal Naval Dockyard for centuries and the study aimed to concentrate upon the origin of the dockyard labour force, the extent of intergenerational job transmission, internal work structure, job security and political attitudes, and the effect of mobility opportunities.

Taking these concerns in more detail, the origins of the dockyard labour force appeared to be obscure. There was speculation over this varying from suggestions of landless individuals driven into the urban area to suggestions that the labour force was partly composed of refugees from prison ships returning from the Antipodes. As late as the 1970s and 1980s the importance of family connections was emphasized with respect to job transmission and it seemed appropriate to assess whether a specific cultural phenomenon had developed in this regard as part of an historical process. Relations between skilled and unskilled workers and the extent of cleavages between them both in the workplace and the wider community, coupled with an analysis of the traditional shipbuilding and ship-repairing skills, were key issues to be investigated. Since the state has always been the employer, the effects of this labour relationship on job security, political attitudes and the extent of a collective solidarity being fostered or retarded by this were also perceived as important issues contributing to the overall objectives of the study.

It should be clear from the above that an ambitious research programme had been planned that was to take a form approaching an historical community study rather than an organizational analysis. The project was funded for up to three years by the author's own institution; the extent of funding enabled a full-time research assistant to be employed for the duration.

Equally ambitious were the proposed methods of enquiry. These were essentially three in kind. First, there was analysis of enumerators' books from a sample of population censuses since 1851 (it was known that these were kept in the Public Record Office – PRO – at Kew and in the local Record Office). This analysis, it was thought, would furnish information that is unavailable in the published census volumes on the levels of dockyard employment, employment between different occupational groups, birthplace of dockyard workers, the source of new recruitment, etc. The second type was records relating to dockyard employment, labour relations and skills to be found in general local histories, Admiralty and Treasury papers (held at the PRO), parliamentary papers, Poor Law records and a sample of local newspapers. And the third kind was the method known as oral history, to be based on interviews with dockyard workers over three generations in order to probe changes in skills, the internal dockyard organization and the criteria for dockyard recruitment.

Almost from the outset of the study, it became clear that too ambitious an exercise had been embarked upon given the time and manpower available. From the point of view of this chapter, examining the use of historical methods, two points arose at this early stage that are relevant. The first is that it was assumed that historical records would be readily available to suit the purposes of the investigation. What we found was that much of what had been assumed to be locally available either no longer existed or was obscurely catalogued in the PRO. As regards the former, much valuable material had been destroyed during enemy action in the Second World War. As far as the latter is concerned, the intricacies of operating the PRO system at Kew were far more difficult than had been imagined. This point will be discussed further below. The second point is that the use of census material proved much more difficult than had been imagined. The common problem of successive censuses changing the kinds of data collected was confronted together with the fact that more recent detailed information from enumerators' books is subject to closure and simply not available even to the bona fide researcher. What information was unearthed proved to take an enormous time to work on: this, coupled with the fact that it was extremely costly to have a research assistant based 250 miles from the research site, partly led to a revision of the original aims of the study.

It was self-evident that a radical re-think of the aims and methods of the study had to be undertaken. Three strategies were adopted to overcome the initial difficulties.

First, it was clear that although the funding for the research was sufficient to employ a research assistant, additional funding was necessary to cover the costs of travelling, subsistence and *ad hoc* office expenses. A successful application was made to the Nuffield Foundation for this money under its Social Sciences Small Grants Scheme. The grant was for an eighteen-month period and was designed to cover the archival phase of the research.

Second, the aims and objectives were significantly altered. The original intention of undertaking an occupational community study with a strong historical influence was focused more specifically so that something approaching an organizational study of the dockyard *per se* was envisaged, with attention centring on technological and historical development covering a period spanning the last century. This decision was made with the historical knowledge that although a naval base had existed since the late seventeenth century, it was not until the nineteenth century that any significant increases in size or technological application took place. With these developments, the RN Dockyard at Devonport became firmly established as one of the foremost shipbuilding and ship-repairing yards for the naval fleet in Britain. This status – although now relating only to repairing and refitting – has been maintained if not strengthened to the present day.

Armed with this knowledge, and with the background information already collected, the areas of concern for the research were reduced to four general topics:

(1) the particular internal organization of the dockyard, including status differentials, division of labour and hierarchical structure;
(2) patterns of remuneration and the reasons for changes from inside contracting to piece-rates and day-wage systems (here Clawson's, 1980, excellent historical analysis was considered extremely valuable);
(3) the effect of technological changes on traditional skills;
(4) the opportunity for and efficacy of unionization in the dockyard.

We shall see below that although these were much more realistic objectives they were still subject to change as the research progressed. It would be curious, in fact, if this were not the case.

Third, there were methodological changes. These were necessary because of the changed nature of the programme and also because of the difficulties that had been initially encountered. The main change was to decide not to undertake the analysis of enumerators' books. As mentioned above, the incompleteness of these records, the laborious and time-consuming nature of their analysis and the move towards a more focused organizational analysis all contributed to this decision. It was not a case of cutting corners or invalidating the ultimate analysis. Rather it was a case of such a method now being redundant: the purpose was no longer justified.

The commitment to official archival records and to oral history techniques remained. Whereas the former could provide 'factual' information, the latter could bring the analysis to life and prevent the potential sterility that official sources often produce. It is to a discussion of the methods eventually employed that we can now turn, before looking at the results of the research and assessing its success.

The chosen methods

In this section, the aim is to provide a general description of the methods employed in the dockyard study although not to relate these methods to the study itself at this stage. The advantages and disadvantages can thus be examined in general terms before turning to an account of how things worked out in practice. In addition to describing the two main methods (historical documents and oral history evidence), the use of a case study approach is also examined.

(i) Historical documents

It is a *sine qua non* that documents provide the 'bread-and-butter' research tool for the historian. It is also the case that social scientists such as sociologists, economists and political scientists are very dependent upon information provided by documents of various sorts, though, of course, not necessarily historical. Both the historian and the social scientist, as discussed above, are concerned, *inter alia*, to understand social life and as such have to interpret any evidence at their disposal within the context of a set of hypotheses they have previously derived. The problem with historical interpretation from documentary evidence is that often there is no way of the researcher knowing the meanings that the producer of the documents attached to them. Indeed, it is often the case that neither the purpose nor the setting of the material is known and can only be guessed at. It is therefore axiomatic to suggest that the more sources of evidence that can be employed, the better. Even so, the researcher is always in danger of interpreting a piece of evidence in the light of his/her contemporary situation and imposing suppositions and assumptions that may be totally unwarranted. The universal problems of any research technique – those of reliability and validity – are therefore more pronounced with the use of historical documents.

One way of overcoming or at least of lessening the potential difficulties is to apply the four tests suggested by Gottschalk *et al.* in asking the following self-explanatory questions:

1 Was the ultimate source of the detail (the primary witness) *able* to tell the truth?
2 Was the primary witness *willing* to tell the truth?
3 Is the primary witness *accurately reported* with regard to the detail under examination?

4 Is there any *external corroboration* of the detail under examination? (Gottschalk *et al.*, 1945, p. 35)

Although such a checklist is useful in assessing the reliability and validity of documentary evidence, there is still the problem that the purposes for which the official documents and statistics were originally gathered do not necessarily coincide with those of the researcher. Indeed it would be rare for this to be the case. Furthermore, the processing and presentation of documentary and statistical evidence is often inappropriate for the aims of a particular study. As indicated earlier, data derived from such secondary sources tend to be somewhat sterile and certainly can only rarely reach the views, beliefs and feelings of individuals and groups. Given the commitment to the principle of multiple methods (Denzin, 1970) the complementary approach of oral evidence can be examined.

(ii) Oral historical evidence

Amongst organization analysts the technique of oral history is relatively unknown. It was introduced here not as an alternative to the 'scientific' lobby of organization researchers but as a genuine attempt to explore the use of a method that could bring some life to the rather barren picture painted by other, more traditional, methods.

A great advantage of using oral history techniques is that previously unexplored or ignored areas of study can be looked at. Spheres of life about which remarkably little is known become accessible. The fact that information is gathered on an individual basis means that the researcher can use his/her own concepts and categories. These might otherwise have been aggregated inappropriately as is often the case with a great deal of secondary statistical sources.

Subjectivity, therefore, lies behind the approach of using oral evidence. Of course, the unwary or unethical might force the data into pre-defined categories and therefore present a view of social and organizational life that is consistent with the researcher's own theoretical position. It must be stressed that any research method is open to such abuse. Indeed, Hindess (1973) suggests that no set of social statistics can exist independently of its means of production, its sets of categories. Behind any statistics lies a conceptual base that influenced their production.

Since oral evidence is uncategorized, the data are available for reassessment in terms of the applicability of the concepts employed. The interpretation can, therefore, be scrutinized by sceptics. Even the researcher may be prompted to reconsider his/her own position since reassessment is a process that naturally produces new ways of thinking, new questions and new approaches. Oral sources, Passerini (1979, p. 91) has suggested, 'like the sphynx . . . force us to reformulate problems and challenge our current habits of thought.'

There is a certain proneness to difficulties and dangers that could render the use of oral evidence inadmissible. In the first instance is the issue of reliability. Certainly the reliability of a respondent's memory is a major worry although Thompson (1979) and Gittins (1979) have suggested that the greatest loss of memory is to be found with a short period recall and that later memory recall is negligible. Even though facts may be recalled, the question of attitudes is more problematic. Distortion of emotions and motives invariably occurs as individuals attempt to harmonize issues.

One of the main aims of the in-depth oral interview is to investigate values. Here the issue of the cultural construction of values is central. Regardless of method, the process of interpretation and reconstruction by the respondent takes place. Thus, any account of the past involves factual events being interpreted through socially constructed values. Using oral evidence makes this process more pronounced and therefore suggests a major advantage. The subjective interpretation common to all reconstruction of the past is possibly more visible with this method. The combination of factual accounts and cultural understanding encourages questioning and interpretation of a kind that does not normally occur with other methods.

The twin problem of validity also needs to be taken into account using this method. In any interview situation the results of the interview are partly determined by the researcher and as such his/her role should be critically examined. The interaction between respondent and researcher can range from a clinical approach to one where the respondent is encouraged to accept the researcher as a confidant and friend (Roberts, 1981). Regardless of the approach, it is virtually inevitable that the researcher will influence the response to a greater or lesser extent.

With respect to the more clinical type of interaction, the researcher is in a more powerful position *vis-à-vis* the respondent. Ordinary everyday conversation tends not to occur insofar as the respondent is encouraged to take long conversational turns whilst the researcher provides short encouraging prompts or even salient symbolic gestures. The respondent can feel obliged to continue because of the brevity or silence of the researcher.

At the other extreme, the friendly personal approach can produce more thoughtful expositions. Again, though, the researcher is likely to influence the views expressed. Clearly, manipulative forces are at work but at least recognizing them can produce a greater and more valid understanding of respondents' views as they express them.

Oral evidence resulting from an interview lasting several hours can lead to problems with regard to selection and presentation of the material. The transcript may imply reduction and manipulation, as Portelli (1980) has suggested. Transcription invariably produces a loss of information, speed, volume and pauses and yet, of course, such features are central to an understanding of meaning.

A professional dilemma is created since the researcher may be fully aware of the mode of delivery of a piece of evidence yet has to refrain from making too subjective an interpretation of the evidence. The decontextualization arising from transcription displays the conflict of whether to present the pure verbal evidence or whether to include interpretive inference. There is no absolute way of resolving this dilemma.

(iii) The case study approach

The organization researcher is no stranger to the use of the case study. Indeed, many of the significant advances in organization analysis over the past forty years have arisen through the employment of the case study technique. It is, therefore, not considered necessary to dwell too long on this methodological issue since the arguments for and against the case study have been rehearsed on many occasions. There is, nevertheless, a criticism that is frequently raised against the use of case studies in social and organization studies – that the possibility of generalizing is minimal. Whilst there is much to support this criticism in terms of the limited ability to move from the particular, a lot depends upon the aims and function of the particular case study.

Certainly if the aim of a study was to confirm a set of hypotheses, it would be dangerous, if not foolhardy, to use a case study approach unless multiple studies could be undertaken. At the level of falsifying or originating hypotheses the case study can be valuable, as shown in the area of deviant case analysis. It is, though, at the level of straightforward discovery that the case study comes into its own. This might mean that a rather descriptive posture is adopted rather than an analytic one. Nevertheless, important insights can often arise from description that can, in turn, lead to the formulation of hypotheses to be subsequently more rigorously investigated. Indeed, Mitchell (1983, p. 204) suggests that 'an illuminating case may make theoretical connections apparent which were formerly obscure'. Furthermore,

> In case studies statistical inference is not invoked at all. Instead the infer-
> ential process turns exclusively on the theoretically necessary linkages
> among features in the case study. The validity of the extrapolation
> depends not on the typicality or representativeness of the case but upon
> the cogency of the theoretical reasoning. (Mitchell, 1983, p. 207)

In this sense, case studies do have a valuable role to play and should not be underestimated as an important research tool. Eysenck's comment, quoted by Glickman (1985, p. 95), summarizes the position very well: 'We simply have to keep our eyes open and look carefully at individual cases – not in the hope of proving anything, but rather in the hope of learning something.'

The study in practice

The role of serendipity and luck in social research should never be underestimated. As far as the dockyard study was concerned, the initial problems encountered with using historical materials were largely overcome by refocusing the objectives as indicated earlier. By chance, information came to light about a series of commissions on the government dockyards that appeared not to have been used in previous dockyard studies by social

historians. These commission reports proved to be extremely valuable since
they contained a wealth of oral evidence on the day-to-day workings of the
organization over the period of the study. In addition to these papers, one
source led to another so that by the completion of the study an enormous
range of material had been consulted. This range included private papers of
various dockyard heads (held at the National Maritime Museum),
Admiralty letters to and from the dockyard and information on wages
systems (held at the PRO); over twenty academic theses were discovered
that were pertinent to dockyard history and access was given to various
trade union and trades council minute books. Many of these items were
unexpected.

A series of long interviews with twelve retired dockyardmen comprised
the oral history part of the study. These interviews lasted for between four
and nine hours each and provided detailed information on work experience
and organizational issues stretching back to the 1920s. The interviews
proved to be an extremely useful resource in terms of bringing the
organization to life.

The study enabled the development of two distinct yet complementary
lines of argument to be pursued. The first was largely historical, putting the
dockyard in the context of the public sector in the nineteenth and twentieth
centuries. In this way there was a divergence from most historical analyses
that tend to deal with the development of communities, workforces,
management and organization in terms of private sector capitalism. The
second was mainly sociological in the sense of casting new light on
phenomena such as bureaucracy, work practices and managerial control.

The particular methodology adopted enabled four specific areas of
concern to be investigated. These can be briefly examined.

(1) Culture and technology

Taking as a basic premise that technology is often imposed by management
in organizations to further physical and ideological control rather than
simply as a means of increasing output or efficiency, technology can be seen
to perpetuate social inequalities. Technology can define organizational
culture; it is experienced culturally and also moulded by the culture within
which it is introduced. Furthermore, technological change can result in
cultural change. It is possible to conceive of a cultural clash where two
technologies – one old and one new – exist side by side. This is precisely
what access to some of the historical records demonstrated as occurring in
the late nineteenth century. What was discovered was that prior to the
building of the Steam Factories, work was a predominantly skilled,
handcraft affair with little scope for mechanization. Furthermore, it became
clear that work culture was taken into the community. These traditions
were rudely threatened by the opening of the Steam Factories since they
brought with them an alien organization of work and alien workers and
managers. Documentary evidence displays the conflict between two
technological cultures. It also shows how a form of assimilation took place

as the new culture was absorbed into the old. In due course, further technological change involving the introduction of iron hulls saw the alignment of the original trades against the encroaching boilermakers, rivetters and platers. The archival material and some of the oral historical evidence suggests that the shipwrights were able to maintain their technological and cultural superiority partly as a result of their relationship with the imposers of technology. It became clear that an adequate understanding of a techno-cultural clash could only occur through a concomitant understanding of the social organization and history of the naval dockyard.

(2) Educating for work

Archival research showed the important role of the Dockyard Schools which admitted dockyard apprentices on entry, taught them for seven years and then made their facilities available to qualified craftsmen keen to improve their position. The Dockyard Schools provided both a technical and an academic education for boys destined to embark on a worklife in the very institution in which they were being educated. Thus, a precise vertical route was forged between school and work. The combination of the two research methods enabled an understanding of the transmission of the basic skills necessary for fulfilling occupational demands and also the attitudes and values required for the successful perpetuation of the dockyard's social relations. The oral history interviews, in particular, were able to highlight attitudes to authority, beliefs concerning work, the everyday organization of work and meanings attached to personal satisfaction. Each of these could be followed from the moment of their production in the schools to their cultural reproduction at work. It was possible to assess the notion of the schools as part of a broader organizational structure, consciously framed to prepare pupils for a worklife in the dockyards, and that structure's reinforcement within the community.

(3) Patterns of unionization

The pattern of union growth throughout the dockyard network displays a marked dissimilarity to the picture portrayed in equivalent shipbuilding and engineering firms in the private sector. Three immediate differences came to light. First, unions entered the dockyards comparatively late. Second, when they did make inroads, they faced a constant battle to gain support and even eradicate suspicion. Third, dockyard unions have shown for the most part a moderate front despite a history of organization and militancy stretching back to the eighteenth century.

It was possible to follow the development of a number of unions in Devonport Dockyard. Each union falls into a certain category – the Sailmakers' Federation is an example of a declining and then dying craft union, the Civil and Public Servants' Association an instance of a burgeoning clerical union, the Shipwrights were the oldest and most powerful combination, and the Amalgamated Society of Engineers represented a 'metal' union. The specialist knowledge gained of the social organization and history of the dockyards was used to interpret and explain the growth of unions. Although no all-embracing model could account for unionization, it was possible to analyse a number of variables relevant to most discussions of union growth in a capitalist society.

(4) Class relations

Events within the naval dockyard during the Falklands conflict, with respect to its effects upon the social relations of production and the nature of the labour force's response, exhibit a striking similarity to equivalent circumstances in every war from the Crimean to the Second World War. This emphasizes the historical continuity and consistency of the dockyards over the course of their existence and points to an unusual pattern of class relations borne of the dockyard's status distinct from orthodox capitalist enterprise – comprising an imperative arm of the capitalist state and functioning within a market – the dynamic of which has always been the suspicion, threat or onset of armed conflict. Again the combination of historical research and oral history interviews enabled the key influences to be described including the institution's naval function, its relationship with the state and its traditionally strong, highly skilled workforce. These have all structured the labour process in a highly individual fashion and acted as constraints within which social relations have been shaped. An ideological paradox has always existed involving the membership of dockyardmen in a labour movement espousing peace alongside the realization that they are part of an organization, their continuing employment within which meant, at times, an aggressive, imperialist Britain. This requires a broader explanation taking into account the singular dockyard milieu. Despite this singularity the analysis of the unusual and enduring dockyard class relations has implications for similar work on class relations in the public sector, in shipbuilding and in industries servicing or serving the armed forces.

Concluding remarks

This chapter has attempted to give an honest and frank account of the difficulties and successes of a research project using, for organization analysts at least, a somewhat different methodology from that which is typical of the field. It has been shown that a number of initial difficulties had to be overcome that were to some extent of the researcher's own making. With the benefit of hindsight it is clear that too ambitious a programme of work was envisaged. A larger research team and more time and money would have been necessary to achieve all that was originally planned. Equally, the difficulties of accessing material from record offices should have been predicted. In the event, the more limited and scaled-down approach proved to be capable of achievement and many interesting, insightful and worthwhile issues came to light from the project.

The author is reminded of a piece of worthwhile advice given him by David Hickson some fifteen years ago, that if one is writing a paper or even a book there is only room to pursue one theme consistently. When it comes to an empirical study of organizations there is some truth in this as well. There is certainly a need to restrict the number of topics that are to be investigated. In the event, as the account of the dockyard study above shows, four specific areas were examined. These were closely related to one another even though they had a certain discreteness in their own right. It would have been difficult to have extended the analysis much further without reducing it to a highly descriptive level.

Mention has been made of the general problems of interviewing. In the case of this project no special problems were encountered that could not have been predicted. Oral history interviewing is a specialist technique. The researcher was fortunate in having a colleague – Diana Gittins – who is recognized as one of the foremost experts in this field and who was able to offer considerable advice and assistance. Nevertheless, the exhausting nature of the technique (for both interviewer and interviewee) should not be underestimated. Similarly, the long process of transcribing the interviews together with attempting to retain the essence of the dialogue, have to be recognized.

There is always a concern as to how far one can generalize from one particular study. The issue of comparability is a problem. In the case of the dockyard study, it was never the intention to prove a set of hypotheses or propositions. The study was more modest. It was concerned to provide description and possibly to aid in the formulation of research hypotheses. In this sense the problems of comparability and prospects for generalization did not raise themselves as major issues, as often happens.

Although the researcher would never claim that the study should or will become one of the 'classics' in organization analysis, it is nevertheless the case that much that is useful has arisen from it. One is modest enough to acknowledge that it might have been undertaken in a rather different way, that mistakes were made. Fortunately, the major difficulties were recognized at an early stage and were capable of remedy; researchers are not always in this fortunate position. The commitment to an historical approach remains. Indeed it is heartening to observe such an approach being incorporated into more and more studies of organizations.

6

IN ANOTHER COUNTRY

Peter Lawrence

In the station restaurant in Essen, West Germany, I once listened (shamelessly) to the conversation at the next table where a German businessman was entertaining two Americans. It was clear from the dialogue that the German was the owner-manager of a family firm, the Americans had just signed him up as supplier, and the lunch was to round off the deal. At one point the Americans urged a cautious, not too hurried approach to some joint undertaking, and one of them quoted the Rome-wasn't-built-in-a-day adage. We have a similar saying in German, responded the host, we say:

> Rome wasn't built in a day.
> That's because the Krauts weren't on that job.

The anecdote is poignant for the study of management in other countries, for the attempt to characterize and compare management styles and systems in different lands. For this enterprise of comparative management steers an uneasy course between the challenge of relating observed behaviour to inferred values on the one hand, and shuffling national stereotypes on the other. This is its charm and danger, a tension that will no doubt be reflected here.

The present account is a personal one in several ways. In part this is a function of age and biography. My fascination with abroad and particularly the European portion thereof owes something to remembering the Second World War as a child and witnessing the reconstruction of Western Europe as an expatriate teenager, and to a history degree which implanted a sense of Europe's cultural richness, plus a sociological training that led to a questioning of cultural generalizations.

It is also fair to say that there is a body of comparative management research which, to generalize, typically relies on central (and hopefully lavish) funding, plus dedicated collaborating teams drawn from various participating countries. The strength of this genre is that it gets the job done, that it produces formally comparable data and findings; perhaps the weakness is that particular entities such as, say, decision-making mode or the formal apparatus of industrial democracy are 'untimely ripped' from the national context, a risk that meaning is sacrificed to comparability.

Whatever the balance sheet, I have not taken part in these studies and cannot write about them with authority. Instead the aim is to exploit a personal research base, which includes various studies of technical, production and personnel managers in West Germany (Lawrence, 1980; Hutton and Lawrence, 1981; Lawrence, 1984), of the character of management in Sweden (Lawrence and Spybey, 1986) and in the Netherlands (Lawrence, 1986), as well as a little first-hand exposure to organizational research in France and a recent exploratory study of management and industrial organization in East Germany, thanks to a British Council Fellowship.

What is more, the thrust of this research is personal in the sense of combining interests. What I have found most fun in the study of management is, first, the comparisons between countries, and second, the work on what managers really do and how to interpret it, the tradition of Carlson (1951), Mintzberg (1973) and Stewart (1976). The personal twist is in crossing the two interests, so that in exploring the nature of management in 'another country' I have given priority to trying to get a picture of what (foreign) managers demonstrably do and why they think they are doing it. This is an emphasis which in turn has implications for methods, but objectives come first.

The ends of understanding

The basic idea that either management or industrial organization might be different in different countries is relatively recent. Until well on into the 1970s the at least implicit assumption was of a universal and monolithic management, at least among the conspectus of advanced Western countries. These assumptions of homogeneity were derived in part from the dual American hegemony, in economic achievement and management literature, but also fundamentally from what might be called 'the logic of industrialization' (Hutton *et al.*, 1977). The essence of the latter is that the universal goals of profit and efficiency would call forth a 'one best way' of both organizing and running companies, any deviations being eliminated by the 'survival of the fittest' mechanism. This idea was given a further thrust in the 1960s by being conjoined to the convergence theory (Kerr *et al.*, 1960). This added a dynamic to the assumptions of universality in industrial organization by positing the advancing homogeneity of industrial societies on the basis of a pluralistic model, a homogeneity even held to be transcending East-West differences in political systems.

In the course of the 1970s these assumptions on the homogeneity of management broke down in the face of a range of studies, comprehending general discussions or analyses of cultural variation, such as Weinshall (1977) and Hofstede (1980), some explicit comparisons of particular aspects of management or industrial organization, such as Glover (1978) and LEST (1977), with occasional monographs on management in a chosen country implicitly characterizing their subject matter from the researcher's standpoint as a national of another country, for instance, Lawrence (1980). The net result is the recognition that both the character of management and the nature of industrial organization may vary by national-cultural context, with a variety of studies in support. In short, comparative management has emerged, at least as a sub-discipline.

So in the light of these developments, what do we want to explain? Of the two possible answers, personal and programmatic, the emphasis here will be on the former. The assignment I find most exciting is trying to produce a general account, an overall characterization, of management in another country – of saying what is different, interesting, and hopefully significant about managers or management in another country, precisely from a British or Anglo-Saxon viewpoint. And such an assignment is most exciting of all if you go to a country of which you have no prior knowledge: this gives the freest rein to sociological imagination.

At the same time I have sometimes embarked on comparative management studies to explore a more limited hypothesis, or knowing already one half of the (national) equation. I know, for instance, what management job advertisements in British papers look like: I once made a collection of similar advertisements from the right newspapers in Switzerland to see if the adverts were the same, and if not, what might be inferred from any differences (Lawrence, 1978). Or again, being familiar with both the literary and industrial reality of 'the problem of the first line supervisor' (Roethlisberger, 1945) in Anglo-Saxonia, I once interviewed a group of personnel managers in West Germany and then some foremen to see if they had 'the problem' too, and if not why not. On another occasion, after spending periods as an observer in a number of manufacturing companies in Germany and observing at first hand the excellent delivery performance (the *non plus ultra* was a production control meeting at a fork lift truck factory in Hamburg where all jobs were on time, so the participants brought forward the completion deadlines on some orders to give themselves a challenge), when I came to repeat these observational studies in Britain I was particularly interested to ascertain the causes of delivery failure in Britain, both intrinsic and contextual (Hutton and Lawrence; 1980).

It is also the case that the distinction between the big broad picture (of management in another country) and the more specific hypothesis of the kind just illustrated may well break down in practice. After arriving in Sweden, for instance, bent on a general characterization, I became fascinated with the idea of the coexistence of capitalist management and long-term parliamentary socialism, and intrigued by the question of what difference this socialist context makes to the functioning of management. In the Netherlands, on another occasion, I was struck by the tension between the accepted internationalism – everyone speaks English, multinationals on every street corner, exports are everything, and the 'we are a small country' (and therefore look beyond our borders) ethic – on the one hand, and the extreme regionalism, provincialism and *verzuiling* (pillarization of society on confessional lines) on the other. This tension set off the question of

whether anyone has ever influenced the Dutch (management) in the way
that the USA has influenced Britain, or Germany has influenced Scandinavia.
At the end of the day the answer is probably no; Holland may be smaller
than Lake Michigan, but it could not be lost there, although the quest for an
answer turned out a serialized illumination of mental bulwarks in the minds
of the Dutch.

But to return to the challenge of 'the big picture', how does one discover,
unpack and decode, the nature of management in another country? How
does one identify key values and related behaviours?

Ways and means

The three approaches I have made most use of in trying to understand
management in other countries are the gathering of background information,
interviews with practitioners, and periods of observation in manufacturing
companies. It is not unusual for researchers to have background information
on a society and its institutions prior to fieldwork, such information being
gained by any amalgam of study, reading, fact grabbing, prior visits or
residence, as well as the 'knock-on' effect of doing several studies in a
(foreign) society. There is probably a word of warning which is relevant
here, and that is that it is possible to know a country very well, without
knowing much about its management or industry. Outside the USA
management and industry are not high-profile institutions, they are not part
of the liberal-humane tradition of knowledge and understanding, and they
are not accessible to touristic acquaintance, even in the superficial way that
a country's culture and politics are. I visited West Germany as a tourist for
years, lived there twice, and even taught in a German university for half a
year, yet when hired by the British Department of Industry to make a study
of engineering management in Germany I found myself starting from
scratch: I did not know anything about the legal status or formal structure
of German companies, little about the vocational education system, nothing
about the way German managers were trained and, since this was my
'square one', had no reason to suppose any of it would be different from
what was observable in my own country.

There is also a certain danger in the attempt to understand the institutions
of another country and this is what might be called 'the fallacy of self-
fulfilling equivalence'. If one expects the newly studied country to be much
the same as one's native country, then there is a temptation to look for
equivalent sets of institutions assuming that matching them is all. It may
lead to false identification or to a missed difference in meaning. French
comprehensive schools, for instance, are different from English comprehen-
sives; they cater for a more restricted age group, collectivize and then
rebifurcate at a different point in the system. Or again, West Germany has
public schools in the English sense of private, fee-paying secondary schools,
which in practice take only the sons and daughters of the wealthy upper
middle class. But they differ from their English 'equivalent' by having
negative prestige connotations; going to a private boarding school in

Germany tends to suggest you were a 'bit of a handful' and your parents
wanted shot of you – it is not a ruling class label.

For any researcher lucky or sufficiently well organized to be in residence
in the foreign country whose management is the object of study there is an
enviable short cut to the years of background reading. This is quite simply
that (foreign national) colleagues in host universities or research institutes
make excellent informants, and spending some time with them can yield a
good understanding of the country's institutions and industrial structure.

Asking questions

When it comes to visiting companies and interviewing managers, whom to
interview is probably more critical than how to do it. Now to some extent it
is a 'non-question' in the sense that what you want to know will dictate the
desired interview sample: if one wants to understand, say, the nature of
financial planning and control in Swiss companies, one has to seek out
finance managers, and so on. And a less obvious variation on this theme is
that even if the task is that of overall characterization of the management in
another country, one will still not end up with a complete picture; this
means that choosing the (type of) interviewees equals choosing the outcome,
making implicit decisions about whether the characterization will be
'intolerably incomplete' without, say, an understanding of product planning
or industrial marketing practices, whether knowing about the quality and
character of top management will contribute more to the characterization
than knowing about the quality of activities of production superintendents
and sales reps. My own view on this last problematic, corporate presidents
versus middle managers, is that management is more differentiated
(between countries) at the bottom than the top, and for that matter more
differentiated at the manufacturing sites than at head office.

Against the background of this qualification that objective dictates type
of interviewee, I would like to indulge in three pieces of special pleading.

First, personnel officers are a good bet. Precisely because they are not
involved in the making, selling, and counting, they have more distance from
their organizations, and sometimes more of an overview. Personnel is also
traditionally a company's link with the environing society; personnel
managers know about the education system, vocational training, labour
laws, and so on, and may also have something more subtle and qualitative,
an appreciation of the values and aspirations which employees bring to the
employing company. Furthermore, in countries such as the Scandinavian
and Benelux ones, West Germany and Yugoslavia, which have a legally based
co-determination system, personnel people will be a critical (managerialist)
source on the functioning of this system and are often directly involved in it.
Until recent legislation, for instance, the personnel officer in a Dutch factory
would act as secretary to the *Ondernemingsraad* or works council.

Second, production managers are a strategic resource for the characterizing study of management in other countries. It is not just that production is

a *sine qua non* function, with most of the typical company's manpower and resources under its control. Production is also a central function, involved in operating chains of the design-to-sales kind, and locked in dependency relations with numerous other functions. Interviewing production managers, therefore, gives a view of the central operation, offers insights into the nature of contingent functions and is a strategic site for gauging the quality of corporate teamwork as well as more formal integration. It is also an area where any nation to nation differences in the nature and degree of informal organization will be most readily apparent.

This derives from several interlocking reasons. Production is *the* function in which blue collar workers are concentrated, it contains the most critical blue collar–management interface, and the managers themselves are involved in 'trading relationships' across departmental and sub-departmental lines.

Third, the objective of characterization is facilitated by dialogue with people having an overview *across* companies, as opposed to the top manager's overview of his own company. In practice this means consultants and sometimes business journalists and writers, or individuals with broad experience in non-executive director roles. People in such positions are valuable for informed generalization and comments on trends, changes and significant developments. They are also much more likely than the typical employed manager to have some international exposure and standard of comparison. And in societies such as Sweden which informally emphasize humility, restraint and not claiming more (knowledge) than one's due, people such as consultants may be exceptionally valuable precisely in their readiness to be opinionated, to generalize without necessarily having proof, to speak of trends which are not publicly verifiable.

On the question of techniques of investigating, two practical considerations may be urged. A pervasive problem with interviewing as a research tool is the difficulty of getting interviewees to admit discrediting things that the interviewer suspects. The particular point here is that this pervasive problem may be enhanced by the international dimension. It is one thing for, say, a production manager to confess to 'one of his own' that they never deliver anything on time, the foremen are worse than useless, the machine down-time is huge and there is a wildcat strike every Tuesday, but it may be rather worse offering such testimonies to some shorthand notebook-toting foreign academic (who obviously has your measure or he would not be asking these questions!). There is no absolute answer to this problem, but if the interviewer suspects a reluctance to 'tell all', there are ways of lowering the threshold. One is to prefix the question by citing the research literature or findings from other studies: we know, you may say, from studies of Japanese subsidiaries in Europe that not all sales departments have explicit market share, volume and revenue targets — how is it in this company? A stronger version of this technique is to admit the fault in your home country and ask for a comparison: in Britain we have two-hour tea breaks, what do you do in Hamburg? Another possible counter is to say, especially if it happens to be true, that you have come across the phenomenon in another company in the same country: the personnel manager over at X told me that all their computer programmers are moonlighting, is this a problem you experience here?

Having said all this, the problem is probably much smaller in reality than one would expect. Only in the intensely patriotic Netherlands have I found it to be a recurrent problem, with stalwart but suspicious denials, and lack of consensus on critical issues.

The second consideration concerns language. If one is interviewing foreign managers in English, there is the residual danger of encountering a respondent whose command is so poor that it conditions what he or she says; that they say not so much what they want in answer to your questions but what they can. If this arises, one has to write off the interview, though thanks to the dominance of English as a world language it is a rare event in my experience.

Much more pervasive is the milder problem of minor misapprehensions together with intimations of uncertainty. One is never quite sure that they have understood the question, or at least its nuances or comparative thrust; one worries that interviewees are responding to the question they think you asked (but you think you asked something different). The problem is compounded by the admirable vagueness of English: there is no other language more suited to the framing of open-ended questions or projective try-ons. Its apotheosis is perhaps the word 'like'. Something as harmless, and as sociologically gainful as, what are members of works councils like in your country, may well have the Swedish personnel manager reaching for his cyanide pills.

There is a lot to be said for interviewing in a foreign language even if your command is not perfect. At least it gives the interviewer control of uncertainty: you know they are replying to the right question; any failure to comprehend is on your side and you can judge whether to throw it away or go for an 'action replay' to get it right.

Finally on the question of language, if one has to interview in English, there is still a lot to be said for knowing some key words in the language of the interviewees, and using them, albeit in the middle of sentences in English. It is important in two instances. First, where mismatches and false equivalents are likely to arise. What, for instance, does the consultant mean by 'technical college': is it where 15-year-olds go for a bit of craft training, or does it produce the nation's (graduate) technical elite? Or again, what does this interlocutor mean by 'supervisor': is it a chargehand or a foreman or a superintendent or indeed anyone with a span of control? In short, it is worth knowing the educational system and work role terms, if nothing else. The second instance is where the interlocutor does not know the equivalents in English, in spite of a good overall command. Foreign managers, for example, often do not know how to render in English the terms relating to the legal status of companies, or to the co-determination system. The interviewer should help them out. Sometimes there is some minor cultural blockage. Dutch managers with a good command of English are more likely to say *agenda* than diary. The interviewer should go along with this: his job is to end up with an enlarged understanding, not to teach other people English.

Work fascinates me, I could watch it for hours

Observation as a method of management research is costly and rewarding. It is difficult to set up observational studies of managers at work: not every manager likes the idea of a foreign academic following him around, sitting in on his meetings, and being a party to all his exchanges; not all companies will allow this anyway.

It is also a fairly demanding assignment for the observer-researcher. You have to go up to ten hours at a stretch in a foreign language, keep your wits about you to make sense of it all, handle it socially and take forty pages of notes a day. And the method really is restricted to countries/languages in which the observer is genuinely competent.

On the other hand, the oft-voiced objection to observation as a research method, how do you know they are not changing their behaviour simply because you are there, is in my view much exaggerated. A number of considerations constrain a manager's ability to change his performance to suit the audience. First, there usually is a substantial unprogrammed element in management work, so that the observed subject has no advance warning of the contingencies he or she will have to deal with and react to, and has to glean and process hot information and take snap decisions. All this makes 'putting on a show' problematic. Second, management work is highly interactive, so that the ability of any individual manager to act differently is constrained by his role set and their interaction expectations; how can you 'put on the style' if the supporting cast do not go along with the performance? And a third consideration which deserves to be urged is that not all national cultures give the same priority to 'putting on a good show' as does the British: impression management is a variable dependent, not an independent variable.

The case for observation as a method is primarily that it is direct. Forms of interrogation, whether interview or questionnaire, are indirect. They represent in the present context attempts to find out about a manager's job and conduct by offering stimuli (questions) where the response is mediated by the respondent's consciousness, whereas in observational studies one is observing that job, that conduct, that action directly and it is the beholder who has the (interpretative) prerogative of consciousness.

Another merit of observation as a method is that it gets one closer to the qualitative things. It helps to answer questions such as: what is the style of management (in this country), do they 'go about things' differently, or to take a small liberty with Ranke, *wie ist es eigentlich?*

Observation is also calculated to yield unprogrammed insights. Most research is dependent on presuppositions (the scientist calls them hypotheses). You think that training is important, so you send round a questionnaire asking about training. Or you think industrial democracy must be an interesting phenomenon from a British viewpoint so you ask people about its functioning in interviews. But what about the things that you would think were important if you ever fell over them?

Observational studies in my case have been limited to West Germany and

Britain, but one or two examples from this spectrum of gains may be helpful. Let us start with something everyone knows about, German authoritarianism.

The view that Germans in authority positions are authoritarian and that those in subordinate positions are authoritarian submissives is one I used to accept without giving it very much thought. Nor does it give rise to hypotheses that it would be especially fruitful to test by interrogative means. But the process of making observational case studies in German companies has convinced me that the popular view is wrong, a conviction that derives from sitting in on a hundred and one meetings in German companies where:

— the tone is much less deferential than in Britain;
— participants do not typically use titles (they do not use Christian names either, but being formal is not the same as being rank-conscious);
— I have noted the vigorous and outspoken contribution of junior participants, including foremen;
— I have observed the prevalence of direct criticism of superiors, whether present or absent, and seeing it accepted as a matter-of-fact phenomenon.

And this is without reference to the 'institutionalized opposition' in the sense of the organs of co-determination.

Or consider delivery punctuality (the delivery of goods and orders to customers on time). One knows from sources such as Turnbull and Cunningham (1981) that German industry has a good record for delivery performance and we might infer from this that they 'take it seriously'. Fine, but what does taking it seriously mean? Again, observational studies offer some answers when the observer sees:

— the endless reminding of people of their time-fixed commitments before the event;
— the better relationship between production and contingent departments/ functions than is normal in Britain;
— the insistent production manager-led spending on the technical infrastructure of the firm;
— the direct involvement of line production managers in the technical facilitation of timely production (you actually see them planning machinery layouts, production aids, and engaging in quality trouble shooting);
— the almost neurotic desire to have reserves, stocks, protection, something to fall back on; if they never run out of anything it must be Germany.

On this last point of the German reluctance to be caught on the hop, an anecdote may be illustrative. One of the observational studies was at a company on the Baltic coast during a blizzard. The town was cut off, supplies became problematic, a state of emergency was declared by the *Land* government. In a dialogue between the production manager and his maintenance boss the latter grimly relayed the fact that without further deliveries their stock of central heating fuel would (only) last until the third week of May. This was on 19 February.

Dimensions of comparison

One of the charms of comparative management is that there is no finite list of variables in terms of which management in different countries may be compared, so that there is a premium on intellectual imagination and research experience, room to 'create from the materials of the human spirit'. What is more, among the dimensions of comparison that do occur in the literature there are marked differences on the specificity-generality continuum. At one end, one may be making useful and specific comparisons, say between the proportions of managers in companies employing more than 5,000 people who are university graduates, while at the other one may be trying to contrast British and American management in terms of its professionalism (which raises questions such as what is professionalism, what are the indicators, how shall we weigh them, does it have non-attitudinal manifestations?)

Nonetheless it may be helpful to offer some dimensions in terms of which management in different countries may be compared, including both the tangible and the less tangible. The ideas discussed in this section are illustrative and emphatically not exhaustive.

The qualifications that managers have in different countries often vary interestingly. First, there is sometimes a difference in level of qualification, certainly in any sample of countries that includes Britain. Second, there are variations in the relative predominance of qualificational types – first degrees in management are not important in France and West Germany (unless one counts the German subject of *Betriebswirtschaftslehre* as management rather than as business economics), but are increasingly important in Britain. Law is unimportant in Britain as a manager qualification subject, but has a traditional importance in Sweden, Germany and the Netherlands. Postgraduate management degrees, MBAs, are vastly more important in the USA than anywhere else, qualified accountants are more important in Britain, and so on. Third, there may be interesting differences in the content of qualifications, even if this is less accessible to survey methods. Law in Switzerland, for instance, is thought of as a more philosophic study, having something of the flavour of 'Modern Greats', than it is in Britain, reflecting the codified versus precedent-orientated legal systems, and the implications for 'heavy learning'. Companies in both France and West Germany could be said to be dominated by qualified engineers, yet there are marked differences of course content and disposition between the products of the *grandes écoles* and those of the *technische Hochschulen*. Or at a more modest level, German foremen get more training than British foremen, but it is craft and technical rather than supervisory (Fores *et al.*, 1978).

The relative prestige of functions – sales, production, finance, and so on – may vary between countries. Staff functions have more standing in the USA than in Europe, and are more likely to lead to, or be part of a journey towards, corporate high office (Booz *et al.*, 1973). Finance has high status in British companies, but not anywhere else. Germans, when asked if there are any *prima donna* functions, either say no or name design. Marketing has higher standing in the USA than anywhere, production has higher standing in Sweden than in Britain, and so on.

Similarly, the formal structure of organizations may vary on a national basis. Franco-German research, for instance, has characterized the French company as a tall, slender pyramid and the West German as a low, squat, broad-based one (LEST, 1977). In a study of financial control systems in British, French and German companies Horovitz (1980) has similarly demonstrated the existence of nationally preferred macro-organizational arrangements for companies. Or again, to take a lower-level example, whether or not the purchasing function is organizationally independent or integrated with production appears to vary on a national basis.

Work roles differ from country to country, while (translated) job titles present an illusion of homogeneity. A German personnel officer is applying the law and servicing the co-determination system; his British colleague is more obviously engaging in the classic functions of personnel management (Lawrence, 1982). A British production manager, to burlesque a little, is a gang boss, trouble shooter, and instant fixer; his opposite number in West Germany is more leisured and technocratic, his critical inputs probably being matters of technical understanding and creativity. When a British production manager says he has always been in production he means he started on the shop floor; when a German says it he means he is a qualified engineer who has alternated between posts in design, engineering, quality assurance and manufacturing.

Management work may be understood on a generalism versus specialism continuum. The Anglo-Saxon tradition is generalist: Americans think they can 'manage anything', the English are proud to be 'good all-rounders'. At the other extreme the Germans have a much more specific understanding of management: one does a specific job, does not change industry, applies a specific training/knowledge/skill basis, uses particularist job titles, not general ones such as 'manager' or 'executive'. And the generalism-specialism dimension is an important determinant of careers, and of attitudes to, and the reality of, inter-company mobility.

The working context varies nationally for managers in terms of the level and nature of industrial relations problems, and with the presence or absence of co-determination. A middle manager in Sweden will have a different approach to the initiation of change from that of his American counterpart (Lawrence, 1983). And indeed the presence or absence of co-determination systems heavily structures the personnel management role, and affects the production management environment as well.

Business strategy is usually treated as an individual corporate variable, in the sense of Company X has these aims and Company Y has those. Yet the study of multinationals (Goldberg and Neghandi, 1983) and even more of subsidiary behaviour in host countries (Doyle, 1986) has suggested some national patterning. Choices as to profits now or profits later, revenue or market share, profitability or growth, initiating or following, yield at least Anglo-Japanese contrasts. We also know that both exporting or manufacturing abroad may be undertaken for a variety of strategic reasons (Mascarenhas, 1986); it may also be the case that further research will demonstrate characteristically national proclivities in the expression of strategic choices.

The pre-eminence of the American contribution to industrial sociology and the influence of classics such as Roethlisberger and Dickson (1939) and Dalton (1959) has led us to take for granted the universality of the informal system and to assume that 'politicking is the normal state of man'. Yet my research suggests a presence or absence continuum for informal organization, with the USA with typically strong, informal organization at one end, Sweden at the other, and the Netherlands in the middle (Lawrence, 1986). One way to test this phenomenon is to ask managers questions of the 'But what do you really do?' kind. The British answer begins, 'Ah, well'; the Germans tell you they have a committee to decide; the Swedes do not understand the question.

End play

While seeking to illustrate the kinds of comparison possible, there has been an effort to stress the open-ended nature of research in comparative management. The value of open-ended questions has been urged, together with the virtue of a methodology that can pick up new impulses and explore them. To end with a footnote on the last idea, I would like to urge the questioning of 'generally accepted' points of view as held by managers in other countries. What they take for granted may be precisely what is most illuminating for the outsider. Swedish managers, for instance, take it for granted that a manager will normally decline a promotion that involves a geographic move. British managers purvey profitability and personal rewards as the driving force. Dutch managers are agreed that it would not be a good idea for their company to be run by an American. Why?

7

CONNOISSEURSHIP IN THE STUDY OF ORGANIZATIONAL CULTURES

Barry A. Turner

There is a story about a farmer's wife who won a national strüdel-making competition in Austria. Asked by a journalist to say how she made strüdels, the farmer's wife looked puzzled. Eventually she said, 'Well, I put on my apron, wash my hands, roll up my sleeves and then I go into the kitchen and make strüdels.' I feel a little of her puzzlement when I am asked to talk about how I study organizations: I find an organization, get into it, and then I study it. Research, like strüdel making, has elements of craft about it, so that some of the knowledge acquired by those who do it is tacit knowledge, embedded in the skills of the craft, and it is sometimes difficult to be explicit about these skills, which are easier to transmit by example and by apprenticeship. I am not trying to suggest that we should avoid trying to talk about them, however. Unquestioned, faulty craft skills may be just as readily transmitted as good ones and discussion may well improve the craft. In this chapter I would like to try to pull out for discussion some aspects of research craft skills.

It might be helpful if I outlined how I would embark upon the study of an organization, or a portion of one, and then reflected upon this sketch of research activity to see what illumination may be extracted from it. For some years I have been concerned to carry out research into qualitative features of organizations, paying particular attention in some work to the cultures which are constituted within organizations, (Turner, 1971) and looking at decision making and safety in organizations in a number of industries, more recently the construction industry (Turner, 1978, 1983). All of this work is based upon the collection of qualitative data. There was a time when this was regarded as an idiosyncratic, not to say archaic way of doing social science, but as understanding has developed of the weaknesses as well as the strengths of surveys and measurement, interest in qualitative methods for the study of organizations has grown (see, for instance, special issues of *Administrative Science Quarterly*, December 1979, and *Journal of Management Studies*, July 1983), especially as such methods have come to be seen to be applicable to matters of urgent practical interest (Peters and Waterman, 1982; Lessem, 1985; Turner, 1986; Pidgeon *et al.*, 1986).

How, then, would I approach the study of an organization? In the crudest outline, I would need to establish first my broad purpose in carrying out the study. I would need an interest in a particular type of organization, and in particular types of activities which might go on within such milieux. I would not normally have a very cut-and-dried set of questions prepared, or a set of strong preconceptions about what I might find. I would want to negotiate entry in a way which would enable me to 'botanize', to observe and begin to sort out and name the social flora and fauna to be found in the setting concerned, so that, in the process, sharper research questions could develop. I would need to gain access to an appropriate organization, or, in some instances, to appropriate documents, negotiating with power holders and 'gatekeepers' as necessary.

Once inside the organization, I would always carry a small notebook, and I would regard myself as always 'on duty', or engaged in research. I would want to supplement even a very formal programme of tape recorded interviews with notes about the physical layout of the organization, the style of decor, the type of people involved, the style of normal interchanges in the canteen, or in the cloakroom, as well as in the office and on the shop floor. This set of notes would constitute a research journal, a chronological record of my activities, written for myself alone. Writing in it every day, I would expect to record observations, plans, methodological and theoretical notes, personal feelings and reactions and speculations about the direction being taken by the research. To get at the cultural aspects of the organization I would also want to talk to people, observe people and to 'be around'.

Typically I would emerge after a period of fieldwork with a set of notebooks, a set of interview records and any ancillary documents I had been offered. Ideally I would like to alternate two or three weeks of fieldwork with a similar period of analysis, for the mental set required when attending to people, and when keeping alert for nuances of behaviour and talk which must be recorded, is completely different from that required for analysis. Alternating fieldwork with analysis not only makes it possible to adjust my way of thinking, but it also helps to keep the problem of analysis within bounds. Six months or more of data collection can completely overwhelm a researcher, so that the research may never be satisfactorily written up. Analysis in this kind of research has the effect, in part, of successively restructuring the way in which the researcher perceives the field of study (Turner, 1981). As you 'botanize', shapes and patterns emerge from the initial confusion, and these patterns become more firmly established during data analysis. In the process, questions can be formulated about the interrelationships between the new cognitions which are developing.[1]

In the analysis period, I would go through my notebooks and interview transcripts, numbering each paragraph for reference purposes. I then set out on 5″ × 8″ file cards the titles of those low-level theoretical categories which I 'see' in each paragraph, noting on the card instances of the recurrence of a particular category at different points in the data. When I have accumulated several instances of a given theoretical category – from six to twelve, depending on the topic – I try to write very clear, formal theoretical definitions of the working category label which I have been using on that particular card, aiming to produce a definition which would be self-explanatory to a newcomer to the research team.

This process of definition writing I find to be very demanding and, at times, curiously enough, very exhilarating. In the process of specifying in abstract terms exactly what are the limits of the particular social category, what social phenomenon it refers to, and what it is *not*, the 'sociological imagination' is stretched. Sometimes, when the elucidation of theoretical possibilities stimulates a rapid flow of suggestions, hypotheses and potential interrelationships within the organization I am studying, this can approach that state of intellectual stimulation described by Glaser (1978, p. 24) as a 'drugless trip'. The two stages of writing definitions and writing about relationships between the theoretical categories generated spill over into each other. The notes and definitions generated constitute a further set of resources which supplies the raw material for written-up versions of the research, in book, article or report form.

All of the processes I have mentioned are iterative and overlapping. There is a starting point, but, once started, there is no logical stopping point in the process itself. The cycle of observation-analysis-theorizing can continue indefinitely, although demands for an article or a report may interrupt it. To qualify this, however, although there may be no necessary logical stopping point, there are personal limits. It is time to move on when you have achieved intellectual closure in an area, when the intellectual energy which fuelled your researcher's curiosity shifts to other areas. Those intellectual issues which are important to you will re-emerge in a new form in your next piece of research.

Let me now try to reflect upon this outline process which I have described. I do not want to dwell on the problems of gaining access to the field, or of carrying out fieldwork, for there is now an adequate if modest body of guidance available already (see, for example, Schatzman and Strauss, 1973; Burgess, 1982; Burgess, 1984a). Nor do I want to elaborate upon the practical details of qualitative analysis, for I have already set these out elsewhere (Turner, 1981, 1983; Martin and Turner, 1986). Instead I would like to take up a number of less evident issues which might be of importance to those wanting to produce good quality organizational research using approaches similar to the one I have outlined.

At an elementary level, the researcher embarking on a qualitative study of an organization needs to be warned that this is a time-consuming exercise. It takes time to gain access, to meet people, to let them tell their stories and to make sure that their telling has included all that you want to know. It takes a long time to transcribe or write up field notes and tape recordings: as a rule of thumb, a one-hour taped interview takes two to three hours to transcribe. But even then, the analysis of non-standardized, non-survey data is in itself a lengthy process. For each study an appropriate approach needs to be devised and implemented, and these tasks cannot be accomplished in a couple of hours.

A second simple caveat is that qualitative research, just as much as any other kind of scientific enquiry, needs to be carried out with meticulous care. Considerations of who was spoken to, of what weight should be given to their comments, of whether their comments are accurately recorded, of the nature of the researcher's relationship to the organization and the members of it, are all important. Most crucial, however, is the question of what kind of analysis the evidence will support if the research is to retain credibility in the scientific community. All of these matters need careful attention.

The last point could perhaps be emphasized even more. Some kinds of research methods have been referred to as 'strong': they possess strong rules for classifying as 'error' any data which does not fit with the method. Wrongly completed, closed-ended answers to questionnaires are like spoiled ballot papers in elections – they are not meaningless, but they have to be discarded because they do not fit the pre-established system. By contrast, in qualitative enquiries, such rules for discarding data as erroneous are very weak. The researcher with few preconceptions about findings has to live with the data collected in all of its complexity and quirkiness. In consequence, very few conclusions can be justified solely by reference to the method used. Generalizations from such a study have to be self-justifying, they have to stand on their own feet. The researcher using this approach is exposed: any theory emerging will reflect the researcher's intellectual grasp, creativity, sensitivity and understanding, as well as the quality of the data-gathering methods used. It is not possible for a poor researcher to hide behind an array of equipment as is often the case with other modes of research.

Turning now to some issues of analysis, the approach which I have been discussing is one intended to produce what is called 'grounded theory'. This term was coined some twenty years ago by Glaser and Strauss (1967) to refer to research which produced 'theory grounded in data'. Approaches like this are sometimes referred to as 'inductive' approaches, since any conclusions are 'drawn out' of a small number of cases, but in fact this loose usage of the term 'induction' is of limited help, since all forms of research, qualitative and quantitative, are based upon a complex admixture of deductive and inductive procedures.

The intention of Glaser and Strauss in formulating this term was to encourage researchers to gather, study and analyse qualitative data in the way which they themselves had done in their studies of American hospital organizations, without being inhibited by the excessive emphasis which was placed at that time upon the acquisition of a grand theoretical schema as an absolute precondition for carrying out research. An orthodoxy which saw major theorists as the only possible source of the theoretical insights which had to be checked by 'proletarian testers' virtually ruled out the qualitative, 'botanizing' approach to research. Indeed, Glaser and Strauss comment that one of their reasons for writing their book *The Discovery of Grounded Theory* was to give qualitative researchers a methodological text to cite when they submitted research proposals, and I have found their book helpful in precisely this way.

Because of its challenge to prevailing research practices, the book was rather coolly received. In my view, however, when the polemic tone is removed they can be seen to be advocating nothing more revolutionary than the application of a non-doctrinaire scientific method to qualitative social science enquiries. To press this point, I consider that the qualitative researcher has no real alternative to pursuing something very close to grounded theory. The details of the techniques may vary, but the shape of qualitative research is limited by a number of necessary constraints. Because of these constraints, and the need for practitioners to select from a limited range of possible ways of dealing with them, comments about many aspects of work using grounded theory will transfer without difficulty to most other forms of non-quantitative social enquiry.

The problems of analysing qualitative data did not, of course, originate in the 1960s. Many social scientists from de Tocqueville and Weber onwards have had to confront such matters in their work. Weber's discussion of 'ideal types' arose out of a need to find an adequate way of dealing with qualitative data, as did Znaniecki's formulation of the approach called 'analytic induction'. In a recent discussion, Znaniecki's approach has been summarized thus:

Analytic induction is intended to maintain faithfulness to the empirical data while abstracting and generalizing from a relatively small number of cases. Its aim is to 'preserve plasticity' by avoiding prior categorization. No definition of a class or category of data precedes the selection of data to be studied as representative of that class. The data analysis begins before any general formulations are proposed. . . . It abstracts from a given concrete case the features that are essential and generalizes them. (Bulmer and Burgess, 1986, p. 251)

I see this summary as applying equally well to grounded theory, even though Bulmer and Burgess separate the two. To study organizations as cultural assemblages from the standpoint of grounded theory, we must abstract and generalize from a small number of cases, preserving 'plasticity' by delaying categorization until our 'botanizing' process is well under way, just as in Znaniecki's approach.

The essential constraints I had in mind when I referred above to the central processes of qualitative research are as follows: the fieldworker looks and listens, interviews and records. A continuous flow of experience presents itself, but for research purposes, it is necessary to divide that potential infinity of material which *could* be collected into sections of data which *are* collected, and then to further subdivide these into segments for manipulation. Agar, in his excellent recent discussion of ethnography, uses Goffman's term 'strip' to refer to the units of data with which an ethnographer works: a strip he regards as 'any bounded phenomenon against which an ethnographer tests his or her understanding' (Agar, 1986, p. 28).

Some procedure must then be devised for recognizing and labelling facets of the 'strip', and it is usually necessary to supplement this with some kind of storage and filing system. To move towards the reinterpretation which must be produced as the outcome of the research, the separated segments will have to be rearranged in a new order in which the researcher can see and offer new patterns of understanding. That is to say, techniques have to be devised which make it possible for the researcher to generate the new empirical or theoretical sequences which will be presented to others as a result of the research. Any novel patterns will need to be scrutinized in order to draw out those general or theoretical conclusions which the investigation will support, and, finally, at those points where aspects of the outcomes are to be passed on to other members of the social scientific community, the researcher's new understandings must be set out in written form for discussion and evaluation.

Every piece of qualitative research must meet these demands, but very little seems to have been written about them in these terms, in part, I suspect, because few individual researchers have felt it sufficiently important to make public their own painfully won solutions to these problems. But even though those who devise them may feel in retrospect that many of these solutions might look rather trivial, in the absence of discussion, later workers will still have to expend time and energy in order to rediscover these techniques or variants of them. Discussion is hampered, too, by the diversity of the subject matter looked at by qualitative researchers, which serves to mask similarities of methods and analysis, so that this, too, ensures that any collective understanding about these procedures grows only slowly.

The qualitative researcher needs to be particularly sensitive to and well versed in the issues of science and scientific knowledge as it applies to the qualitative enterprise. Or, perhaps, it would be better to say that the qualitative researcher needs to be especially aware of questions which surround the kind of *knowing* that is central to such research. The exposure to people in the field, the 'botanizing', the detailed reflection and analysis necessitated by grounded theory and other qualitative approaches, makes the researcher aware at first hand of the demands of 'attending to' events and of perceiving that multiplicity of features which will, eventually, serve as a basis for theoretical categorizations. The researcher has to learn how to get to know the phenomena in question, and to develop the associated skills of knowing.

Even in the physical sciences, some people seem to be more able than others at observing in a way which connects with the development of knowledge. There is a section in Leonardo da Vinci's notebooks about the flight of birds (da Vinci, 1952, pp. 92–103) in which he describes his observations of the way that birds adjust and trim their wing and tail feathers on take-off and landing, and then comments on the ways in which these movements vary subtly from species to species. These field observations are made coherent in a logical and illuminating discussion. But even with the benefit of this discussion, my own poor powers as a biological observer are shown up by the difficulties I experience when I try to see, to attend to the subtle differences and variations set out so perceptively by da Vinci. In the field of biological medicine, Hans Selye (1964) urged his graduate students to develop their perception in experimental work by *contemplating* their experimental animals, so that they could get to know them and perceive a *gestalt* of characteristics which would be much more difficult to notice or interpret if considered individually and separately. By such means, Selye himself identified the pattern of subtle features displayed by rats under stress, enabling him subsequently to discover and treat the 'stress syndrome' in human beings.

Differences in the skills of knowing are displayed, then, in the natural sciences, and we might expect the difference between those who are good and bad at such things to be wider in the social sciences. Goffman, for example, was clearly a good 'knower', spotting events and incidents which enabled him to generate a vast range of insightful and transforming concepts, even though, as various commentators have pointed out, he shrank from building these into extensive theoretical systems (Gouldner, 1971; Ditton, 1980). Everett Hughes, too, seems to be a skilled perceiver of social phenomena who was also able to develop at Chicago a mode of training which ensured that his graduate students such as Geer, Becker and Polsky, after their apprenticeship, constituted a second generation of skilled social observers (Becker *et al.*, 1968). Warren Bennis has expressed succinctly his own view of how he tries to be a good observer of organizational processes: 'I record as far as possible every homely, quotidian detail in the belief that to look closely is to be surprised' (Bennis, 1973, pp. 9–10). To be surprised is to experience a breakdown of one schema and to have to construct another (Turner, 1978, chapter 8; Agar, 1986); it is to learn at a level higher than the most basic one (Bateson, 1973); it is to extend our understanding.

In shifting towards a discussion of the skills of knowing which a researcher can bring to bear on a situation, it is clear that we are starting to talk not only about what is to be observed in organizational research, but also about the observer. This shift in emphasis should make it clear that we cannot treat the process of data gathering simply as a mechanical one, with the researcher acting like a human tape recorder, trying to transcribe anything offered in a passive manner. We know from a decade or more of ethnomethodological enquiry and discussion that social and organizational life is a continuously achieved process, that social encounters are creative constructions, occasions to be 'brought off' by those participating in them. The social researcher in the field is not exempt from these insights, and, even though those trained in a strongly positivistic tradition may find difficulty in accepting that 'the facts' are not independently waiting 'out there' to be gathered in, if they are to succeed in qualitative research, they will need to recognize that when such social research takes place, there will be an overlapping and a partial fusing of the horizons of knowledge of at least three parties: the observer, the observed and the scientific audience. Evidently, the role of the observer in such a relationship cannot be a passive one.

The philosopher Michael Polanyi was concerned with this relationship between the observer and that which was to be observed when he wrote, in a discussion of *natural* science:

> . . . the discovery of objective truth in science consists in the apprehension of a rationality which commands our respect and arouses our contem-

plative admiration. . . . (S)uch discovery, while using the experience of our senses as clues, transcends this experience by embracing the vision of a reality beyond the impressions, a vision which speaks for itself in guiding us to an ever deeper understanding of reality. (Polanyi, 1958, pp. 5–6)

Observations such as this, of course, take us into deep water, and even Polanyi himself admitted that to make such statements would seem like the wildest return to Platonism. But his 'post-critical philosophy' does take up a position close to this, in which he directs our attention to the role of the 'intellectual passions' in knowing. Purely descriptive grounded theory, purely descriptive qualitative analysis, that which plays back one everyday account of the data collected, has little of interest to offer. If new practitioners are to produce something more, they have to learn not only to attend very closely to the data, but to do so with.something which is close to what Polanyi calls 'intellectual passion'.

Polanyi writes of human intellectual powers and their:

passionate participation in the act of knowing . . . manifested in the appreciation of probability and order in the exact sciences and . . . even more extensively in the way the descriptive sciences rely on skills and connoisseurship. At all these points the act of knowing includes an appraisal and this personal coefficient, which shapes all factual knowledge, bridges in doing so the disjunction between subjectivity and objectivity. (Polanyi, 1958, p. 16)

The good qualitative researcher needs, therefore, to become a connoisseur in the realm of social knowing, developing skilful knowing as an *addition* to analytic comprehension. Rather than merely absorbing knowledge, the connoisseur pours his or her attention into the 'subsidiary awareness of particulars', passionately participating in the act of knowing and at the same time appraising the quality of that which is known. Polanyi contrasted his advocacy of such connoisseurship with what he called Mach's 'telephone directory' view of scientific theory, a view of theory as a 'convenient contrivance for recording events and computing their future course' (Polanyi, 1958). Good qualitative research in organizations should not produce 'telephone directory' accounts of organizational behaviour, but accounts observed by a connoisseur.[2]

Following Polanyi, the philosopher Solomon has elaborated at much greater length upon the place of the passions in philosophy and in life (Solomon, 1976). Drawing upon his work (pp. 18ff.) I find it helpful to think of the researcher as bringing a distinctive 'perspective' to an enquiry, a perspective which does not deny the possibility of achieving a degree of objectivity in investigation, but one which equally does not deny the presence and the significance of the values, the passions, and the subjectivity of the observer. There is no real alternative to this, for research is a human activity, carried out by human beings, who cannot relinquish their values and passions. If we find a discussion of research in these terms novel, it is not because we are importing such matters *into* qualitative organizational studies, but because discussion of such matters can be more easily suppressed in quantitative, positivistically orientated work. In admitting the presence and the importance of the observer's 'perspective', we acknowledge that the first-person standpoint is *not erroneous*. Solomon observes that the recognition of subjectivity as one element of our perspective allows us to accept that we view the world personally and self-consciously, with an awareness of just *who* is doing the research, or carrying out whatever other activity. But objectivity, too, has to be an element of our perspective if we are to avoid both solipsism and fantasy. Objectivity is not a mechanical recording of the world 'in the way that it is', but it is an achievement, an overcoming of biases and prejudices. Our lives, as much as our researches, are a dialectic, a 'conversational' movement between subjectivity and objectivity which continues as we put meaning *into* things.[3] As Schatzman and Strauss have commented, the data do not speak for themselves: they only hint at something *if* you are able to hear (Schatzman and Strauss, 1973, p. 118).

The researcher intending to develop a grounded theory of organizational culture or organizational behaviour needs, therefore, to acknowledge the importance of seeking out, acquiring and interpreting data through a unique personal perspective in which the subjective and the objective are in constant interplay. The researcher needs also to become accustomed to this idea, that a competent researcher puts meaning into the field. Isherwood's narrator, in his short novel *Goodbye to Berlin* (1940, p. 1), said of himself, 'I am a camera,' precisely in order to detach himself in a dispassionate and amoral fashion from the events surrounding him in Berlin in the 1930s. When a social scientist appears to aim for such an avoidance of humanity, what emerges is an account which also has an amoral character: the disregard for aspects of human rights and dignity in an American mining setting, for example, are chronicled in Vaught and Smith's (1980) study in such a deadpan manner as to raise doubts about such a dehumanized objectivity being presented as social science.

A consequence, then, of encouraging investigators to participate in the act of knowing and to develop skill and connoisseurship in knowing is that they are likely to supplement their analytic understanding with what Polanyi variously calls 'personal knowledge', 'tacit knowledge' or 'craft knowledge' of that which they seek to understand. In its nature, the essence of this 'personal knowledge' is difficult to express articulately: as Polanyi comments, 'We know more than we can say.' But personal knowledge nonetheless provides a background of experience and expertise which enables us to appraise that information which we wish to absorb and employ explicitly. In the light of this tacit knowledge, we treat, as Polanyi puts it, 'the experience of our senses as clues' to an array of possible theoretical accounts which would express our deepened understanding. Ravetz (1971) has shown the importance of tacit or craft knowledge which is passed on from one natural science researcher to another. It serves to establish schools of scientific enquiry and to unify traditions of investigation. I know of no detailed discussion of these effects in social science, but I would expect them to be at least as strong, if not more so.

One hint of the kind of device which might be adopted by a researcher anxious to avoid the production of merely a 'telephone directory' account of an organization under study is Schatzman and Strauss's idea of looking for 'conceptual leverage'. In the process of trying to analyse organizational data, the process of actively discovering relevant classes of things, persons and events, and significant relationships between them, the analyst will want to search for appropriate 'conceptual levers': that is to say, for appropriate thinking devices which both distance the analyst from the data and provide a new perspective on it. A wide array of conceptual levers could be devised. The most common are provided by approaches which require the analyst to interrogate the data, either substantively by reference to the concepts and frameworks already existing in appropriate disciplines, or logically, by asking experimental, comparative, historical, analogical or functional questions about the data.

A corollary of our concern with the contribution made to research by the individual qualitative researcher is a recognition that the mode of analysis adopted by an investigator is likely to be affected by personal style and personal preference. Thus one of my colleagues wrote of another who was trying out qualitative research and grounded theory for the first time:

> My colleague had been very adamant about sticking 'close to his data' and he, for his own reasons, has to see everything as neat and orderly. He is very smart but also *very* cautious and that old background in the verification (and experimental) mode of research lingers on. . . . I feel my own limitations regarding what a final product *should* look like. I think my own uses of grounded theories have turned out to be largely empirical summaries rather than real theory. . . . Really this last step is, to me, the toughest for everyone. I can see that students of mine are almost but not quite taking it, and I can point this out and encourage them to do so. But I find it *very difficult* to take myself. I flat out do not know how to do it myself. Does this seem surprising? Is there anything I can do to learn how? Even Glaser and Strauss's work fails to help – because, in many ways, their work strikes me as mostly well-organized description within a 'discovered' conceptual framework. . . . I have learned a lot trying to write about grounded theory and I have learned that I really do not know very much about the last stages of the process. Even in teaching grounded theory, I realized that I emphasize the early parts of the process and basically neglect the later ones. It is high time I moved on a notch. (personal communication)

Reading these reflections on personal experience in carrying out qualitative research, and thinking about the different attitudes I have encountered when collaborating with others in grounded theoretic exercises, or in trying to teach students this way of dealing with qualitative data, I am struck by the relevance of the individual's characteristic mental set as carried through into their research work. Those who, for example, are orderly, fastidious and neat in their dress, demeanour and mental habits are likely to find the removal of order threatening. The intellectual world benefits greatly from those order-giving drives which are intent on establishing 'cognitive ownership' of an area, but this mental set may not be conducive to the production of good qualitative research.[4]

A low tolerance of ambiguity is likely to be a characteristic displayed by those who want to have things cleared up, sorted out and neatly stacked, while those with a higher tolerance of ambiguity can live more readily with uncertainties and obscurities without distress. Lowe (1977) in an illuminating thesis on research practice, commented that, although the conclusion of her thesis had been delayed while she took two years off to complete a pottery course, the practical experience which she gained in reducing chaos to order made her better equipped to complete her thesis when she returned to it. In a psychological exercise requiring students to type out a passage while deliberately mis-spelling every word, a small number of those involved, those with low tolerance of ambiguity, felt dizzy and ill as they tried to type and were unable to complete the task (Perls *et al.*, 1973, pp. 75–82). An extreme intolerance of ambiguity was reported by Luria in his discussion of a remarkable 'memory man' (Luria, 1968). While this man had no discernible limits to his memory, his understanding proceeded in a very literal manner, and the synaesthesia which helped him to remember long lists of words caused him physical discomfort when he was confronted by the ambiguities of puns and of poetry. We may conclude that, notwithstanding his prodigious powers of memory, this individual would have made a poor qualitatiye researcher!

These references to 'chaos' and 'ambiguity' arise here because of the recurrent problem which any qualitative researcher has in dealing with masses of non-standardized data. In the absence of pre-constructed categories for data, the material gathered is difficult to subdue. Researchers often fear that they are being overwhelmed by it, and they have to learn both to live with that threat *and* to find strategies for extracting from the collected data propositions about the organization in question which are sustainable and communicable.

Whether the researcher uses file cards, data slips or computer entries to record how the data 'strips' are divided into categories, an initial difficulty is likely to be the embarrassing number of such categorizations. Two research workers wrote to me to indicate the difficulties which they faced when, after six months of continuous joint fieldwork, their initial analyses had yielded 513 category cards to one and 526 to the other. The researcher faced with such a volume of material is likely to be dealing with an excess of low-level concepts which are not at all well articulated in regard to one another. Sets of ideas may be extracted from such a conglomeration of material by strategies such as:

1 clustering the data and creating hierarchies of related concepts so that *sub-sets* may be manipulated and analysed at any one time, rather than the whole set;
2 limiting the number of people involved in generating categories from the original data: a group of people may help a researcher to commence data analysis, as in Glaser's 'seminars' (Glaser, 1978,

pp. 33–5), but the regular involvement of more than two people in the generation of categories from an extensive set of qualitative data multiplies the number of categories emerging and raises the risk that the analysis may be swamped;

3 progressively digesting the data gathered: successive bouts of data gathering and retreat from the field to analyse data are likely, as we have already noted, to help to produce a structured perception of core concepts which should certainly number less than one hundred, and which may be considerably less than that.

Bailyn, in a discussion of the problems of analysis of survey data (Bailyn, 1977), offered the observation that such analysis needed to be pursued by the retention of an appropriate degree of complexity in the work. Some time ago I transferred this general injunction from survey work to the qualitative area (Turner, 1981, p. 229) without considering in much detail how the researcher might assess what was 'an appropriate degree of complexity'. This point is important because at too high a level of complexity in the data, the analyst is overwhelmed while at too low a level of complexity, the theorizing is sterile, and 'nothing happens.' Very little emerges in the nature of interesting theoretical accounts or propositions when there is a paucity of interlinked conceptual relationships which offers only a low level of analysis. One of the major virtues of qualitative research is that it does not try to reduce the world to a few simple categories, but offers instead theoretical accounts which are multi-faceted. This quality makes it more likely that they will offer to the reader and the practitioner an adequately complex map of the portion of the social world which is under investigation.[5]

This concern about a requisite level of complexity in analysis might be worth linking with Miller's (1956) long-established observation that the maximum number of variables which can be held in short-term memory is 'seven plus or minus two'. This might be worth considering as a possible rule of thumb for assessing complexity in the theoretical analysis emerging from a qualitative analysis of an organization. Let me propose that a theoretical sub-system under analysis should have between five and nine major elements in order to yield an interesting outcome. If this is so, then the theorist with more elements than this should consider whether it is helpful to cluster, simplify or concentrate material until the theoretical field is occupied by the requisite five to nine components to be related. Equally the theorist with fewer than five elements should seek to expand the scope of the sub-system under analysis. The image of adjusting the degree of magnification of a microscope is one which I find helpful in thinking about this process. A cursory examination of a number of texts and theses suggests that diagrams and classificatory tables in many social science writings do, in fact, conform to this precept. It is worth noting again that all of this discussion of scope, of focus and of levels of complexity arises as much, if not more, from the capabilities and limitations of the researcher as from the constraints of the area under investigation.

Students and practitioners who use a qualitative approach in their investigations of organizations are engaged, as social scientists, not in an individual quest, but in a communal one. They do not carry out their studies primarily to achieve personal enlightenment. The best organizational study in the world counts for nothing if it is not written up to be made available to other members of the scientific community, or to members of the organization who are engaged in pursuing improvements. Clearly, the communication of research results is as much an integral part of the social scientific process as are the other stages we have discussed.

The qualitative researcher has many potential advantages when faced with the task of writing up research. The complexities, ambiguities and overlapping perceptions we have been discussing can make fascinating reading. And yet, while facile reviewers can temper their praise for the 'rich' data of a qualitative study with dismissive comparisons with novel writing, the social scientist is not a novelist. For good communication, it *is* necessary to tell a story to your audience, but, as Schatzman and Strauss point out, the social scientist has to tell a story which makes clear the classes of social events dealt with, the connective categories which link them and the locative categories which specify their intensity and scope (Schatzman and Strauss, 1973, pp. 110ff.). Priorities are selected as the data are examined to determine which portions are to be used, and this selection has to be done in a way which offers up propositional statements. In telling the story of the research, all of these elements must be manipulated to achieve the necessary communication, but the links must be made with care, tying them in a defensible manner to the data collected.

Social researchers are much criticized for their poor use of language, often with some justification, but the qualitative researcher should be better placed than most to overcome the pedestrian, jargon-laden style of much writing on social analysis. If a study has been carried out by a researcher who has developed some degree of connoisseurship in the skills of social knowing, the written accounts should be able to convey to the reader something of that experience of knowing. Two contemporary qualitative researchers who seem to me to be able to write with an authentic and an authoritative voice about their fieldwork are Willis in his study of a group of boys in a comprehensive school (Willis, 1977), and Hockey in his recent account of the socialization of private soldiers into the British Army (Hockey, 1986). Both of these accounts reveal writers who have put their energy into experiencing their field of study, and who have then, through the resultant 'connoisseur's accounts', conveyed both their knowledge and their energy about knowing to the reader.

In a helpful manual on the work of writing, Elbow (1981) makes a distinction between writing with 'no voice', writing with 'voice' and writing with 'real voice'. Writing with no voice is, as Elbow comments, like much sociology: dead, mechanical and faceless writing, which lacks sound, rhythm, energy and individuality, whereas writing with voice has the elements of texture, fluency and life. The competent researcher needs to develop, professionally, skills in writing which will enable him or her to communicate research findings with 'voice'. Then, occasionally, although it is more difficult in research than in 'creative writing', it may also be possible to write with what Elbow calls 'real voice', when the accounts of a portion of the organizational world can be rendered in words which do not merely communicate well, but which have the power and magic to command the attention of the reader.

Conclusions

Those aspects of research practice which are easiest to codify are those furthest from the dynamic centre of the research process. In trying to reflect upon my own dealings with organizational research, particularly that concerned to generate grounded theory, it has seemed to be important to try to write about aspects of the 'craft skills' involved. This has necessitated a concern with the researcher rather than with the subject area of the research, and it draws attention to the element of appraisal as well as of cognition which seems to be involved in skilful knowing. In seeking to delineate the nature of Polanyi's 'connoisseurship' in research, we become concerned with the researcher's perspective which must recognize an interplay between objectivity and subjectivity in the interactions of research. The personal style and mental set of the researcher are not irrelevant to the manner in which organizational research is carried out, especially, although not exclusively, in the stages of data analysis and theory construction. These mixtures of personal and collective concerns carry through into the final stage of research when the researcher has to communicate accounts of the research to those studied, to the scientific community or to the wider public. All of these aspects of qualitative research into organizational activities involve the development of personal skills by the researcher. Important elements in transmitting such skills are example and apprenticeship, but these should not be the only mode of transmission: the activities involved would benefit from more examination, so that a critical analysis of research skills can be built up to supplement the more tacit training processes.

Acknowledgments

I am grateful to Andy Deseran, Patricia Y. Martin and Nick Pidgeon for comments on earlier drafts of this chapter. Preliminary versions of these ideas were presented to seminars at the School of Social Work, University of Alabama, Tuscaloosa and at the Dipartimento di Politica Sociale, University of Trento. The assistance of the Consiglio Nazionale delle Ricerche of Italy in the preparation of this paper is gratefully acknowledged.

Notes

1 The following account derives largely from the work of Glaser and Strauss set out initially in their book *The Discovery of Grounded Theory* (1967). The topic is dealt with more explicitly later in this chapter.

2 As a point of reference for Polanyi's discussion of connoisseurship it is salutary to recall his reminder of the elements of judgment associated with the classification of a particular insect as a new species. The British Museum holds 15,000,000 insect specimens which may be used as comparators to assist with this task.

3 Blaikie and Stacey (1984) have developed the idea, which some of my colleagues have found helpful in their research, of regarding qualitative research as a series of dialogues of the researcher with the researched, with colleagues and with the academic community, as well as within the researcher's own consciousness.

4 The reader interested in developing thoughts about personal style in research might like to compare the 'intellectual texture' of Bott's study of conjugal family roles – the careful, competent, detailed casework – with Gluckman's provocative and stimulating treatment of her material in the introduction to the second edition of Bott's book (Bott, 1971).

5 Compare this with Ashby's discussion of the Law of Requisite Variety for systems which attempt to map salient features of the world around them (Ashby, 1952).

8

THE ASTON RESEARCH PROGRAMME

Derek Pugh

Introduction

In 1961 the Industrial Administration Research Unit of the Birmingham College of Advanced Technology (later to become the University of Aston in Birmingham) was formed. The Unit consisted of myself as Senior Research Fellow, David Hickson (Research Fellow), Bob Hinings and Graham Harding (Research Assistants). We worked under the general aegis of Tom Lupton, the then Head of Department, who had a government grant to support the work which was also supported by a research fellowship from the college itself. We were a strange bunch in a strange place!

The college was moving away from being a technical college towards a higher academic level; 'Dip. Techs' said to be the equivalent of degrees had been started, new posts of 'Reader' were introduced, and research was stated to be important. The recent appointment as Head of Department of an academic social science researcher, not as might have been expected an engineer or manager, showed which way the wind was blowing. We didn't know it yet, of course, but it was to become a gale which was to blow us as part of the 1960s Robbins development into being a university within five years.

The situation gave the Research Unit a number of advantages. The college had been teaching managers, supervisors, and shop stewards since the war and had built up a status and a bank of goodwill which meant that the 'field' was extremely receptive when it came to fieldwork. Our colleagues not really knowing what research was, and not rating it highly anyway, on the whole allowed us to get on with it. The fact that Tom Lupton had brought the grant from his previous post at Manchester but that no researchers had moved with him meant that we newly recruited members of the unit felt free to review the objectives and methods of the research *de novo* – particularly as Lupton had large managerial responsibilities as the head of what we should nowadays call the largest business school in the country, which restricted his involvement in the actual research.

The research approach

With this degree of research freedom before us, we started by reviewing the field. To do that we went into an ivory tower – which like most research ivory towers was a basement in a nearby slum! Conceptually, though, it was an ivory tower, since in it we sat and argued for one whole year about what we should study. I know of no other research group which has had that degree of preparation, so one cannot think in terms of causal relations, but I incline to the view that this may be why Aston, in its own terms, was so very successful. The physical situation was most helpful. We only had one room so we were all in it together. We were away from the main college so we could concentrate on the work in hand free from distraction, and we were neglected by all except Tom Lupton who provided the protection of authority together with academic tolerance and encouragement.

We had another advantage here in that the group was consciously set up as an interdisciplinary one. Tom Lupton was an anthropologist and so brought his concern with the firm as a culture whose norms of worker behaviour were influenced by its product, its markets, and its methods of payments. David Hickson's interests were in worker performance; what was the whole range of factors affecting restriction of output, for example? I was a social psychologist discovering sociology and concerned with how task allocation affected attitudes and conflicts as in the relationships between production and inspection supervisors and workers. Bob Hinings brought mainstream sociological scholarship; Graham Harding, an experimental psychologist, brought a sceptical view of theory and a down-to-earth knowledge of the local situation.

Our integration was enhanced by the participation of everyone in this design phase. Nothing had been decided and therefore each member had a full opportunity to make whatever contribution he could. As things became clearer, this effect was further supported by job rotation. That is, although interviewing in a particular organization always remained with one researcher because he had established the personal contacts, tasks such as reading up a particular literature or analysing particular information were moved from person to person round the group. Thus while it is possible to look back and say that the conceptualization and measurement of a particular variable owed more to one particular researcher than anyone else, it is not possible to say that any particular piece of work belonged to any one person.

We had a clean sheet to work on, practically a *tabula rasa*, and this is very rare. We began by surveying the literature as fully as we could. One thing was very striking, particularly to those of us from a psychological background: how much the writing at that time depended upon single case studies of what was happening in particular organizations, and what a dearth there was of systematic comparative study. Some of these single case studies were extremely insightful but they were non-comparative and therefore – by a peculiar paradox – were presented as applying to *all* organizations. The best one I still use in my teaching, along with, I dare say, a lot of other people: Gouldner's (1955) study of a gypsum mine. It is a one-case study, of one mine, in one state, which uses one technology, at one particular time. From this Gouldner produced a theory of what he called three types of bureaucracy, but which are better thought of as three modes of bureaucratic functioning, viz: mock, representative, and punishment-centred. It is extremely intuitive and insightful, but we do not know whether it applies to any other gypsum mines, let alone to coal mines, car factories or government departments.

We felt that there were enough one-case studies and that we wanted to identify precisely and comparatively what factors affected differences between the workings of organizations. Since we took such a wide brief, we started widely. 'What factors affect behaviour in organizations?' we asked. We spent time brainstorming all the factors we could think of, from 'an individual worker's machine is adjusted' to 'a general strike is called' by way of 'a new payment system is installed' and 'the queen visits the factory'. The factors, including psychological, sociological, economic and cultural ones, ranged as widely as we could make them.

We collected lists of such factors and classified them by levels of analysis: organizational, group, and individual. Then we began to realize that the worker works in an organization with a management control structure, and this had not been included in the potential explanations. This thought became more and more central. After all, size could be comparatively easily measured, ownership could be traced, and technology could be categorized, but there were no suggestions as to how to compare systematically the structure of one organization with that of another. This became more and more difficult and more and more interesting, and eventually the effort to do it produced the decision to study first at the organizational level, then to add the group level, and finally to add the individual level of analysis – accepting always that the aim was to study the three levels simultaneously.

'Comparative study' meant, for those of us with experience in differential psychology, standard questions and classifiable answers. We wanted to develop concepts that could be systematically applied as variables across organizations and which would discriminate between them; that is, we wanted to measure – in as far as anything is measureable in the social sciences – concepts that anyway were scaleable. In the event we carried out a lot of statistical work to establish the scaleability, reliability and validity of our measures. All of these things it seemed obvious to us needed to be done: the development work of using the methodology of individual psychology applied to questions of organizations, environments and groups.

The research strategy

The research strategy we adopted may therefore be summarized as being based on five main assumptions:

1 In order to find which organizational problems are specific to particular kinds of organizations and which are common to all

organizations, comparative studies need to include organizations of many types.

2 Meaningful comparisons can only be made when there is a common standard for comparison, preferably measurement.

3 The nature of an organization will be influenced by its objectives and environments, so these must be taken into account.

4 Study of the work behaviour of individuals and groups should be related to the study of the characteristics of the organization in which the behaviour occurs.

5 Studies of organizational processes of stability and change should be undertaken in relation to a framework of significant variables and relationships established through comparative study.

We wanted to generalize and develop the study of work organization and behaviour into a consideration of the interdependence of three conceptually distinct levels of analysis of behaviour in organizations: (1) organizational structure and functioning, (2) group composition and interaction, and (3) individual personality and behaviour. We were also concerned with the interrelationships of each of these levels. Thus, for example, we aimed to study group composition and interaction in relation to particular organizational structures.

We intended to undertake a comparative analysis to establish the significant variables at each level and their relationships, and then to develop at each level a processual analysis within the framework thus established. Initially we were interested in conducting an analysis at the first level of organizational structure and functioning that could be used as an empirical research tool.

The study of the structure and activities of an organization must also be conducted in relation to its other characteristics and to the social and economic context in which it is found. We thus developed a list of contextual variables in order to relate them to the variables of organizational structure and functioning. Thus we identified the effects of various patterns of these independent variables on organizational structures and functioning.

At the next level of analysis, group composition and interaction, a new set of variables was to be investigated and related to the contextual and structural variables established earlier. Later we wished to study individual behaviour and personality in relation to context, structure and group behaviour. In this way we hoped to establish systematic comparative relationships across organizations between these various levels of analysis.

As a first approximation for comparative study, we assumed one-way causality from the larger to the smaller unit. But this was clearly a great oversimplification, and a full analysis has to take account of two-way interactions and feedback loops. Studies of this type cannot be done on a cross-sectional basis; they must be longitudinal, taking account of dynamic processes over time. Only in this way will data on rival causal hypotheses be obtained. Such process studies would then be carried out within a framework of established meaningful stable relationships.

Thus the overall strategy of the Aston approach is to conduct nomothetic studies to produce generalizable concepts and relationships, and then to conduct idiographic studies moderated by and developed from a generalized framework that can give proper balance to the common and specific aspects of a particular organization's functioning.

Since 1961 a considerable number of studies have been conducted within this framework, which has become known as the Aston programme. It is not the purpose of this chapter to report in detail about the research findings of the approach. Most of the studies are collected and reprinted in an Aston series of Research Monographs, of which the first four volumes have appeared: Pugh and Hickson (1976), Pugh and Hinings (1976), Pugh and Payne (1977), Hickson and McMillan (1981). These form the most convenient source of material of the work of the programme as it was developed. Pugh (1981a) is a useful short overall review which includes some later developments.

Organizational level analysis

Our initial study sought to develop valid and reliable measures of organizational structure and context. We utilized a sample of forty-six organizations offering an extremely varied range of manufacturing and service operations in Greater Birmingham, each of which employed at least 250 people. We included manufacturing firms that made strip steel, toys, double decker buses, chocolate bars, injection systems and beer, and service organizations such as chain stores, municipal departments responsible for clearing roads and teaching arithmetic, transport undertakings, insurance companies and a savings bank.

This diversity was a mark of the fieldwork cooperation that we received. In so many of these organizations managers, supervisors, and shop stewards had been on courses at the college and this was the first time that research cooperation had been requested. The argument that we needed to do the research in order to develop the teaching that we were giving was very acceptable. I used the word 'sample' in the paragraph above advisedly. The forty-six organizations were a stratified random sample by size (number of employees) and type of product or service (Standard Industrial Classifications) of the employing organizations in the area. This is very unusual at the organizational level, where the word 'sample' is usually a euphemism for an assorted group of firms who have agreed to collaborate. We had two refusals of the original group who were randomly substituted – a 92 per cent response rate.

Our methods of data collection underlined the comparative, relatively objective nature of what we wanted to know; that is, we were using our interviewees as 'informants', not 'respondents' (Pugh and Payne, 1977). There were structured interview schedules for several main executives, containing objective questions such as: 'Are there written operating instructions for direct workers?' We directed specific questions to executives who were responsible for particular areas and then received formal confirmations of their responses. For example, we may have asked the production manager about written operating instructions and then requested an actual set of instructions as evidence. Finally, we gathered information from public records and other sources to obtain measures such as an index of individuality of ownership.

We arranged individual item responses into a previously developed (Pugh *et al.*, 1963) scheme and then into cumulative measures that characterized the organization. The following organizational variables were measured.

CONTEXTUAL VARIABLES

Origin and history: private versus public foundings and the history of changes in ownership and location.
Ownership and control: public versus private ownership and the number and type of owners.
Size: number of employees, net assets, and market position.
Charter: the nature and range of goods and services.
Technology: the degree of integration in work processes.
Interdependence: the extent of dependence on customers, suppliers, and trade unions.

STRUCTURAL VARIABLES

Specialization: the degree of division into specialized roles.
Standardization: the degree of standard rules and procedures.
Formalization: the degree of written instructions and procedures.
Centralization: the degree of decision-making authority at the top.
Configuration: long versus short chains of command and role structures, and percentages of 'supportive' personnel.

These measures varied widely in number, type, complexity and sophistication. For example, location was assessed by one relatively crude measure, number of operating sites; however, the main standardization scale had 128 dichotomous items that formed two subscales based on factor analysis. When possible, we used factor analysis within the main variables to confirm their existence as factors and to identify and make operational subsidiary factors. We also applied general dichotomous or Guttman procedures to relevant scales to confirm internal validity. Thus there were 132 fully operational measures for characterizing organizations, which ranged from simple dichotomies to large multi-item scales (Levy and Pugh, 1969).

We then examined interrelationships separately within the sets of contextual and structural variables and also studied the relationships between contextual variables (treated as independent variables) and structural variables (treated as dependent variables) (cf. Pugh and Hickson, 1976).

The findings of the initial Aston study can be summarized as follows.

1 The division of labour (specialization), the existence of procedures (standardization) and the use of written communication and role definition (formalization) are highly related and can be summarized by a single structural dimension called 'structuring of activities'. This dimension is primarily related to the size of the organization, and secondarily to its

technology. Large organizations with automated and integrated technologies will have more specialists, more procedures, and will use written means of communication and role definition. Size is quite clearly the most important factor here.

2 The locus of authority (centralization) is negatively related to specialization, and a number of measures of centralization can be summarized by a single structural dimension called 'concentration of authority'. This is primarily related to the dependence of the organization on other organizations. Those organizations which are dependent on other organizations by virtue of ownership ties or economic integration will centralize many decisions.

3 Various aspects of role structure such as the number of employees in the direct line hierarchy, the span of control of the first-line supervisor, and so on, are related and can be summarized by a single structural dimension called 'line control of workflow'. Organizations with integrated and automated technologies will control work by means of procedures and specialists outside the line chain of command, and vice versa.

These findings gave us a set of hypotheses for testing in further studies. Looking back, I would regard the basic achievement of the Aston programme as putting all this range of variables into one conceptual framework and attempting, successfully I think, to arrive at the relative importance of them. Before then, in relation to structure, for example, we had those who were stressing the importance of size, and others insisting that ownership or technology were the most important in determining management forms. We stressed the need to take a comparative approach and to determine the relative importance of all these factors.

The biggest disappointment that I have in terms of the content of the Aston work is the awareness *now* of the enormous impact of size. We are sometimes characterized as size theorists, but that is not because of a priori thinking – the data show it. If you look at the conceptual framework it is obvious that we were prepared to look at the relative weights of all possible determinants of structure. My own personal hypothesis was that they were all probably more or less equal, and I'm somewhat disappointed that size appears to take up about 50 per cent of the variance of structuring, and dependence is such a large contributor to centralization.

The research team process

I find it useful to identify three common institutional approaches to doing research.

The first regards carrying out research essentially as individual training and development in order to lead to a teaching post. The short-term nature of most research jobs provides a strong institutional framework for this approach. Researchers are mostly young, without the necessary knowledge, experience or status to teach with authority, and they do research until they have grown up to be big and strong enough to be an adult and thus to teach. We might, somewhat cynically, call this the 'kindergarten' concept of research. It is the most common in British social science. Researchers are considered as second class citizens on limited term contracts, and most are anxious to obtain normal teaching appointments.

The second approach sees research as an opportunity for a teacher who has otherwise become stale to renew his batteries by taking a sabbatical period of research in the course of which he would acquaint himself with the current developments in the field. Then, refreshed in body and mind, he would return to be a better teacher. This might be called the 'riviera' concept of research.

The third approach sees it as axiomatic that all academic lecturers do research. After they have done their lectures, tutorials and marking, seen individual students, participated in their professional association's activities and (in some cases) carried out their consultancy (which are all more programmed activities and therefore, according to Simons's law, will come first), they will also do their research, perhaps on Thursday afternoons from 3.30 till 6 o'clock. It is implicit in this approach that the research can be continually taken up and put down, with something to show for the period in between, so that this might be called the 'academic knitting' concept of research. Many mute inglorious Miltonic academics are hoping to get enough Thursday afternoons to finish their project and its accompanying book.

Good research is certainly carried out under these three approaches (and this is a compliment to the calibre of the academics involved rather than to the institutional setting), but it is apparent that they are unlikely, by themselves, to be adequate to sustain a long-term integrated programme of work as envisaged by the Aston group. In this case, it was crucial to the research team process that the group included two relatively senior academics (David Hickson and myself) who from 1961 to 1968 saw the carrying out of the programme as their primary academic task. We had both gone through the 'kindergarten' research stage and were employed in permanent posts. I was on long-term secondment from a lectureship; David Hickson was appointed to a lectureship which involved teaching, but he and I were able to create a perception of his role as being a special one in which the research came first. Our security needs being satisfied, we were able, as Maslow (1943) would have predicted, to concentrate on self-actualization through the carrying out of the research programme. It is a sad commentary on the prevalence of the three approaches to research outlined above that only very rarely do academics in the social sciences get such opportunities at that stage in their careers (from early to late thirties), although this is much more common in the physical and medical sciences.

So David and I were able during this period to form a permanent nucleus of stability and commitment to the programme. We were joined by Bob Hinings, whose commitment, gained by membership of the first generation, enabled him, even when he moved to a teaching post in the neighbouring University of Birmingham, to make a much more sustained research contribution than is possible on the individual 'academic knitting' approach.

In 1963 the moving away of the first two research assistants (in financial terms only in the case of Bob Hinings) allowed the recruitment of the 'second generation Aston Researchers': Keith Macdonald, Christopher Turner and, in 1964, Theo Nichols. Since the conceptual framework and the research strategy had by then been worked out, their main contribution was to the operationalization of the concepts, and data collection and analysis. It is striking how this task, important though it is, has the effect, with the inevitable feeling of working on 'somebody else's research', of setting limits to academic long-term commitment. None of this generation of researchers, for example, is continuing to do work in the field, in contrast to the first generation nucleus, and the third generation to be discussed below. The contribution of the second generation to the second and subsequent stages of the Aston programme was enormous, but their absence from the crucial first stage of problem formulation and design makes the contribution of Aston to them less clear. The need for all researchers to be involved in all stages of a research project, though not always possible, is clearly preferable and this underlines the point made above, that research bodies should not expect proposals to be too closely detailed when they are inevitably being designed before all the people who work on them have been appointed.

In 1965 the original government grant was due to come to an end, and proposals and justifications had to be put to the University of Aston to carry out the undertaking it had made on the acceptance of the grant in 1960, to continue to support the research work from its own resources if the work was still regarded as important and timely. In the inevitable bureaucratic complexities to which this type of decision is subject (and bureaucrats, being in permanent jobs, have all the time in the world), it was literally less than two weeks before the official date of ending of the grant that the decision was announced. By this time, of course, only the permanent nucleus of Hickson and myself remained. In an expanding social science market all three members of the second generation had obtained permanent teaching appointments elsewhere. This is a common problem with fixed-term grants where researchers on contracts are not in a position to stay until the end of the grant, but have to look for jobs for anything up to a year before. This argues for longer-term commitments of grant awards, perhaps a rolling system, and certainly longer notice of decisions than is currently the case. The existence of the permanent nucleus funded on a different basis was a necessary condition of the continuation of the Aston programme.

But still, the answer was: yes. The University of Aston agreed to take over the funding of the work. This considerable inflow of institutional support was the second necessary condition for continuation. Such decisions to continue research work begun with outside funds were surprisingly infrequent even in the 1960s (and are virtually impossible now). The decision of the university authorities to provide support at a crucial time makes clear how appropriate it is that the programme has become internationally known as 'the Aston Studies'.

The decision to provide three research posts to replace those supported by the grant paved the way for the entry of the third generation of Aston researchers. Kerr Inkson, Roy Payne and Diana Pheysey were appointed to these posts. In addition, I obtained an SSRC grant for a replication and extension of the original study, to which John Child was appointed, with Will McQuillan as research interviewer. The group now entered a new phase of its activities: new projects were designed, the previous conceptual frameworks were extended, new concepts developed and operationalized and new data collected and analysed. All the members of this generation were thus involved in all the stages of the research process, which meant that their psychological investment and the longer-term commitment it generated were greater. All but one of the members of this generation continue to work in the field of organizational studies with concepts developed from this work.

But this phase of the group's work developed its own problems. After considerable debate it was decided that the whole group could not work on a single integrated project, and that the programme could best be developed by sub-groups working on three projects in parallel. One project was carried out by David Hickson and Kerr Inkson (developing short-form measures of the variables), a second by Roy Payne and Diana Pheysey (whose work was concerned with relating structure to group and individual behaviour), and a third by John Child and Will McQuillan (who were carrying out a national replication and relating the structures to organizational performance). I was the 'link-man' and officially a member of each sub-group. By this fractionating of my task, I took on a 'director's' role which was not easy to maintain with three tightly knit sub-groups of pairs. The amount of time I could spend within each group compared with the other members was obviously limited; it was not possible for me to be involved in fieldwork in these circumstances, which limited my contribution and, still more, my credibility. With problems of the psychological ownership of the work defence mechanisms come into play, and I inevitably overestimated my contribution to the three projects, as the sub-groups underestimated it.

These are very well-known problems in the management of research, and the problems of the research director who is forced to 'leave the bench' (or, in this case, the field) are well documented in the natural sciences. We can only report that Aston suffered from them too, and that I am now of the opinion that no social scientist who has pretensions to being a researcher, and not a research manager only, should allow himself to get into this position. If there are to be sub-groups, then every member of the team should be clearly identified with one of them (although there should be secondary links with others) and every member should be in a position to carry out fieldwork.

The final phase of the Aston group as such occurred from 1968 onwards with the splitting of the permanent nucleus. For various and quite independent reasons, in that year Child, McQuillan and I went to the London Business School (Payne following a year later), while Hickson and Hinings went to the University of Alberta. The position was now quite reversed from that of early 1965. There was now institutional support in terms of posts available, but no permanent nucleus to continue an integrated programme. Researchers were appointed who had their own research projects, and as there was no integrated thrust, the institutional support began to crumble. Researchers were not replaced and posts were allowed to lapse or were allocated to other sections of the department. The Industrial Administration Research Unit was continued as an entity, but more as an administrative convenience than as an integrated work group. In 1973, with the general reorganization of the department, the title lapsed, but it had by then in any case ceased to function in terms of the original concept. The two crucial conditions of a permanent nucleus and institutional support were no longer present. (Later, with the setting up of the ESRC Work Organization Research Centre, there was a resurgence of research at Aston, I am glad to say.)

The development of the Aston programme

Once a research study has been carried out a number of things can happen. Perhaps the most likely, as with most research studies, is that it will be neglected, forgotten apart from occasional references usually by the author himself. This did not happen with the Aston studies. They generated considerable interest and continue to do so after two decades – as is demonstrated by their presence in this current collection of papers. They are continually being cited and several papers have been featured as 'citation classics' by the Institute of Scientific Information based on the references in the *Social Sciences Citation Index*. The work is regularly referred to in most textbooks in the subject.

This interest is not, of course, all adulatory. A number of papers have appeared purely concerned with critiquing the study – which I take to be the highest form of academic accolade. The most cogently comprehensive is Starbuck (1981) – but see also my rejoinder Pugh (1981b).

I consider that there are three reasons why the work itself and the interest in it continues. The first is the most obvious: the concepts used are central to the study of organizations and researchers in this field continually have to struggle with them. The concepts are dealt with in an innovative way and the empirical results are interesting and challenging in themselves. The remaining two reasons are, perhaps, not so usual.

The second reason is that through our publications the group made the methodology completely explicit and the methods openly available. Not for us the all too frequent couple of paragraphs on method then on to the content. The items used, the questions asked, and the analyses carried out have been fully published so that it is comparatively easy for others to utilize the methods developed. Thus studies have appeared based entirely on published methods from, for example, India (Shenoy, 1981), Jordan (Ayoubi, 1981), Finland (Routamaa, 1980), as well as the expected Britain (e.g. Grinyer and Yasai-Ardekani, 1980) and America (e.g. Kmetz, 1978). There is an Aston databank at the SSRC (now ESRC) Data Archive at the University of Essex, established under John Child's direction, where all the data sets using the Aston methodology are available for comparative analysis.

The third reason is the group basis of the original research. Many of the succeeding papers are follow-ups by members of the group and their new collaborators – the 'fourth generation' of Aston researchers. Thus in addition to work at Aston, work has been and is being carried out in collaboration with earlier Aston generations, at the London Business School, the Universities of Birmingham, Bradford, Sheffield and the Open University in the UK, and a large number of countries abroad including Canada, Poland, Egypt, Germany, Japan, the USA and Sweden. Lex Donaldson of the Australian Graduate School of Management, formerly a colleague of mine at the London Business School and thus a fourth generation Aston researcher, has presented the first worldwide meta-analysis of Aston data based on the databank (Donaldson, 1986). At the Open University, I have been collaborating with Gordon Redding of the University of Hong Kong on a study of Chinese businesses in South East Asia (Redding and Pugh, 1986) and with Isobel de Val Pardo of the University of Valencia on a study of the effects of new technology on management structures in Spain. The group basis gives a stability and continuity to research which it is virtually impossible for a single individual to maintain.

Overview of the Aston programme

So the Aston programme has carried on away from the original Aston study both in time and distance. Replications and extensions are being undertaken at the organizational level both in Britain (cf. Pugh and Hinings, 1976) and worldwide (cf. Hickson and McMillan, 1981). The framework was used in studies of organizational performance (Child, 1976) and the group level of analysis has developed with studies of role, group and organizational climate in relation to structure (cf. Pugh and Payne, 1977). Longitudinal and processual studies of organizational change and functioning within the framework have begun (Pugh, 1981a).

I would summarize the achievements of the approach in broad terms under the following points.

(1) The development and application of a useful heuristic framework of stable, meaningful variables applied to organizational functioning and behaviour. The framework enables reliable and valid comparative measures to be made, is publicly available for use by other researchers, and is applicable to a wide range of types of organization in a large number of countries.

The existence and use of this framework is in itself a contribution to organization theory that develops by the interplay of nomothetic and idiographic approaches. The demonstration that a nomothetic comparative approach can be carried through rigorously with interesting results is important if we are to develop through a descriptive to an analytical discipline.

(2) At the organizational level of studies, that is, organizational environment, context, structure and performance, the relationships between context and structure have been sufficiently consistent to warrant a predictive approach. This approach has been viable when applied to

industry, public services, non-work organizations, and so on, and when applied to manufacturing organizations in a range of different countries.

The stability of these relationships, which of course is considerable but by no means complete, provides an important orientation point for studies of variations, which will need to include additional predictor variables.

(3) At the group level of analysis, relationships are less clear and less well explicated. But dimensions of organizational climate have been established. The conceptual similarity between results based on objective structural measures and perceptual climate measures is very encouraging and has provided the basis of convergent validity of both types of measures.

However, the percentage of variance predicted by subjective methods at the group level of analysis is considerably less than that at the organizational level, even when it is in the predicted direction. This is partially due to the probable lower reliability and validity of subjective measures, but it is also due to the fact that individual-level variables such as aspects of personality have not yet been sufficiently included in the framework and in the studies. Very much more needs to be done to find out what influences the way managers see their role.

Conclusions

The Aston programme has been part of a development during the past two decades whose major impact on the study of organizational behaviour has been the need to 'take the structure seriously'. A major component of the reaction against the traditional management theories on the part of behavioural scientists who established their own particular approach to organizational functioning was to neglect or downgrade the organizational structure in favour of individual motivation, interpersonal relationships, group processes, and so on. This in effect gave less importance to the authority structure of an organization. One important impact for practice that the Aston studies have had is in helping to change this approach, in particular in the Organizational Development movement (see Huse, 1975; Strauss, 1976). Workers in that field are now much more aware of the importance of authority structures and power allocations within an organization and the way in which these may limit the possibilities of change via development of interpersonal relationships and revised attitudes. The OD movement itself is much more realistic in this way about what can be achieved.

The Aston programme has also been part of the movement to establish a 'contingency approach' to these issues. This movement supports the idea that there are organizational structures or methods of communication that are more appropriate to some situations and less appropriate to others. The concept that each particular situation will have its own more appropriate style sounds reasonable and sensible, but the actual working out of what is appropriate continues to be a necessary research activity to which the Aston approach has contributed.

9

RUMINATIONS ON MUNIFICENCE AND SCARCITY IN RESEARCH

David J. Hickson

These ruminations could as well have been called 'tales of two teams'. For they are a personal chewing over of memories of two research teams, end-on in my own life but otherwise unrelated, the first in conditions of munificence and the second in conditions of scarcity. In the first, there was both as much money and, for the central participants, as much time in each twenty-four-hour day as could be made use of; in the second, both were hard to come by and never enough. The first team, which studied power, was in Alberta, Canada; the second, which studied decision making, was in Bradford, England.

It has to be said, even though it should be obvious, that these tales are told here in the manner in which they linger in a particular person's memory, my own. Ruminations are solitary. Other members of the same teams would tell the same basic stories, but would do so from the points of view of their own careers and feelings. My point of view is that of the originator of each team who set the balls rolling on two very different pitches, and was the only member who belonged to both.

Further, whilst these tales are one man's truth, they are not even for me the whole truth. They emphasize money and time, but there is more than this to research and there was more than this to the contrast between Alberta and Bradford. It has often been contended by members of both teams that what was attempted at Bradford was of a greater scale and complexity, so that differences in the nature of what was being done, as well as in the resources to do it, must go into the understanding of what took place. Doubtless that is so, but it is something that must await the telling somewhere else at some other time.

AN ALBERTA TALE
Munificent money

On second thoughts, perhaps it was not I but Charles Lee, a Texan enjoying the wide spaces of Western Canada around the boom city of Edmonton, who rolled the ball on to the pitch in Alberta. As Chairman of the Organizational Behavior section of the Faculty of Business Administration and Commerce, University of Alberta, he wrote to me in 1967 enquiring whether I would be interested in moving there to build up research. I was startled to find this letter out-of-the-blue on my desk in the room we all shared in the Research Unit at the University of Aston (Derek Pugh looks back on those days in Birmingham in chapter 8).

We did not intend the Aston team to break up, but we had more than once mused over the seven-year-bust-up tendency in other research groups. If they survived that long then around about that point they seemed to finally disintegrate, if not in name then in any real concerted work. We were on that point but getting along well. Maybe instead of being broken up by some uncontrollable influence we could engineer a controlled separation and then re-group? So my reply to the surprise letter did not say no. It outlined what might be needed for a couple of years to set up a research team. In the correspondence that followed all the possible needs in posts and money were matched by what was likely to be available. The Province of Alberta was – and still is – riding high on its mineral resources, especially oil, and Canada as a whole was doing well. To such munificence I could not say no. It was a chance to launch fresh research. It set off two years' concentrated effort, 1968 to 1970. Well, twenty-two months' working time, given the travelling to and fro and holidays.

I approached Bob Hinings, then at the University of Birmingham a few miles from Aston, but still working with us, to join the Albertan adventure (adventure it was, since at that time neither of us had ever been to North America, nor flown so far). Years afterwards the attractions of Alberta claimed him once more and he returned there permanently. A couple of months after Bob and I arrived in Canada, Hans Pennings joined us from the Netherlands. Charles Lee was already there, of course, and so was the fifth team member, Rodney Schneck, our only Albertan, immensely tolerant of this foreign body in his homeland. But then Albertans are used to people of many origins.

Later on there was Charley McMillan from the far end of Canada, whose talents were spotted by Rod Schneck, but he is the main character of a different story that will be alluded to here only in passing.

Held in common

We were high up in the umpteen-storey Tory Building, a disconcerting label to English eyes, but which had been the name of an Albertan celebrity and benefactor. In academic terms each research group should begin its research anew as far as that is humanly possible, but we did carry over some principles of team construction from the Aston experience. First and foremost, interpersonal competition should be minimized and cooperation maximized by holding in common what the team accomplished. This was achieved by agreeing that the names of all members should be on every publication, and be omitted only at the request of an individual who for some unforeseeable reason wished to come off. That would apply irrespective of whether individual contributions to the collective effort were more conceptual or more empirical or more in the final writing. All are vital to the end result. The writing cannot take place unless something has been done to write about, and what is done remains just a personal pastime if it is not communicated to others.

This did leave open for negotiation the question of whose should be the first names in the order in any lists of authors, but nevertheless it removed manoeuvring over who did what with an eye to ensuring future places on publications.

The blunders that can still be made could not be more vividly instanced than by what Bob Hinings and I later did. When the literature on power in organizations (the team's theoretical focus) had been reviewed it occurred to us that there might be a publisher for an edited selection, a reader on power. To our minds this was an incidental by-product of the research, and of little consequence. We saw journal papers as the real prize. Because we did not want to divert attention from this goal we did not involve the others in the notion of a book, but in an odd half hour or so had a list of possible contents typed out and mailed to publishers.

When what we had done so naively became known, it nearly shattered the team. To our colleagues who, unlike us, were aware of the money that could be made from book sales in North America, a book and not journal papers seemed at first sight the greater prize. Worse, here was I, the very enunciator of the held-in-common principle, ignoring it in order to line my pockets on the side. For hours we talked it out, but who knows whether complete trust was ever wholly regained. Perhaps it was fitting that no such book ever came into being.

A second team-building principle was a room in common. We did not ask for separate capacious offices, though they were there for the asking, but for a room large enough for desks for three or four, with a linked secretary's room. Common purpose and mutual stimulation do not come only from prearranged discussions or meetings for seminars. They come also from casual chats, passing comments that set someone else's mind going, mugs of coffee and tea drunk sitting on a desk edge, getting a sandwich together. These happen day by day in the normal course of things, above all fostered by constant contact working in and out of the same four walls.

Munificent time

The team did have to work against the difficulty that the original tenured Alberta faculty members had inevitable commitments and obligations due to their already established positions in the department. They could not abruptly drop these. Nor could they uproot themselves from their accustomed personal rooms and move into the research team room. They did everything they could by also having 'research desks' in the team room, which certainly helped, but we could not wholly overcome the difficulty. Those who moved in from outside, unencumbered by prior relationships, could fling themselves totally into the common effort. Those who were already there could not do so to quite the same degree.

For the newcomers, time was munificent. Not endless, since a two-year contract had been agreed, but as much each day as mind and body could give. We taught just one course each for a short academic year, and beyond that there were no research students to be supervised, no administrative jobs, no committee memberships, nothing to distract from or detract from the common aim. A comparatively undisturbed mental and emotional concentration was possible.

Bob Hinings's presence fulfilled a third team-building principle, that a minimum base for a viable team is two research-minded, full-time, fully committed members right from the beginning. They can hold on to the aims even if others are subjected to competing pressures, and in the last resort they can ensure continuity even if all goes awry.

The research task

Apart from a relative munificence of money and time, the team had another factor in its favour. It knew where it was going. It was going to explain power in organizations. It did not know what was meant by power, whose power was to be explained, nor what the explanation might be, but everyone could get down to work quickly on these questions without a long preparatory casting around to define the central aim. That aim had to be set in the initiating transatlantic correspondence during which a firm statement of the general objective was required so that funds could be applied for. It was premature insofar as research aims should be formulated by everyone, all together, and anyone who cannot participate in this is liable to be proportionately that less committed. However, this was offset by the team having a sense of direction right from the start.

In setting the general aim I had brought out a thought that had been at the back of my mind for years. In 1963, the Routledge edition had appeared of Blau and Scott's *Formal Organizations*, which seemed then to us at Aston the first thoroughgoing textbook in our field, an affirmation that a new subject, organization theory or the sociology of organizations, or what-you-will, was emerging. On page 175 a footnote had announced a forthcoming book by a Frenchman, not then much known beyond France, Crozier. The text said that 'Crozier suggests that bureaucratic formalization eliminates many areas of uncertainty. Power accrues to those who can control the remaining areas of uncertainty.' Although I did not really understand what this might mean, it had intrigued me, and when subsequently *The Bureaucratic Phenomenon* (1964) became available, I had seized on it. So for Alberta I proposed that we follow Crozier's lead. Hence the mixed European and North American team in Alberta owed its aims to Michel Crozier in Paris and to a footnote by Peter Blau and Dick Scott in Chicago.

Bob Hinings and I wanted to spell out theory more explicitly than had been done at Aston. So the five of us set out to search our minds, and those of everyone who had published anything relevant, for reasons why in organizations some had more power than others. Lawrence and Lorsch had just published encouraging results on 'subsystems' (Lawrence and Lorsch, 1967), and this view of organizations as interdepartmental systems fitted neatly with Crozier's idea, which had arisen from the tactics of the maintenance departments in French tobacco factories.

We worked out the rudiments of what was eventually published as a 'strategic contingencies theory', and went forth to test it in breweries, and in packaging factories, small organizations with virtually identical departments, a sampling that also owed a lot to Crozier. Because he had a set of small, simple, identical factories, a pattern of power repeated again and again had been plain to see, and we followed this example. We did not choose alcohol just because his study had been tobacco! We did so because of the peculiarities at that time of the Albertan liquor market. There were tight governmental controls. Alcohol was sold only from government liquor stores, windowless and advertless buildings in which a form filled in at the counter produced the required bottles from featureless shelves out of reach of the customer. Advertisements anywhere of any kind were carefully restricted. Though they were allowed on buses, for example, if they did appear and showed a glass then the glass must not touch the lips. The number of salesmen each brewery could employ was laid down. Only three companies were allowed to have breweries in the province, and imports over the provincial border were strictly limited.

So here were easily comprehended small organizations, with a simple product and technology, in the same highly defined market conditions. If there was any uncertainty, and if the theory worked, then it and the power should both be easily recognizable. Indeed, they were recognizable, subject to the conditions the theory states. In particular, there was the mystique of the brewer blending the hops so as to produce a standard beer despite uncertain crop variations.

Later, some small breweries in the United States and packaging manufacturers in British Columbia were added. Personally, I would have preferred chocolate factories! As it was, the others in the team got all the free beer samples that were going, and all I got were endless bought-in lunches of fast food spare ribs during interviews in one brewery, tasty at first but wearing week after week!

The project design demonstrates the advantages of a deliberately selected sample under controlled conditions when there is a clear theory. It became a textbook example of a hypothesis-testing design. And it worked. We did know what we were doing as much as anyone can in the research world. We had taken our initial theoretical inspiration from Crozier, but we did not look to any particular source for methods of data collection and data analysis. We tried to develop these for our particular research problem and sample. It is a mistake to believe in a method and repeat it whatever the problem. Methods should be devised to suit the task in hand. Naturally, accumulated experience is brought to bear with its preconceptions and predilections, and we worked within the structural functionalist approach, but we sought fresh ways of empirically getting at uncertainty and at the other major concepts, centrality and substitutability. We tried to get everything two ways, by open-ended interview and by questionnaire, so that variables were represented by two separate cross-checking sets of data.

Achievement

This was a team that realized its full potential. Of course, there was more to be done and more that we would have liked to do. Maybe other individuals might have done more, and they would certainly have done different. But this group of individuals did all that it could in twenty-two months. It achieved a drawing together of its ideas into a single explanation, it evolved this in interaction with empirical experience, and it published papers that have been cited by others.

Munificent money and time provided conditions in which the work could be driven forward with single-minded determination. Munificence created confidence and allowed concentration. Since the individuals who made up the team were confident of the two years they had wanted, and had got, they could concentrate on what they were doing and give to it all they respectively had.

The strain of the effort was still very great. There were the stresses in the team, due to the different degrees of concentration possible and to mistakes like the never-to-be power reader. There was also a little of the 'second generation' effect which Derek Pugh has described in chapter 8. Things are never quite the same for anyone who was not there in the first days and weeks when so much was still open, unthought of, unshaped. Coming later means coming into a situation already partly shaped. The 'second generation' then tends to leave earlier as the far end draws near. This was the fate of Hans Pennings who, having been unable to be present on day one, was first to move on as the conclusion of the project approached. Derek Pugh reports that those at Aston who were in this position did not continue to work in organizational research, but clearly this does not indicate some immutable law since Hans has continued to do so with distinction.

When the two years expired, Charles Lee and Rod Schneck stayed on to sustain Alberta in this academic field, but the team dispersed and the Research Unit as such came to an end. It was not continued in the same form. Its visible symbols, the common room, the secretary's office, and the filing cabinets, faded away. Research is so much the creation of individuals, within the situation and the thinking of their day. It does not march on regardless. It is not bureaucratizable.

Personal links persisted, of course. These included a relationship with Charley McMillan, mentioned earlier, who had joined the group to carry through a second project, a structural type comparison of American, Canadian and British factories. It led to him afterwards moving to Bradford to tackle a similar British, Japanese and Swedish comparison. In turn this brought a contact with Runo Axelsson in Sweden who had a decisive influence on what else then transpired at Bradford.

A BRADFORD TALE

Those at Bradford were not lucky enough to live in the comparatively secure confidence that sustained those at Alberta. The environment was not the same. Scarcity – relative scarcity – ruled. It called for a supreme determination to keep on whatever the adversities.

I went to Bradford from Alberta in 1970, with a brief to help build up the research side. Bradford Management Centre was still in its formative phase, and research activity was only just getting going. After a while Charley McMillan followed to undertake the cross-national comparison. Alongside this funds were fortuitously won from the Department of Health and Social Security for research staff to study local health centres. Again a Dutch link was forged when Ad Teulings applied for a temporary vacancy and came to Bradford for eighteen months. He and I had long discussions about possible research on power, and these and the arrival of Stewart Clegg amongst the first doctoral candidates kept my interest in power alive. Indeed, it was lively for Stewart and I had many stimulating and fruitful exchanges about what power did and did not mean.

Scarce money

With hindsight, the omens did not show the favour they had showed at Alberta. There were hindrances and delays from the start. On the same principle as before, that prolonged team research should be based on a minimum of two fully committed members, I wanted to recruit an experienced research-minded colleague. Moves to do so were twice frustrated, first when the departure of the Management Centre's founding Director created a temporary uncertainty, then by inapposite university appointments procedures.

At last things were on course when Richard Butler was attracted home from the United States in 1973 to make the stipulated pair. Neither he nor I knew the nature of what was ahead – a protracted research programme which required endurance from everyone involved, including the two of us who began it. As the Foreword to the ultimate book thirteen years later says, it was 'an uphill struggle to carry through large-scale, long-term research on small-scale, short-term grants' (Hickson *et al.*, 1986, p. xi). The principle of having two members with secure jobs who could hold on when all around were losing theirs, and to whom the others less fortunate could hold on, was fully borne out, though rather it had not been so tested.

The general economic and political omens also contrasted with those in oil-rich Alberta. The British economy was feeling the effects of the oil price increases by the OPEC producers. Suspicious political glances were being cast at the SSRC, the Social Science Research Council, and it had to be circumspect in what it did. Research pay-offs had to be foreseeable, and be not too long coming. It was a climate of opinion best evidenced by the subsequent change of title from SSRC to ESRC, the Economic and Social Research Council.

Nevertheless, we succeeded in obtaining a grant from the SSRC for a Research Fellow, for two years. We were pleased. In absolute terms this could be considered a good start. Yet it was half what we believed to be necessary for the magnitude of the work our intentions entailed. We had hoped for the security of an assured run of years. Our ideal was five years. So in relative terms the signal it gave was not so much of success as of an instant scarcity climate, an insecurity, which was to persist throughout.

As little as one year can be enough for a small-scale project re-using known concepts, whereas we were trying to think ourselves into an area where concepts were fuzzy and methods virtually non-existent. We found that it called for undistracted concentration, and the confidence to spend time on thoroughly clarifying concepts. Two years became inadequate, as we had feared. Although it sounds ample, and it can be sufficient for research which already has an explicit starting point and does not need further money beyond that, as the Alberta experience showed, the timetable it imposed on us was cramped. For the first month or two a new group has to shake down together. Then, if further funds are desired, work must commence inside six months on drafting a proposal, assuming submission of the proposal at the mid-point of the two years so that there is a chance of revising it if requested to do so and still obtaining money in time. And also assuming that unbroken employment is to be afforded to those contract researchers who have given themselves to the initial thinking and planning and to whom the research belongs as much as or more than to anyone else. Thus before anything much can be done on which to base a further proposal for money, that proposal has to be written. The group is distracted from the work on which it needs to concentrate by trying to dream up a persuasive proposal for a future before it has created a present.

All the time that a decision on new money is awaited the insecurity grows. Thought becomes pressured. The minds of contract members are in some measure diverted on to job vacancies elsewhere, and how long they can risk hanging on.

At Bradford, a self-reinforcing series of short-term research grants awarded to Richard Butler and me began. There were grants or grant extensions of two years, eighteen months, fifteen months, twelve months and four months, and finally a Personal Research Grant to myself for five months. At various points Graham Astley, David Cray, Geoffrey Mallory and David Wilson fell off at the end of one grant or another, the latter two even working for nothing in gaps between grants.

Conceptualizing and methodological consideration had again and again to be crumpled into shorter horizons than they demanded. There was never time to hammer things out as far as they possibly could be. Proposals for further money were always having to be concocted before we felt ready to do so. Therefore, each successive research proposal, whilst all right as far as it went, lacked that fuller assurance which ultimately comes from having worked ideas through and through as far as they can be taken. So, in their turn, our academic peers who toiled away for the SSRC and read these proposals never felt we deserved backing at any greater length. The sequence of proposals and grants reiterated itself round and round.

In all, we received SSRC grants on and off across nine years, including the gaps. To our peers with the SSRC it must have seemed like a series of generous acts of faith, constantly demonstrating goodwill despite a repeated lack of results. In all it ultimately did amount to a funding that was substantial in proportion to the total they allocated. But to us it was incessant insecurity and frustration, and a latent awareness that it was suppressing the potential that we thought was there to be had. The same amount of money awarded in longer grants might have got better value for money. We once reckoned that over the entire period Richard and I spent one quarter of our available time and attention not on research but on applying for money.

Scarce time

The core members of the team did not have the same freedom from other obligations as their equivalents had at Alberta. I had gone to Bradford to a Chair, as these positions are quaintly called. I found that this carried other furniture with it as well. Committees and policy discussions were always cropping up, not excessively as Chairs go, but nonetheless dislodging thoughts from their research focus.

Furthermore, as part of the creation of a research image, and as part of our contribution to the Management Centre, Richard and I took on the supervising of doctoral candidates. This was congenial enough, often stimulating, but whilst one is talking about or thinking about someone else's research you cannot have your mind on your own. For the same reasons we became Vice-Chairman and Chairman respectively of the doctoral programme, a most apt and complementary activity, but nonetheless another activity. Also for the same reasons, as well as for my own personal interest in it, I followed the doctoral chairmanship by accepting the editorship of *Organization Studies*, again a most pertinent occupation but a preoccupation nevertheless.

Desirable though all such commitments are if a research-orientated milieu is to be maintained, they fraction time and attention. We could never give our all to the main project to the extent that our Research Assistant and Research Fellow on contracts could, and this was a strain within the group.

The strain had been signified early on, before this project itself began, when I had attempted to join research staff in a common research room. All our desks were there, mine too. My allocated Professor's room opposite, measured out in the decreed number of square feet to encompass a Chair, was declared commonly available for anyone to retreat to for solitary work.

Tolerated for a while, my presence became intolerable. The interruptions to whatever was being done in the research room from calls and callers to me became too frequent. I had to move out to the Professor's room opposite. My time for research was too scarce. I was different. Though we successfully bore onwards from Alberta the principle of everyone's names being on common publications unless any individuals wanted theirs off, we could not sustain the common room.

The meaning of the word 'professor' is very different in Europe from its meaning in North America, of course. I knew this, but coming from Canada where we were all professors in title, I still had to learn its status divisiveness in Britain the hard way. In this, Britain and most of Europe lags behind.

There also were clear gaps between tenured members of the team and the others in age and experience, as well as in status. These criteria all cut through the group at the same point, whereas in Alberta they had criss-crossed around the group. So a second earlier attempt to overturn the realities had also failed. We had once decided to have a research group Chairperson, and had chosen Arthur McCullough, one of the forerunners to the project. It was a non-job. Requests and decisions had come to me anyway.

It is difficult for a Professor with a capital 'P' to get it right. If a Professor plays too large a part in research group affairs the potential of other members may be squashed out, should undue attention be paid to what he or she says. Play too small a part and the group misses what it could gain from contributed experience.

The research task

I had come from 'intraorganizational power' at Alberta, and Richard had come from work in interpersonal influence at Chicago, so we saw the new project heading somewhere into power and influence. This time there was not a specific antecedent such as Crozier had been for the Albertan team, but a general fashion to be followed. In 1973/74 the world of organization studies was just discovering *inter*organizational relationships anew. So why not study organizational power?

However, Runo Axelsson arrived from Sweden as the first Research Fellow. He applied for our advertised vacancy and was successful. David Wilson came as a Research Student. Runo was fresh from a jointly authored dual doctorate thesis, an academic novelty in itself, on decision making in colleges in Sweden. To him it was obvious that power or influence, whatever it is, is exercised when decisions are made.

Although Runo could not stay the full course and returned home because of the insecurity of his appointment and personal circumstances, he was crucial to all that transpired. As the point he made sank in, we turned away from the interorganizational literature and towards decision making as our subject for research. In any case, we realized that decision making must be heavily affected by interorganizational influences, as we later were able to show.

We found that whilst a composite picture of what decision making might be like could be sketched from the brilliant writings of the progenitors, no one had so far sorted out any different kinds of decision making. So scarcity notwithstanding, we set out to find ways of conceptualizing decision

making processes among organizational elites, and to find explanations for
any similarities or differences that we might come across.

Graham Astley, British but returning from the United States, succeeded
Runo, and he saw clearly the distinction in the literature between the
technical or task aspect of a decision and its political aspect. Our attempts
to explain decision-making processes were thereafter shaped by this
distinction.

We began fieldwork with six intensive case studies, progressing to a
second phase using interviews with multiple informants for each case. We
were well into this phase when once more we failed to obtain longer-term
funding. We again had to review our plans. We had to so conduct the
fieldwork that if this were the last money of all, when it ran out we would
have enough time to make sense of what we had and would not be left with
incomplete, unusable data. We were embarked on a large sample, which
subsequently reached 150 cases of decision making from thirty organizations, in order to cover enough variation to be able to differentiate and
explain. The crunch choice was whether to reduce either the number of
cases, or the number of interviews per case. We chose to reduce the
interviewees, which is why there was a third phase of cases that are the
accounts of single principal informants and of those others whom they
contacted for information. Long afterwards corroborations of one feature
by another in the data, and by what was comparable in other published
research, showed this to have been a valid choice, but nonetheless it was a
regrettable necessity.

Since scarcity also forged repeated crisis choices between thinking some
more or dashing out for more data while there was still time, some of us
crying forwards and others crying that forwards would be retrograde, the
concepts were not wholly defined nor the theory weaving them into an
explanation wholly spelled out until the very end. The clarity of concepts
attained comparatively quickly in Alberta, which accelerated work there,
was not attained until later in Bradford. The defining of concepts and theory
requires concentration in a less pressured situation, and not until someone
did have a chance for that were the last kinks ironed out. It was I who had
that chance. I was fortunate enough to obtain a year's Fellowship in
1982/83 at the Netherlands Institute for Advanced study in the Humanities
and Social Sciences. Our debt to the Dutch for it is immeasurable. At NIAS I
found that our theory had confused statements of phenomena, such as
decision problems and decision processes, with the variable qualities of
those phenomena. When this was sorted out the steps in the argument
which had seemed all right, but not yet quite right, became clear and it could
form the theme for the book which followed.

Sometimes some among us wondered whether studying processes was not
more difficult than studying structures. Look at all that had been done on
organization structure in the 1960s. It seemed easier to get a grip on
structure. As we were finding it so hard to conceptualize processes and to
grasp them empirically, surely they must be more elusive? This could be
right, but to me it is not. Research always looks easy in retrospect, when the
results are on neatly printed pages, to those who did not have to think of it

in the first place. To study process is indeed to describe movement, but since all creation is in ceaseless flux I have never been really sure where process ends and how structure can differ from it in the final analysis.

Turning points

The lowest point was when we applied for a five-year Programme Grant from the SSRC and failed to get it. We got more months, not more years. Looking back on this eventuality, it can clearly be seen to have ensued from the lack of a secure period to think through what we planned to do sufficiently well, apart from any personal failings of mine or anyone else which there may have been.

Always juggling thinking time against fieldwork time against research-grant-proposal-composing time, we were at a stage when we had done most on the six initial intensive case studies. These therefore came over confidently and well to the SSRC visiting party, especially given David Wilson's capabilities in expounding what he had been largely responsible for since, within our allocation of tasks, it was he who had concentrated on them. The rest of the work, which was incomplete, and our future intentions, which were aspirations, must have seemed wishy-washy by comparison. It is easier to be convincing about what you have already done and so know well than about what you are doing or are about to do, even though it is the latter that are supposed to be under scrutiny.

Graham Astley's contract came to an end and he moved on, disappointed and despondent as we all were, another 'second generation' member unable to stay right through. His thoughtful contribution to organization theory has continued from the United States, like that of Hans Pennings of the Alberta group.

Geoff Mallory and David Wilson somehow managed to stay, with Richard and I, until the turnaround came. It arrived on another short grant in the person of David Cray from Wisconsin. His arrival brought new energy, and galvanized the team into further efforts when all might have appeared spent. The project surged ahead, a surge that eventually carried it to a successful conclusion.

However, the interminable insecurity again took its toll when David Cray, as the end of the grant that paid him approached, had to follow Graham Astley across the Atlantic, though not to the United States but to Canada. Richard and David Wilson switched by agreement to the study of strategies in voluntary organizations. But the fresh momentum that had been gained was enough. It carried Geoff Mallory and David Cray through final and indispensable data analyses on computers on opposite sides of the Atlantic, and me through final siftings of the evidence and book writing in Holland and at home in Yorkshire, alongside Geoff who as the surviving sheet anchor man at Bradford defied all the difficulties of successive 'generations'.

Achievement

Much was achieved, all the greater in the circumstances. An exceptionally wide empirical study was accomplished. Strategic decision-making processes, social processes, were holistically typified by characteristics they revealed over time so that differences among them can be recognized. The duration of processes, the consequentiality of what is being decided, and the influence of interests, were described. Which kind of process is most likely to happen was explained by the complexity and politicality of the matter under decision. Whether that process is due more to the matter under decision or to the organization in which it happens was examined. Journal papers, book chapters, and a book were published.

But for me the achievement might have been better still. Of course, such thoughts are about might-have-beens, and there always will be might-have-beens. There can never be a research project where more might not have been achieved in one respect or another had the fates been different. With puny research instruments, our human selves, all research is necessarily bad research, and the question is merely how bad it is. Yet in this instance there were more than a dozen years between preparatory discussions and the publication in 1986 of the book which gives the bulk of the results. Perhaps we could have worked more speedily and effectively. It is hard to say. But stop-go financing sapped confidence, distracted attention, and held productivity below what it could otherwise have been.

TALES' END

Both tales show clearly the benefits of researcher mobility from project to project and from nation to nation. The Alberta and the Bradford projects both gained from the variety of individuals they drew together. In Alberta we were from three scattered preceding locations and from four nations, Britain, Canada, the Netherlands and the United States. In Bradford we were in all from nine preceding locations and again from four nations, three the same as in Alberta, Britain, the Netherlands and the United States, and one different, Sweden.

Obviously these locations and nations were all within an international research culture in which the individuals drawn together had an acceptable degree of homogeneity in values and methodological assumptions. Equally obviously to the individuals themselves, they were far from identical. They brought differing preferences and, most important, they brought different bunches of concepts from their previous experience. The interactions between these preferences and these concepts determined what research problem was lighted upon, how it was perceived, and how it was approached methodologically. Both teams added perfectly to the evidence that effective research requires heterogeneity on a basic homogeneity. It requires argument but not dispute, variety but not confusion, novelty but not strangeness. Probably most of the ideas that go into it, perhaps all of them, are expressions of age old thoughts in a contemporary form, but each new mix has in it the possibility of a fresh and more currently relevant compound.

Both Alberta and Bradford also show how likely it is that there will be a constant internal strain in a team between those who can give the research virtually all their time and attention and those who cannot. In the more usual situation such as at Bradford, those who can are likely to be those who are on short-term contracts, the most insecure, and they rightly feel that everything they have is at stake, whereas those who cannot give so much time and attention risk either treading heavily when they do not know enough of what they are treading on, or feeling awkwardly diffident because they know less than they are expected to. A solution in the case of externally funded research might be to pay some or all of the salaries of tenured staff so that they can be released from their teaching and administrative obligations. This is puzzlingly rare when it ought to be commonplace.

The big difference between the two teams, as it seemed to me and with increasing hindsight continues to seem, was in their relative munificence and scarcity. Both tales tell of achievement. A great deal was accomplished. The question I have ruminated upon was whether at Bradford yet more could have been accomplished, given a better situation in which to do it. Of course, the munificent Alberta team did not float lightly along without a care in the world. There were only two years. Individual member had many worries over what they were doing and should do with their lives. Yet, relative to what was attempted, there was security and confidence enough for concentrated mono-purpose effort. The Bradford team made the same personal effort but, relative to what they attempted, did not have that degree of security and confidence.

This does not imply that researchers should have all the money in the world for an indefinite period. They need neither opulence nor infinity. In funded research there is always the challenge of getting something done by a given date. There is always the compulsion to guess at the incalculable so as to fit it into a finite number of years. On balance, and only on balance, this may have more advantages than disadvantages. But it is challenge enough, together with the overriding academic challenge, without it being taken to a degree where the disadvantages of the insecurity overwhelm any stimulus from the challenge. Notably, researchers with longer-term aspirations need enough time to fully think out what they are to do, before they are diverted into composing further proposals for funds, or into precipitate fieldwork because they dare not delay it any longer. The outstanding problem is how to assess who most needs and deserves that munificence.

APPENDIX: SOME SELECTED ALBERTA AND BRADFORD TEAM PUBLICATIONS TO DATE
Alberta

Hickson, D.J., Hinings, C.R., Lee, C.A., Schneck, R.E. and Pennings, J.M. (1971), 'A strategic contingencies theory of intraorganizational power', *Administrative Science Quarterly*, 16, pp. 216–29.

Hinings, C.R., Hickson, D.J., Pennings, J.M. and Schneck, R.E. (1974), 'Structural conditions of intraorganizational power', *Administrative Science Quarterly*, 19, pp. 22–44.

Bradford

Astley, W.G., Axelsson, R., Butler, R.J., Hickson, D.J. and Wilson, D.C. (1982), 'Complexity and cleavage: dual explanations of strategic decision making', *Journal of Management Studies*, 19, pp. 357–75.

Hickson, D.J., Butler, R.J., Cray, D., Mallory, G.R. and Wilson, D.C. (1985), 'Comparing one hundred and fifty decision processes', in J.M. Pennings (ed.), *Organizational Strategy and Change*, San Francisco, Jossey-Bass.

Hickson, D.J., Butler, R.J., Cray, D., Mallory, G.R. and Wilson, D.C. (1986), *Top Decisions: Strategic Decision Making in Organizations*, Oxford, Blackwell, and San Francisco, Jossey-Bass.

Hickson, D.J. (1987), 'Decisions at the top of organizations', *Annual Review of Sociology* (to appear in 1987 issue).

Mallory, G.R., Butler, R.J., Cray, D., Hickson, D.J. and Wilson, D.C. (1983), 'Implanted decision making: American owned firms in Britain', *Journal of Management Studies*, 20, pp. 191–211.

Wilson, D.C. (1982), 'Electricity and resistance: a case study of innovation and politics', *Organization Studies*, 3, pp. 119–40.

Wilson, D.C., Butler, R.J., Cray, D., Hickson, D.J. and Mallory, G.R. (1982), 'The limits of trade union power in organizational decision making', *British Journal of Industrial Relations*, XX, pp. 322–41.

10

SOME REFLECTIONS UPON RESEARCH IN ORGANIZATIONS

Martin Bulmer

The contributors to this book demonstrate that the field of organizational studies is a flourishing one in which to reflect about research methodology. My role – as someone not working in that field but with an interest in research methods generally – is to offer some constructive comments on the issues raised in earlier chapters. The original question put to me by the editor was whether research in formal organizations, and on people who work in them, throws up special problems and considerations which are in some sense unique. There are relatively few issues of research method within organizations which are unique to them. What is clear, however, is that several major issues are sharply highlighted by studies of organizations. These I shall review in this chapter.

Organizations as settings for research have a number of special features. They are bounded institutions to which one must seek, negotiate and gain access. Once admitted, the researcher must establish a workable and convincing role in which to gather data by various kinds of interview, observation and from documentary sources. Research within organizations, because it involves interaction between the researcher and people working within a formal structure, may also raise more sharply ethical issues in research. The researcher is likely to be interested in different levels within the organization: the organization as a whole; divisions or sections within it; departments; individuals working within departments. The collection and analysis of data thus raises problems of the appropriate level of aggregation, and problems of moving between these different levels in analysis. Certain types of organizational research use the comparative method, providing an opportunity to reflect upon its value as a research strategy.

These methodological issues will now be examined, starting with more specific aspects of the research process and concluding with more general issues. Access to the research site is of key importance in organizational research, an issue addressed by several contributors. Buchanan and colleagues discuss this most explicitly, and offer useful specific advice which is unexceptionable. Whether it is generally possible to use friends and relatives may be doubted, but their other four points are well taken. Their conclusion that 'negotiating access . . . is a game of chance, not of skill' is an oversimplification when stated so baldly. Indeed, Crompton and Jones suggest that the presentation of one's project to managers and unions requires careful preparation and considerable finesse, which is certainly not to be left to chance. They emphasize, for example, the importance of securing support from employee organizations as well as management, both in their gatekeeping role and as providers of information. Effective initial presentations can help to overcome resistance at key points, and any suspicion which the identification as 'social scientist' or 'sociologist' may convey. This problem needs to be addressed directly, as Crompton and Jones suggest. One strategy is to describe oneself as a management scientist or organizational analyst. Michael Useem's fascinating study of corporate business leaders in Britain and America, *The Inner Circle* (1984), was facilitated by presenting the project as one concerned with leadership in business rather than a sociological study of an elite group.

Crompton and Jones also emphasize the value of informal contacts within the organization in gaining access. Buchanan and colleagues almost elevate this into a principle. Certainly the researcher is dependent upon all means available to try to gain access. Perhaps for this reason, there is little discussion in these chapters of sampling problems in the selection of organizations. Pugh's comment is apposite. 'Sample' in this context 'is usually a euphemism for an assorted group of firms who have agreed to cooperate.' The possibility of failing to secure cooperation must be anticipated, and may be much more common than might be inferred from published studies which concentrate upon describing how they did gain access. Beynon documents several examples of such refusals. Reeves and Harper (1981) suggest that in organizational studies one must expect a fairly high refusal rate and generally not to be informed about the reasons for the refusal.

Indeed there is a need for more guidance on issues of access and negotiating entry, a generally neglected topic. *The Access-Casebook*, edited by Colin Brown and others (1976), provides some guidance, but too much autobiographical reminiscence about the course of research projects and not enough on gaining entry. Too little attention is given, also, to the merits of an even-handed stance compared to entry via management or via unions. Donald Roy (1970) describes a research project undertaken with union cooperation, while S.M. Miller (1952) points to the dangers of over-identification with the union side in such a situation. Huw Beynon directly addresses some of the political issues raised by research access, and describes one project undertaken from a committed point of view. He points out, however, that neither management nor unions are unitary, that there is a delicate balance to be made between different parties on each side, while ultimately academic detachment is needed to weigh up conflicting evidence which is collected.

It may also be questioned whether his discussion of the miners' strike, interesting though it is, is typical of the contexts in which most organizational research is undertaken. In the literature there is some guidance on how to approach large corporations (Lawton, 1970), hospitals (Mauksch, 1970) and the military (Little, 1970), and some clues to how to interview elite members which include comments on entry and introduction (Moyser and Wagstaffe, 1987). But generally the available guidance is sparse. Several chapters suggest or hint at important features of approaching an organization: openness and honesty on the part of the person making the initial contact; a clear explanation of the purpose of the study, free from jargon of any kind; persuading the organization that the researcher is trustworthy; a clear statement of the benefits likely to follow from the research, both for the organization and more generally; responsiveness to objections which may be raised by the organization; and tenacity in the face of adverse reactions. More work on access issues is needed.

When one turns to field relations in the process of settling into an organizational setting and collecting data, a much more extensive literature is available as guidance. Ever since Adams and Preiss (1960), specialist material has been appearing on field research methods (cf. Agar, 1980; Burgess, 1982, 1984a; Hammersley and Atkinson, 1983). None of the contributors says much about the role that they played in the field. One may assume that it was the conventional, overt, participant-as-observer, role (in the case of those doing observational studies) (cf. Gold, 1958). None of the researchers played a covert role (cf. Bulmer, 1982a), though there are examples of organizational studies done in this way (cf. Cavendish, 1981). Nor did any of the authors act as a consultant, a role with its own stresses and strains, as Lisl Klein (1976) has described.

The contributors' experiences suggest various areas that deserve further exploration. One is the question of whom to contact within an organization. Lawrence argues the case for approaching the personnel staff because they have more distance from an organization and more of an overview. Production staff are also critical, particularly in continental countries. His reminder of the significance of people in intercalary roles both within and outside organizations is also timely. The expertise and experience of those such as management consultants and government inspectors has as yet been little drawn upon (to my knowledge) in British studies of organizations.

Different papers emphasize the common importance of personality, gender and 'tone' in maintaining field relations. As Buchanan and colleagues emphasize, 'getting on' within the organization depends upon personality, and the researcher's personality is likely to be scrutinized more closely in this type of setting than in others in which he or she may be engaged (for example, in an informal group or a local community). Members of organizations become adept at judging the personalities of those with whom they work closely, and the same applies to researchers with whom they come into contact. Their points about the necessary attributes of the researcher are well taken. Even a matter as simple as appropriate dress should be attended to, since inappropriate clothes may have a quite disproportionately negative effect.

Gender is not malleable, and thought needs to be given, as Crompton and Jones suggest, to the appropriate composition of the research team in relation to the gender of the workforce. Men may be more forthcoming with men, and women with women, in some situations. In some organizational cultures with men predominating, such as the police, it may be quite difficult for women to conduct effective research without being relegated to the sidelines. 'Tone' is more difficult to define, but it is the important ability of the researcher to tune in to the environment being studied and pick up clues despite preconceptions that they may have. Lawrence provides a clear example of revising his views on German 'authoritarianism' on the basis of first-hand observation in German companies.

Language is part of the art of fitting into a setting. Speaking the same language as those with whom one interacts is important. Edward Shils (1985) has commented on the apparent reluctance of British sociologists to study the higher echelons of their society, and one may speculate that the social origins of some social scientists may have handicapped them in Britain's boardrooms. Certainly foreign scholars, such as Useem (1984) in the City and Heclo and Wildavsky (1974) in Whitehall, seem to have found it easier to gain an *entrée*, perhaps because of their foreignness and the fact that they could not be pigeonholed within the British class system. On the other hand, foreignness can be a drawback, as the distinguished American political scientist found who had to undertake an intensive study of the game of cricket in order to understand the metaphors being used in parliamentary debate. Lawrence rightly emphasizes the importance in research abroad of being able to speak the language (cf. also Bulmer and Warwick, 1983, pp. 145–82 and Deutscher, 1968). Even within one's own society, different speech patterns can be a barrier to communication and need careful attention (Deutscher, 1984).

Several chapters properly stress the importance of autonomy in field relations within organizations. Researchers must safeguard their own independence, by, for example, insisting that managerial staff do not sit in on interviews, or handpick employees whom the researcher will interview. Beynon describes attempts by personnel in the organization to persuade him to reveal to them information given him by others, which he had to resist. These matters require tactful handling, but are not negotiable. At the same time, the researcher must recognize the responsibilities, both to withdraw in an orderly fashion from the setting, with appropriate acknowledgments to those who assisted, and in fulfilling obligations to feed back results of the research to the organization studied, preferably in as lucid and intelligible a fashion as possible. Buchanan and colleagues are right to point out that failure to do this can hamper or prevent future research by others at the same site. They might have added that a research bargain effectively met may smooth the path of those who follow, and even stimulate demand for further research on the part of the organization studied.

For some types of data collection, researchers in organizations are likely to use tape recorders. More attention needs to be given to the presence of a recorder as influencing the course and outcome of an interview. Buchanan and colleagues suggest that the tape recorder is now 'accepted technology'. While this may be so, it could still affect the outcome of the interview in subtle ways. Sometimes, for example, more interesting material is revealed when the machine is switched off. Turner rightly emphasizes the value of the notebook for recording information. As a general comment, however, it is disappointing that more attention is not given, first, to the problems of recording and preserving data in situations other than the structured interview, and second, the almost complete omission of any discussion of how one develops analyses out of non-standardized data sources. Particularly in field research, the volume of material produced is very great, and there are acute problems of categorization, compression and interpretation (cf. Becker, 1970).

Two more general observations on the field relationship may be made which are not direct criticisms of the authors. One is the need to consider the use of systematic social observation using multiple observers within organizations. Pugh describes an impressive body of research across different types of organization. What of the strategy of studying a single case or a few cases, but instead of relying upon a single observer using multiple observers in an effort to gain more reliable knowledge? What has been termed 'systematic social observation' (cf.Reiss, 1976; McCall, 1984) is being used for the study of a variety of organizational settings. A.J. Reiss, for example, carried out a major study of the police in which as many as thirty-six observers undertook eight-hour turns of duty daily for two months with police on patrol in a particular city (1971b). Reiss indeed argues that such a strategy is more appropriate the more organized the setting.

> The degree to which any activity is organized affects its amenability to systematic observation. The more formally organized is the activity or process, the more open to systematic observation [it is]. (1971a, p. 7)

The second comment concerns the value of methodological reflection about studies conducted in particular settings, by research practitioners in those areas. An unusual example is the review by G.J. McCall, *Observing the Law* (1978), dealing with crime and the criminal justice system. R.W. Habenstein's *Pathways to Data* (1970) includes essays on a variety of settings by authors with first-hand experience. Such accounts are of particular value to the new researcher starting in a field, as well as in apprising more experienced workers to other experience which they may draw upon. The essays collected here represent a useful start to such an overview for the field of organizational studies, even if they do not say enough about some of the particular methodological difficulties which may be encountered within organizations.

Ethical issues arise in organizational research and are alluded to in one or two papers. Buchanan and colleagues, for example, suggest that researchers should grant the organization being studied the right to correct information about them in the research report, and in effect would grant them the right to censor publication. In my view, this is an unacceptable position, for the reasons set out two paragraphs below. Such a judgment on my part requires that ethical issues arising in the negotiation of research access be considered more fully. There is little value in propounding *ad hoc* ethical nostrums in the absence of an overall view of the researcher's rights and obligations.

The researcher gaining entry to a setting has the responsibility to explain fairly and openly to the organization being studied what is the purpose of the enquiry. There is also a responsibility to show members of the organization draft material in order to allow the correction of factual inaccuracies. There is the further obligation in any material that is published to safeguard the organization from revelations that could be harmful to its commercial activities or its reputation. The commonest device for achieving this end is the use of anonymity in naming the organization and possibly not too closely identifying the locality in which it is situated. Beynon quotes Donald Roy on the importance of anonymity.

On the other hand, the researcher should retain to themselves the right to publish material gathered in the course of the study. Buchanan and colleagues are too glib about the problems which can arise if censorship is exercised, which in the last resort may prevent publication. Maurice Punch's account of what he calls '*publicatio interruptus*', the vicissitudes of his attempt to get his study of Dartington Hall School published after he had given the school and its trustees the right of veto over publication, should be a cautionary tale (1986, pp. 49–70). If financial support and sponsorship are accepted, from an outside source – for example, by an organization for a study of itself – and if the study is research, rather than consultancy, the investigator should retain the right to publish the results independently of the organization, subject to suitable confidentiality safeguards as to the identity and locale of the study.

It would be naive to ignore the fact that research in organizations may give rise to other ethical issues. Crompton and Jones refer to the issue of identification with management or with unions already discussed. The detachment of the investigator from the setting is itself a variable in the research. Some investigators believe that it is possible to do adequate research from a strongly committed standpoint. Beynon's study of Ford (1973) is a case in point, involving strong reliance on trade union and worker sources and little cooperation from the firm or access to the plant. His chapter here justifies such an approach, but it is not without its difficulties, for example in preventing the researcher from making their own observation of conditions within the workplace.

Another issue concerns the need to ensure the verifiable accuracy of statements made to the researcher. There are several grounds for favouring interviewing with more than one person present (cf. Bechhofer *et al.*, 1984), but in particular circumstances it may be a necessary strategy on ethical grounds. Braithwaite describes research on corporate crime and the Australian pharmaceutical industry where two interviewers were used, in part, 'so that there would be two witnesses to any statement which might later be renounced in a libel suit' (1985, p. 136).

The proper behaviour in certain situations may give rise to problems. Melville Dalton, in a thoughtful article reflecting upon the research for *Men Who Manage* (1959), revealed that he had made use of personal relationships to gain research data. For example, he provided counselling about her boyfriend problems to a secretary he knew, in return for confidential information about managerial salaries to which she had access and which he could not otherwise obtain (Dalton, 1964, pp. 65–9). Simon Holdaway (1982) describes the problems of doing covert research upon police behaviour within police stations while himself being a serving policeman. Pseudo-patient studies in the medical field have involved researchers masquerading as patients (Bulmer, 1982b; Rosenhan, 1982). The use of deception in research is a wider issue (cf. Bulmer, 1982a), which also bears on types of harm in social research (Warwick, 1982). Such ethical issues, because of the tightly structured environment, can arise particularly sharply in organizational research and need to be kept in mind.

At this point two omissions among methodological issues raised in the papers may be noted. Sampling receives scarcely any attention. Pugh describes a design based upon a probability sample, noting how rare such designs are in organizational studies. This is amply borne out in other papers, where there is scarcely any discussion of selection of units or of representativeness. Undoubtedly this reflects the difficult problems of access, but one might have expected more comment.

More serious is any sustained attention to the level of analysis of data appropriate in organizational studies, an issue facing both qualitative and quantitative researchers. There are echoes here of debates about methodological individualism and holism (cf. O'Neill, 1973) and of macro v. micro levels of theoretical analysis (cf. Knorr-Cetina and Cicourel, 1981), but the issue is more specific. In analysing the organization, does one focus upon properties of the whole, and of intermediate levels, or upon individuals within it? This is a familiar theme of the literature (e.g. Blau, 1957). Robert Weiss (1968) has pointed out the limitations of analyses in terms of variable relationships compared to the importance of under-standing the organization of living systems, and looks at the total system. Perhaps there is an analogy to be drawn between community studies and organizational studies, in that common problems exist of how to trace the relationships which exist between different parts of the system and demonstrate the influence of different parts upon each other. To what extent could network analysis be applied to organizational relationships (cf. Bulmer, 1985)?

Quantitative survey researchers are also aware of these problems, but relatively little progress has been made in developing new methods to grasp the complexities of wholes. *Union Democracy* (Lipset, Trow and Coleman, 1956) is now an ancient study, and Coleman's seminal article (1958) on the use of survey methods to study social organizations is thirty years old. There are two distinct issues. The need to collect and analyse data about different levels of the hierarchy is there, and at least implicitly recognized in several chapters, particularly that on the Aston programme. But there is also the need to collect and analyse data on relationships within an organization and avoid the atomism inherent in conventional survey approaches. Marsh (1982, p. 61) has pointed out that statistical procedures for both types of analysis are still relatively underdeveloped. Coleman identified four promising techniques: pair analysis, partitioning of cliques, establishing the boundaries of homogeneity, and contextual analysis.

Of these, emphasis on context is the only one represented in this book, and then as a metaphor rather than an analytic technique. Crompton and Jones describe their attempts to use data of this type. Lawrence makes the point that understanding institutions in another culture requires the clear understanding of the context in which they operate. Perhaps attention to context is usually implicit rather than explicit, but it deserves more attention.

An American doyen of organizational research, George Homans, has recently observed that

> field studies of small groups seem [to be thought] almost a waste of time. Where are now such studies as that of the Bank Wiring Room in the Western Electric researches (Roethlisberger and Dickson, 1939), of Whyte's *Street Corner Society* (1943), of Peter Blau's *The Dynamics of Bureaucracy* (1955)? I can think of some, but in no such quantity or quality. The decline of these studies has had unfortunate results. Science beings, as L.J. Henderson used to say, with the scientist's acquiring an intuitive familiarity with the facts (see Barber, 1970, p. 67). In our field, this can only be acquired by the scientist's watching and talking to people at first hand, and field studies alone provide the opportunity. Science, of course, does not end there, but it certainly begins there. (Homans, 1986, pp. xv–xvi)

A most valuable feature of the essays as a whole is their salutary emphasis upon the value of first-hand empirical enquiry as a *sine qua non*. Turner quotes with approval Warren Bennis: 'to look closely is to be surprised.' Dunkerley emphasizes the value of detailed case studies in generating ideas and testing generalizations. Crompton and Jones comment on the preponderance of a priori reasoning on a slight empirical base in certain areas of stratification research, and assert the necessity of grounding general propositions in empirical data.

Data alone, however, no matter how extensive or rich, are inadequate without adequate theory. The role of conceptualization and hypothesis formulation is rightly emphasized in the preceding chapters. Dunkerley stresses the importance of making one's theoretical model explicit and then seeking to test it by means of empirical research. Turner considers that the qualitative researcher has little alternative to pursuing a strategy of developing grounded theory. Hickson describes a different, hypothesis-testing, design which 'demonstrates the advantages of a deliberately selected sample under controlled conditions when there is a clear theory'. The relationship between theory and research in organizational studies may also benefit from discussions couched in wider terms. Miles (1983) provides some suggestive ideas from a qualitative approach, while recent discussions of analytic induction (Bulmer, 1979; Mitchell, 1983; Hammersley and Atkinson, 1983) are clearly applicable to field research. Lieberson's (1985) recent discussion of the logic of survey research is a challenge to think through the inferential basis of quantitative strategies. More thought needs to be given to the logic of designs involving comparisons between organizations. In this respect some of the literature on evaluation research – for example Sinclair and Clarke's (1981) discussion of cross-institutional designs – is likely to provide useful ideas.

The present collection illuminates the relation between theory and empirical data in three specific ways. First, attention is directed to the importance of clarifying the theoretical assumptions used in enquiry. Lawrence provides an example, in his questioning of whether the informal system exists. Normally taken for granted as an aspect of organizations on the basis of Roethlisberger and Dickson (1939), Blau (1955) and Dalton (1959), he suggests variations in its presence or absence between societies. A conundrum of criminological research some years ago, as to whether the Mafia exists, also illustrates the need to clarify assumptions. The phenomenon John Landesco (1929) studied sixty years ago in Chicago continues to arouse controversy, with the nature of the criminal confederation of Sicilian origin arousing the sharpest controversy (cf. Mack, 1970; Cressey, 1972). So extensive are the business activities of the Cosa Nostra in Italy and the United States that it repays study as an organizational phenomenon as well as a criminal network. (It also incidentally illustrates the potential theoretical pay-off of cross-fertilization between different fields of enquiry.)

A second valuable perspective bringing together theory and empirical data is a diachronic view, pursuing change over time. Dunkerley's chapter exemplifies this *par excellence*, though he has set himself a considerable challenge in the attempt to use life history materials. Dunkerley indicates the potential for this type of analysis, drawing on his own earlier theoretical work.

The papers collected here also testify to the fruitfulness of the comparative method as a means of theorizing in organizational research. There are at least three dimensions to this: the study of variation within a single organization; the study of different organizations within the same society; and the study of similar organizations within different societies. Buchanan and colleagues use the first strategy to some extent (cf. also Miles, 1983, pp. 128–31), Pugh the second, and Lawrence the third with notably illuminating results, particularly given the Anglo-centrism of much British social science. Useem's study of top British and American directors (1984) is also a valuable exemplar of the third approach, as are earlier studies such as Form's (1976) analysis of the situation of car workers in four societies. This is not the place for a discussion of the comparative method, but if such comparisons are built into a research design, the investigator may gain more purchase on the phenomena to be explained and the processes at work than a single case study would allow. Consider, for example, Lawrence's observations about management education and the academic backgrounds of managers in different countries. This in turn needs to be related to characteristics of the educational system and the relative standing of different occupations, in determining the flow of manpower into management positions (cf. Weiner, 1981 for Britain).

A final methodological observation of a general kind concerns the relative positions of qualitative and quantitative research reflected in these chapters. Crompton and Jones's argument appears the most convincing:

Quite simply, in organizational research it is not a mutually exclusive decision between quantitative and qualitative methodology. In reality it is very difficult to study organizations without using both sorts of methods. [And] in any event, quantitative data always rest upon qualitative distinctions.

Different investigators may have different preferences, and lean in one direction or another, but there are no general principles which can be adduced in favour of one or another style of research. Moreover the range of methods of data collection represented here does not divide easily into quantitative and qualitative. Research procedures described here include informal interviewing, oral history techniques, documentary research and cross-national informant interviewing. These do not fit easily into the contrast between large-scale surveys and small-scale ethnography often implied in comparing quantitative and qualitative research. More attention needs to be given to the solemnizing of methodological marriages (cf. Sieber, 1973; Warwick, 1983). As Bryman (1984) has shown, a good deal of nonsense is propounded by would-be philosophers of social science and general methodologists about the fit between particular general sociological orientations and particular methods. As he shows, the fit is not nearly so neat as they suppose. The value of a collection of reflections by practising researchers such as this lies in part in puncturing some of these overblown armchair reflections.

This is not to say that the task of combining different methods is an altogether easy one. Despite clarion calls to 'triangulation' (cf. Webb *et al.*, 1966) and demonstrations in classic studies such as *Union Democracy* (Lipset *et al.*, 1956) or *Patterns of Industrial Bureaucracy* (Gouldner, 1955) that different methods can be combined effectively, the precise ways in which such combinations can be effected needs more attention. Fielding and Fielding (1986) have recently provided some pointed observations on linking qualitative and quantitative data, drawing upon their work in police organizations. They quote Donald Campbell (Fielding and Fielding, 1986, p. 91):

'The polarity of quantitative versus qualitative approaches to research or social action remains unresolved, if resolution were to mean a predominant justification of one over the other. . . . Each pole is at its best in criticisms of the other, not in the invulnerability of its own claims to descriptive knowledge.' (quoted from Campbell, 1974)

In conclusion, some remarks on the value of an organizational perspective upon organizational research itself may be offered. Several chapters throw interesting light upon problems of research management and the appropriate institutional structure within universities for ensuring continuity of research effort. Pugh and Hickson, as befits authors associated with larger-scale research, have most to say about this. One generalization suggested seems to be the importance of cohesion and morale among a research team, exemplified in the early Aston research which unusually managed to bind together teaching and research staff in a highly motivated group. The ecology of the workplace and the lack of status distinctions within the group seems to have contributed to its effectiveness. One of the drawbacks of the pyramidal structure within British departments is, as Hickson observes, that accession to a Chair usually draws the incumbent out of research into administration. The amount of resources available seems to be less significant than the way in which research is organized and the involvement of younger staff. Hickson's contrasts between relative scarcity in Britain and munificence in oil-rich Alberta are well-drawn. In addition, one may hypothesize that in times of retrenchment and job famine, academic teams may hold together longer than at times when opportunities are more plentiful, provided continued research funding can be secured.

The conditions which foster the institutional endurance of organizational research groups are difficult to pin down. Pugh suggests that even the most successful groups are likely to have a finite life – seven years, it is suggested, is a critical point – and the need for younger staff to find permanent employment is an underlying factor leading to turnover. Arguably one of the critical factors, which both Aston researchers discuss, is the relationship between tenured teaching staff and contract research staff. The Aston model succeeded in part because teaching staff devoted considerable effort to organized research and became highly involved in it. This is comparatively unusual, and too often there are centripetal tendencies which push teachers and organized research apart (Bulmer, 1983). A different model, exemplified by Everett Hughes's influence at the University of Chicago, centred upon cadres of able graduate students working under a stimulating senior teacher with an overarching vision (cf. Becker *et al.*, 1968). For this to succeed, of course, a necessary condition is an adequate supply of students, a condition unlikely to be achieved in contemporary Britain. In both the Aston and Chicago cases, however, a 'collegial' form of organization of the research team appears to have borne fruit, though Pugh discusses the problems of being pushed into a more bureaucratic role as research director. Indeed he suggests that it was a mistake to allow this degree of role differentiation to develop.

All in all, the chapters in this book advance the study of organizations in Britain and provoke reflections about the appropriate methodology to pursue. Certain topics and questions are not adequately addressed, but many are. The practising researcher and the apprentice researcher – whether graduate or undergraduate – will find much of value to reflect upon after reading these accounts.

BIBLIOGRAPHY

Abrams, P. (1982), *Historical Sociology*, Shepton Mallet, Open Books.

Adams, R.N. and Preiss, J.J. (eds) (1960), *Human Organization Research: Field Relations and Techniques*, Homewood, Illinois, Dorsey Press.

Agar, M.H. (1980), *The Professional Stranger: An Informal Introduction to Ethnography*, New York, Academic Press.

Agar, M.H. (1986), *Speaking of Ethnography*, Sage University Paper Series on Qualitative Research Methods (Vol. 2), Beverly Hills, Calif., Sage.

Argyris, C. (1960), 'Creating effective relationships in organizations', in Adams and Preiss (eds) (1960), *q.v.*

Ashby, W.R. (1952), *Design for a Brain*, New York, Wiley.

Astley, W.G., Axelsson, R., Butler, R.J., Hickson, D.J. and Wilson, D.C. (1982), 'Complexity and cleavage: dual explanations of strategic decision making', *Journal of Management Studies*, 19, pp. 357–75.

Atkinson, P. (1981), *The Clinical Experience*, Farnborough, Hants, Gower.

Ayoubi, Z.M. (1981), 'Technology, size and organization structure in a developing country: Jordan', in D.J. Hickson and C.J. McMillan (eds) (1981), *q.v.*

Bailyn, L. (1977), 'Research as a cognitive process: implications for data analysis', *Quality and Quantity*, 11, pp. 97–117.

Ball, S.J. (1983), 'Case study research in education: some notes and problems', in M. Hammersley (ed.), *The Ethnography of Schooling: Methodological Issues*, Driffield, Humberside, Nafferton Books.

Ball, S.J. (1984), 'Beachside reconsidered: reflections on a methodological apprenticeship', in Burgess (ed.) (1984b), *q.v.*

Barber, B. (ed.) (1970), *L.J. Henderson on the Social System*, Chicago, University of Chicago Press.

Bateson, G. (1973), 'The logical categories of learning and communication', in G. Bateson (ed.), *Steps to an Ecology of Mind*, St Albans, Granada.

Bechhofer, F., Elliott, B. and McCrone, D. (1984), 'Safety in numbers: on the use of multiple interviewers', *Sociology*, 18, pp. 97–100.

Becker, H.S. (1970), 'Problems of inference and proof in participant observation', in *Sociological Work: Method and Substance*, London, Allen Lane.

Becker, H.S., Geer, B., Riesman, D. and Weiss, R.S. (eds) (1968), *Institutions and the Person*, Chicago, Aldine.

Bell, C. and Encel, S. (eds) (1978), *Inside the Whale*, Sydney, Pergamon.

Bell, C. and Newby, H. (eds) (1977), *Doing Sociological Research*, London, Allen & Unwin.

Bell, C. and Roberts, H. (eds) (1984), *Social Researching: Politics, Problems, Practice*, London, Routledge & Kegan Paul.

Bennis, W. (1973), *The Leaning Ivory Tower*, San Francisco, Jossey-Bass.

Berk, R.A. and Adams, J.M. (1970), 'Establishing rapport with deviant groups', *Social Problems*, 18, pp. 102–17.

Beynon, H. (1973), *Working for Ford*, Harmondsworth, Penguin.

Beynon, H. and Wainwright, H. (1978), *The Workers' Report to Vickers*, London, Pluto Press.

Blaikie, N.W.H. and Stacey, S. (1984), 'The generation of grounded concepts: a critical appraisal of the literature – a case study', paper presented to the ISA European Symposium on Concept Formation and Measurement, Rome, 1984.

Blau, P.M. (1955), *The Dynamics of Bureaucracy: A Study of Interpersonal Relationships in Two Government Agencies*, Chicago, University of Chicago Press.

Blau, P.M. (1957), 'Formal organizations: dimensions of analysis', *American Journal of Sociology*, 63, pp. 58–69.

Blau, P.M. (1964), 'The research process in the study of *The Dynamics of Bureaucracy*', in Hammond (ed.) (1964), *q.v.*

Blau, P.M. and Scott, W.R. (1963), *Formal Organizations*, London, Routledge & Kegan Paul.

Bloor, M. (1983), 'Notes on member validation', in R.M. Emerson (ed.), *Contemporary Field Research: A Collection of Readings*, Boston, Little, Brown.

Blum, F.H. (1952), 'Getting individuals to give information to the outsider', *Journal of Social Issues*, 8, pp. 35–42.

Boddy, D. and Buchanan, D.A. (1986), *Managing New Technology*, Oxford, Basil Blackwell.

Booz, Allen and Hamilton Report (1973), English translation, 'German management', *International Studies of Management and Organization*, Arts and Science Press (Spring/Summer).

Bott, E. (1971), *Family and Social Network*, 2nd edn, London, Tavistock.

Bottomley, B. (1978), 'Words, deeds and postgraduate research', in Bell and Encel (eds) (1978), *q.v.*

Bowen, E.S. (1954), *Return to Laughter*, London, Gollancz.

Braithwaite, J. (1985), 'Corporate crime research: why two interviewers are needed', *Sociology*, 19, pp. 136–8.

Braverman, H. (1974), *Labour and Monopoly Capital*, New York, Monthly Review Press.

Bresnen, M.J. (1986), *A Study of Forms of Project Organisation and Matrix Management: Case Studies from the Construction Industry*, unpublished PhD thesis, University of Nottingham.

Bresnen, M.J., Wray, K., Bryman, A., Beardsworth, A.D., Ford, J.R. and Keil, E.T. (1985), 'The flexibility of recruitment in the construction industry: formalization or re-casualization?', *Sociology*, 19, pp. 108–24.

Broadhead, R.S. and Rist, R.C. (1976), 'Gatekeepers and the social control of research', *Social Problems*, 23, pp. 325–36.

Brown, C., De Monthoux, P.G. and McCullough, A. (eds) (1976), *The Access-Casebook: Social Scientists Account for How to Get Data for Field Research*, Stockholm, Teknisk Hogeskolelitteratur.

Brown, R. (1982), 'Work histories, career strategies and the class structure', in A.

Giddens and G.M. Mackenzie (eds), *Social Class and the Division of Labour*, Cambridge, Cambridge University Press.

Bryman, A. (1984), 'The debate about quantitative and qualitative research: a question of method or epistemology?', *British Journal of Sociology*, 35, pp. 75–92.

Bryman, A., Bresnen, M., Ford, J., Beardsworth, A. and Keil, E. T. (1987a), 'Leader orientation and organizational transience: an investigation using Fiedler's LPC scale', *Journal of Occupational Psychology*, 60, pp. 13–19.

Bryman, A., Bresnen, M., Beardsworth, A.D., Ford, J. and Keil, E. T. (1987b), 'The concept of the temporary system: the case of the construction project', in *Research in the Sociology of Organizations: Volume 5*, Greenwich, Conn., JAI Press (in press).

Buchanan, D.A. and Boddy, D. (1982a), *Organizations in the Computer Age*, Aldershot, Gower.

Buchanan, D.A. and Boddy, D. (1982b), 'Advanced technology and the quality of working life: the effects of word processing on video typists', *Journal of Occupational Psychology*, 55, pp. 1–11.

Bulmer, M. (1979), 'Concepts in the analysis of qualitative data', *Sociological Review*, 27, pp. 653–77.

Bulmer, M. (ed.) (1982a), *Social Research Ethics: An Examination of the Merits of Covert Participant Observation*, London, Macmillan.

Bulmer, M. (1982b), 'The research ethics of pseudo-patient studies', *Sociological Review*, 30, pp. 627–46.

Bulmer, M. (1983), 'The social sciences', in J.W. Chapman (ed.), *The Western University on Trial*, Berkeley, University of California Press.

Bulmer, M. (1985), 'The rejuvenation of community studies? Neighbours, networks and policy', *Sociological Review*, 33, pp. 430–48.

Bulmer, M. and Burgess, R.G. (1986), 'Do concepts and indicators interrelate?', in R.G. Burgess (ed.), *Key Variables in Social Investigation*, London, Routledge & Kegan Paul.

Bulmer, M. and Warwick, D.P. (eds) (1983), *Social Research in Developing Countries: Surveys and Censuses in the Third World*, Chichester and New York, Wiley.

Burgess, R. (ed.) (1982), *Field Research: A Sourcebook and Field Manual*, London, Allen & Unwin.

Burgess, R.G. (1984a), *In the Field: An Introduction to Field Research*, London, Allen & Unwin.

Burgess, R.G. (ed.) (1984b), *The Research Process in Educational Settings: Ten Case Studies*, Lewes, Falmer Press.

Burgess, R.G. (1984c), 'Autobiographical accounts and research experience', in Burgess (ed.) (1984b), *q.v.*

Burgess, R.G. (ed.) (1985), *Field Methods in the Study of Education*, Lewes, Sussex, Falmer Press.

Burgess, R.G. and Bulmer, M. (1981), 'Research methodology teaching: trends and developments', *Sociology*, 15, pp. 477–89.

Burns, T. and Stalker, G.M. (1966), *The Management of Innovation*, London, Tavistock.

Campbell, D. T. (1974), 'Qualitative knowing in action research', Kurt Lewin Award Address, New York, Annual Meeting of the American Psychological Association.

Carlson, S. (1951), *Executive Behaviour*, Stockholm, Strömberg.

Cavendish, R. (pseudonym) (1981), *Women on the Line*, London, Routledge & Kegan Paul.

Chandler, A.D. (1962), *Strategy and Structure*, Cambridge, Mass., MIT Press.

Cherns, A.B. and Bryant, D. T. (1984), 'Studying the client's role in construction management', *Construction Management and Economics*, 2, pp. 177–84.

Child, J. (1976), 'Managerial and organizational factors associated with company performance', in Pugh and Hinings (eds) (1976), *q.v.*

Clarke, M. (1975), 'Survival in the field: implications of personal experience in field work', *Theory and Society*, 2, pp. 95–123.

Clawson, D. (1980), *Bureaucracy and the Labor Process*, New York, Monthly Review Press.

Clegg, S. and Dunkerley, D. (eds) (1977), *Critical Issues in Organizations*, London, Routledge & Kegan Paul.

Clegg, S. and Dunkerley, D. (1980), *Organization, Class and Control*, London, Routledge & Kegan Paul.

Cohen, M.D., March, J.G. and Olsen, J.P. (1972), 'A garbage can model of organizational choice', *Administrative Science Quarterly*, 17, pp. 1–25.

Coleman, J.S. (1958), 'Relational analysis: the study of social organizations with survey methods', *Human Organization*, 16, pp. 28–36.

Cressey, D.R. (1972), *Criminal Organization: Its Elementary Forms*, London, Heinemann.

Crichton, C. (1966), *Interdependence and Uncertainty: A Study of the Building Industry*, London, Tavistock.

Crompton, R. and Jones, G. (1984), *White-Collar Proletariat*, London, Macmillan.

Crozier, M. (1964), *The Bureaucratic Phenomenon*, London, Tavistock.

Dalton, M. (1959), *Men Who Manage*, New York, Wiley.

Dalton, M. (1964), 'Preconceptions and methods in *Men Who Manage*', in Hammond (ed.) (1964), *q.v.*

da Vinci, L. (1952), *The Notebooks of Leonardo da Vinci*, ed. I.A. Richton, Oxford, Oxford University Press.

Davis, J.A. (1964), '*Great Books and Small Groups*: an informal history of a national survey', in Hammond (ed.) (1964), *q.v.*

Day, G., Caldwell, L., Jones, K., Robbins, D. and Rose, H. (eds) (1982), *Diversity and Decomposition in the Labour Market*, Aldershot, Gower.

Denzin, N. (ed.) (1970), *Sociological Methods: A Sourcebook*, Chicago, Aldine.

Deutscher, I. (1968), 'Asking questions cross-culturally: some problems of linguistic comparability', in Becker *et al.* (eds) (1968), *q.v.*

Deutscher, I. (1984), 'Asking questions (and listening to answers): a review of some sociological precedents and problems', in M. Bulmer (ed.), *Sociological Research Methods: An Introduction*, London, Macmillan.

Dingwall, R. (1980), 'Ethics and ethnography', *Sociological Review*, 28, pp. 871–91.

Ditton, J. (ed.) (1980), *The View from Goffman*, London, Macmillan.

Donaldson, L. (1986), 'Size and bureaucracy in east and west: a preliminary meta-analysis', in Redding (ed.) (1986), *q.v.*

Douglas, J.D. (ed.) (1972), *Research on Deviance*, New York, Random House.

Doyle, P. (1986), 'A comparative study of Japanese marketing strategies in the British Market', *Journal of International Business Studies*, 17, pp. 27–46.

Edwards, R. (1979), *Contested Terrain: The Transformation of the Workplace in the Twentieth Century*, London, Heinemann.

Elbow, P. (1981), *Writing With Power: Techniques for Mastering the Writing Process*, New York, Oxford University Press.

Fielding, N. and Fielding, J. (1986), *Linking Data*, Sage University Paper Series on Qualitative Research Methods (vol. 4), Beverly Hills, Calif., Sage.

Finch, J. (1984), '"It's great to have someone to talk to": the ethics and politics of interviewing women', in Bell and Roberts (eds) (1984), *q.v.*

Fleming, M.C. (1980), 'Construction', in P.S. Johnson (ed.), *The Structure of British Industry*, London, Granada.

Fores, M., Lawrence, P. and Sorge, A. (1978), 'Germany's front line force', *Management Today* (March).

Form, W.H. (1976), *Blue-Collar Stratification: Autoworkers in Four Countries*, Princeton, New Jersey, Princeton University Press.

Freeman, J. (1986), 'Data quality and the development of organizational social science', *Administrative Science Quarterly*, 31, pp. 298–303.

Freilich, M. (ed.) (1970), *Marginal Natives: Anthropologists at Work*, New York, Harper & Row.

Friedman, A. (1977), 'Responsible autonomy versus direct control over the labour process', *Capital and Class*, 1, pp. 43–57.

Fuller, M. (1984), 'Dimensions of gender in a school: reinventing the wheel?', in Burgess (ed.) (1984b), *q.v.*

Gallie, D. (1978), *In Search of the New Working Class*, Cambridge, Cambridge University Press.

Gans, H.J. (1962), *The Urban Villagers*, New York, Free Press.

Gittins, D. (1979), *Fair Sex*, London, Macmillan.

Glaser, B.G. (1978), *Theoretical Sensitivity: Advances in the Methodology of Grounded Theory*, Mill Valley, Calif., Sociology Press.

Glaser, B.G. and Strauss, A.L. (1967), *The Discovery of Grounded Theory*, Chicago, Aldine.

Glickman, M. (1985), 'Case studies', in A. Kuper and J. Kuper (eds), *The Social Science Encyclopaedia*, London, Routledge & Kegan Paul.

Glover, I.A. (1978), 'Executive career patterns: Britain, France, Germany and Sweden', in M. Fores and I. Glover (eds), *Manufacturing and Management*, London, HMSO.

Gold, R. (1958), 'Roles in sociological field observations', *Social Forces*, 36, pp. 217–23.

Goldberg, W. and Negandhi, R. (1983), *Governments and Multinationals: The Policy of Control versus Autonomy*, Cambridge, Mass., Oelgeschlager, Gunn & Hain.

Golde, P. (ed.) (1970), *Women in the Field: Anthropological Experiences*, Chicago, Aldine.

Goldthorpe, J.H. (1973), 'A revolution in sociology?', *Sociology*, 7, pp. 449–62.

Goldthorpe, J.H. (with Llewellyn, C. and Payne, C.) (1980), *Social Mobility and Class Structure in Modern Britain*, Oxford, Clarendon Press.

Goldthorpe, J.H. and Payne, C. (1986), 'Trends in intergenerational class mobility in England and Wales 1972–1983', *Sociology*, 20, pp. 1–25.

Gordon, D.M., Edwards, R. and Reich, M. (1982), *Segmented Work, Divided Workers*, Cambridge, Cambridge University Press.

Gottschalk, L., Kluckhohn, C. and Angell, R. (1945) *The Use of Personal Documents in History, Anthropology and Sociology*, New York, Social Science Research Council.

Gouldner, A.W. (1955), *Patterns of Industrial Bureaucracy*, London, Routledge & Kegan Paul.

Gouldner, A.W. (1971), *The Coming Crisis of Western Sociology*, London, Heinemann.

Goyder, J. and Leiper, J.M. (1985), 'The decline in survey response', *Sociology*, 19, pp. 55–71.

Grinyer, P.H. and Yasai-Ardekani, M. (1980), 'Dimensions of organizational structure: a critical replication', *Academy of Management Journal*, 23, pp. 405–21.

Gullahorn, J. and Strauss, G. (1960), 'The field worker in union research', in Adams and Preiss (eds) (1960), *q.v.*

Gyllenhammer, P.G. (1977), *People at Work*, New York, Addison Wesley.

Habenstein, R.W. (ed.) (1970), *Pathways to Data: Field Methods for Studying Ongoing Social Organizations*, Chicago, Aldine.

Hammersley, M. and Atkinson, P. (1983), *Ethnography: Principles in Practice*, London, Tavistock.

Hammond, P.E. (ed.) (1964), *Sociologists at Work: Essays on the Craft of Social Research*, New York, Basic Books.

Hammond, S.K. (1981), *Multinational Tactics in a Traditional Coal-Mining Community – Conflict in Spennymoor*, unpublished MA thesis, University of Durham.

Haraszti, M. (1971), *A Worker in a Workers' State*, Harmondsworth, Penguin.

Heclo, H. and Wildavsky, A. (1974), *The Private Government of Public Money: Community and Policy Inside British Politics*, London, Macmillan.

Hickson, D.J., (1987), 'Decisions at the top of organizations', *Annual Review of Sociology* (in press).

Hickson, D.J. and McMillan, C.J. (eds) (1981), *Organization and Nation: The Aston Programme IV*, Aldershot, Gower.

Hickson, D.J., Hinings, C.R., Lee, C.A., Schneck, R.E. and Pennings, J.M. (1971), 'A strategic contingencies theory of intraorganizational power', *Administrative Science Quarterly*, 16, pp. 216–29.

Hickson, D.J., Butler, R.J., Cray, D., Mallory, G.R. and Wilson, D.C. (1985), 'Comparing one hundred and fifty decision processes', in J.M. Pennings (ed.), *Organizational Strategy and Change*, San Francisco, Jossey-Bass.

Hickson, D.J., Butler, R.J., Cray, D., Mallory, G.R. and Wilson, D.C. (1986), *Top Decisions: Strategic Decision Making in Organizations*, Oxford, Blackwell and San Francisco, Jossey-Bass.

Higgin, G. and Jessop, N. (1965), *Communications in the Building Industry*, London, Tavistock.

Hindess, B. (1973), *The Use of Official Statistics in Sociology: A Critique of Positivism and Ethnomethodology*, London, Macmillan.

Hinings, C.R., Hickson, D.J., Pennings, J.M. and Schneck, R.E. (1974), 'Structural conditions of intraorganizational power', *Administrative Science Quarterly*, 19, pp. 22–44.

Hockey, J. (1986), *Squaddies*, Exeter, Exeter University Publications.

Hoffman, J.E. (1980), 'Problems of access in the study of social elites and boards of directors', in Shaffir *et al.* (eds) (1980), *q.v.*

Hofstede, G. (1980), *Culture's Consequences*, Beverly Hills, Calif., Sage.

Holdaway, S. (1982), '"An inside job": a case study of covert research on the police', in Bulmer (ed.) (1982a), *q.v.*

Homans, G.C. (1986), 'Fifty years of sociology', *Annual Review of Sociology*, 12, pp. xiii–xxx.

Horovitz, J.H. (1980), *Top Management Control in Europe*, London, Macmillan.

Huse, E.F. (1975), *Organization Development and Change*, St Paul, Minnesota, West Publishing.

Hutton, S.P. and Lawrence, P.A. (1980), *Production Management and Training*, Report to the Science Research Council, Swindon.

Hutton, S.P. and Lawrence, P.A. (1981), *German Engineers: Anatomy of a Profession*, Oxford, Oxford University Press.

Hutton, S.P., Lawrence, P.A. and Smith, J.H. (1977), *The Recruitment, Deployment and Status of the Mechanical Engineer in the German Federal Republic*, Report to the Department of Industry, London.

Isherwood, C. (1940), *Goodbye to Berlin*, London, Readers Union.

Johnson, J. (1975), *Doing Field Research*, New York, Free Press.

Jongmans, D.G. and Gutkind, P.C.W. (eds) (1967), *Anthropologists in the Field*, Assen, Van Gorcum.

Kahn, R. and Mann, F. (1952), 'Developing research partnerships', *Journal of Social Issues*, 8, pp. 4–10.

Kamata, S. (1983), *Japan in the Passing Lane*, London, Allen & Unwin.

Kaplan, A. (1964), *The Conduct of Inquiry: Methodology for Behavioural Science*, San Francisco, Chandler.

Kerr, C., Dunlop, J. T., Harbison, F. and Myers, C.A. (1960), *Industrialism and Industrial Man*, Cambridge, Mass., Harvard University Press.

Klein, L. (1976), *A Social Scientist in Industry*, Aldershot, Gower.

Kmetz, J.L. (1978), 'A critique of the Aston studies and results with a new measure of technology', *Organization and Administrative Sciences*, 8, pp. 123–44.

Knight, K. (1976), 'Matrix organization – a review', *Journal of Management Studies*, 13, pp. 111–30.

Knorr-Cetina, K. and Cicourel, A.V. (eds) (1981), *Advances in Social Theory and Methodology: Towards an Integration of Micro- and Macro-Sociologies*, London, Routledge & Kegan Paul.

Landesco, J. (1929), *Organized Crime in Chicago: Part III of the Illinois Crime Survey*, Chicago, Illinois Association for Criminal Justice.

Lawrence, P.A. (1978), 'Executive head hunting', *New Society*, 44, 25 May.

Lawrence, P.A. (1980), *Managers and Management in West Germany*, London, Croom Helm.

Lawrence, P.A. (1982), *Personnel Management in West Germany: Portrait of a Function*, Report to the International Institute of Management, West Berlin.

Lawrence, P.A. (1983), *Swedish Management: Context and Character*, Report to the Social Science Research Council, London.

Lawrence, P.A. (1984), *Management in Action*, London, Routledge & Kegan Paul.

Lawrence, P.A. (1986), *Management in the Netherlands: A Study in Internationalism*, Report to Technische Hogeschool Twente, Enschede, Netherlands.

Lawrence, P.A. and Spybey, A. (1986), *Management and Society in Sweden*, London, Routledge & Kegan Paul.

Lawrence, P.R. and Lorsch, J.W. (1967), 'Differentiation and integration in complex organizations', *Administrative Science Quarterly*, 12, pp. 1–47.

Lawton, W.C. (1970), 'Sociological research in big business', in Habenstein (ed.) (1970), *q.v.*

Lessem, R. (1985), *The Roots of Excellence*, London, Fontana.

LEST (Laboratoire d'Economie et de Sociologie du Travail) (1977), *Production de la hierarchie dans l'entreprise: recherche d'un effet social Allemagne-France*, Aix-en-Provence, LEST.

Levy, P. and Pugh, D.S. (1969), 'Scaling and multivariate analysis in the study of organizational variables', *Sociology*, 3, pp. 193–213.

Lieberson, S. (1985), *Making it Count: The Improvement of Social Theory and Research*, Berkeley, Calif., University of California Press.

Linhart, R. (1981), *The Assembly Line*, London, John Calder.

Lipset, S.M. (1964), 'The biography of a research project: *Union Democracy*', in Hammond (ed.) (1964), *q.v.*

Lipset, S.M., Trow, M.A. and Coleman, J.S. (1956), *Union Democracy: The Internal Politics of the International Typographical Union*, Glencoe, Illinois, Free Press.

Little, R.W. (1970), 'Field research in military organizations', in Habenstein (ed.) (1970), *q.v.*

Lockwood, D. (1958), *The Blackcoated Worker*, London, Allen & Unwin.

Lowe, A. (1977), *Facts and Frameworks: Aspects of the Research Process*, unpublished MA thesis, University of Birmingham.

Luria, A.R. (1968), *The Mind of a Mnemonist*, trans. L. Solotaroff, New York, Basic Books.

McCall, G.J. (1978), *Observing the Law: Field Methods in the Study of Crime and the Criminal Justice System*, New York, Free Press.

McCall, G.J. (1984), 'Systematic field observation', *Annual Review of Sociology*, 10, pp. 263–82.

Mack, J.A. (1970), 'Does the Mafia exist?', *New Society*, 16, 30 July 1970.

Mallory, G.R., Butler, R.J., Cray, D., Hickson, D.J. and Wilson, D.C. (1983), 'Implanted decision making: American owned firms in Britain', *Journal of Management Studies*, 20, pp. 191–211.

Marsh, C. (1982), *The Survey Method: The Contribution of Surveys to Sociological Explanation*, London, Allen & Unwin.

Martin, J. (1981), 'A garbage can model of the psychological research process', *American Behavioural Scientist*, 25, pp. 131–51.

Martin, P.Y. and Turner, B.A. (1986), 'Grounded theory and organisational research', *Journal of Applied Behavioral Science*, 22, pp. 141–58.

Mascarenhas, B. (1986), 'International strategies of non-dominant firms', *Journal of International Business Studies*, 17, pp. 1–26.

Maslow, A.H. (1943), 'A theory of human motivation', *Psychological Review*, 50, pp. 370–96.

Mauksch, H.O. (1970), 'Studying the hospital', in Habenstein (ed.) (1970), *q.v.*

Messerschmidt, D.A. (ed.) (1981), *Anthropologists at Home in North America: Methods and Issues in the Study of One's Own Society*, Cambridge, Cambridge University Press.

Miles, M.B. (1964), 'On temporary systems', in M.B. Miles (ed.), *Innovation in Education*, New York, Teachers College Press.

Miles, M.B. (1983), 'Qualitative data as an attractive nuisance: the problem of analysis', in J. van Maanen (ed.), *Qualitative Methodology*, Beverly Hills, Calif., Sage.

Miller, G.A. (1956), 'The magical number seven plus or minus two: some limits on our capacity for processing information', *Psychological Review*, 63, pp. 81–97.

Miller, S.M. (1952), 'The participant observer and "over-rapport"', *American Sociological Review*, 17, pp. 97–9.

Mintzberg, H. (1973), *The Nature of Managerial Work*, New York, Harper & Row.

Mintzberg, H. (1979), 'An emerging strategy of "direct" research', *Administrative Science Quarterly*, 24, pp. 582–9.

Mitchell, J.C. (1983), 'Case and situation analysis', *Sociological Review*, 31, pp. 187–211.

Moore, R. (1977), 'Becoming a sociologist in Sparkbrook', in Bell and Newby (eds) (1977), *q.v.*

Moyser, G. and Wagstaffe, M. (eds) (1987), *Research Methods for Elite Studies*, London, Allen & Unwin.

National Economic Development Office (1978), *How Flexible is Construction? A Study of Resources and Participants in the Construction Process*, London, HMSO.

Newby, H. (1977), 'In the field: reflections on the study of Suffolk farm workers', in Bell and Newby (eds) (1977), *q.v.*

Nichols, T. and Armstrong, P. (1976), *Workers Divided*, London, Fontana.

Nichols, T. and Beynon, H. (1977), *Living with Capitalism: Class Relations and the Modern Factory*, London, Routledge & Kegan Paul.

Nicholson, N. (1976), 'Negotiating research into industrial relations', in Brown *et al.* (eds) (1976), *q.v.*

Oakley, A. (1981), 'Interviewing women: a contradiction in terms', in Roberts (ed.) (1981), *q.v.*

O'Neill, J. (ed.) (1973), *Modes of Individualism and Collectivism*, London, Heinemann.

Palm, G. (1977), *The Flight From Work*, Cambridge, Cambridge University Press.

Partridge, H. (1986), *Fiat and Labour in Turin*, unpublished PhD thesis, University of Durham.

Passerini, L. (1979), 'Work ideology and consensus under Italian fascism', *History Workshop Journal*, 8, pp. 79–93.

Perls, F.S., Hefferline, R. and Goodman, P. (1973), *Gestalt Therapy*, New York, Brunner/Mazel.

Peters, T.J. and Waterman, R.H. (1982), *In Search of Excellence*, New York, Harper & Row.

Pettigrew, A.M. (1979), 'On studying organizational cultures', *Administrative Science Quarterly*, 24, pp. 570–81.

Pettigrew, A.M. (1985), 'Contextualist research and the study of organizational change processes', in E. Lawler *et al.* (eds), *Doing Research that is Useful for Theory and Practice*, San Francisco, Jossey-Bass.

Pfeffer, J. (1981), *Power in Organizations*, Boston, Pitman.

Pfeffer, R. (1979), *Working for Capitalism*, New York, Columbia University Press.

Pidgeon, N., Blockley, D. and Turner, B.A. (1986), 'Design practice and snow loading – lessons from a roof collapse', *Structural Engineer*, 64A, pp. 67–71.

Platt, J. (1976), *Realities of Social Research: An Empirical Study of British Sociologists*, London, Sussex University Press.

Polanyi, M. (1958), *Personal Knowledge: Towards a Post Critical Philosophy*, London, Routledge & Kegan Paul.

Polsky, N. (1971), *Hustlers, Beats and Others*, Harmondsworth, Penguin.

Portelli, A. (1980), 'The peculiarities of oral history', *History Workshop Journal*, 9, pp. 24–41.

Powdermaker, H. (1966), *Stranger and Friend: The Way of an Anthropologist*, New York, Norton.

Prandy, K. (1986), 'Similarities of life-styles and occupations of women', in R. Crompton and M. Mann (eds) (1986), *Gender and Stratification*, Oxford, Polity Press.

Pugh, D.S. (1981a), 'The Aston Programme perspective', in Van de Ven and Joyce (eds) (1981), *q.v.*

Pugh, D.S. (1981b), 'Rejoinder to Starbuck', in Van de Ven and Joyce (eds) (1981), *q.v.*

Pugh, D.S. and Hickson, D.J. (1976), *Organizational Structure in its Context: The Aston Programme I*, Aldershot, Gower.

Pugh, D.S. and Hinings, C.R. (eds) (1976), *Organizational Structure – Extensions and Replications: The Aston Programme II*, Aldershot, Gower.

Pugh, D.S. and Payne, R.L. (eds) (1977), *Organizational Behaviour in its Context: The Aston Programme III*, Aldershot, Gower.

Pugh, D.S., Hickson, D.J., Hinings, C.R., MacDonald, K.M., Turner, C. and

Lupton, T. (1963), 'A conceptual scheme for organizational analysis', *Administrative Science Quarterly*, 8, pp. 289–315.

Punch, M. (1986), *The Politics and Ethics of Fieldwork*, Beverly Hills, Calif., Sage.

Pyke, F., Hudson, R. and Sadler, D. (1984), 'Undermining Easington', Report for Easington District Council, Durham.

Ravetz, J.R. (1971), *Scientific Knowledge and Its Social Problem*, Oxfords, Clarendon Press.

Redding, S.G. (ed.) (1986), *The Enterprise and Management in South East Asia*, Hong Kong, University of Hong Kong Press.

Redding, S.G. and Pugh, D.S. (1986), 'The formal and the informal: Japanese and Chinese organization structures', in Redding (ed.) (1986), *q.v.*

Reeves, T.K. and Harper, D. (1981), *Surveys at Work: A Practitioner's Guide*, London, McGraw-Hill.

Reiss, A.J. (1971a), 'Systematic observation of natural social phenomena', in H. Costner (ed.), *Sociological Methodology 1971*, San Francisco, Jossey-Bass.

Reiss, A.J. (1971b), *The Police and the Public*, New Haven, Conn., Yale University Press.

Reiss, A.J. (1976), 'Systematic observation surveys of natural social phenomena', in H.W. Sinaiko and L.A. Broedling (eds), *Perspectives on Attitude Assessment: Surveys and their Alternatives*, Champaign, Illinois, Pendleton.

Roberts, H. (ed.) (1981), *Doing Feminist Research*, London, Routledge & Kegan Paul.

Roethlisberger, F.J. (1945), 'The foreman: master and victim of double talk', *Harvard Business Review*, 23, pp. 283–98.

Roethlisberger, F.J. and Dickson, W.J. (1939), *Management and the Worker*, Cambridge, Mass., Harvard University Press.

Rosenhan, D. (1982), 'On being sane in insane places', in Bulmer (ed.) (1982a), *q.v.* (originally published in *Science*, 19 January 1973).

Routamaa, V. (1980), 'Organizational structuring: an empirical analysis of the relationships between structure and size in form of the Finnish shoe and clothing industry', *Acta Wasaensia*, 13, Vaasa School of Economics, Finland.

Roy, D. (1955), 'Efficiency and "the fix": informal intergroup relations in a piecework machine shop', *American Journal of Sociology*, 60, pp. 255–66.

Roy, D. (1960), 'Banana time: job satisfaction and informal interaction', *Human Organization*, 18, pp. 158–68.

Roy, D. (1970), 'The study of southern labour union organizing campaigns', in Habenstein (ed.) (1970), *q.v.*

Ruby, J. (ed.) (1982), *A Crack in the Mirror: Reflexive Perspectives in Anthropology*, Philadelphia, University of Pennsylvania Press.

Sayles, L.R. and Chandler, M.R. (1971), *Managing Large Systems*, New York, Harper & Row.

Schatzman, L. and Strauss, A.L. (1973), *Field Research: Strategies for a Natural Sociology*, Englewood Cliffs, New Jersey, Prentice-Hall.

Schwab, D.P. (1985), 'Reviewing empirically based manuscripts: perspectives on process', in L.L. Cummings and P.J. Frost (eds), *Publishing in the Organizational Sciences*, Homewood, Illinois, Richard D. Irwin.

Scott, W.R . (1965), 'Field methods in the study of organizations', in J.G. March (ed.), *Handbook of Organizations*, Chicago, Rand McNally.

Selye, H. (1964), *From Dream to Discovery: On Being a Scientist*, New York, McGraw-Hill.

Serber, D. (1981), 'The masking of social reality: ethnographic fieldwork in the bureaucracy', in Messerschmidt (ed.) (1981), *q.v.*

Shaffir, W.B., Stebbins, R.A. and Turowetz, A. (eds) (1980), *Fieldwork Experience: Qualitative Approaches to Social Research*, New York, St Martin's Press.

Shenoy, S. (1981), 'Organization structure and context: a replication of the Aston Study in India', in Hickson and McMillan (eds) (1981), *q.v.*

Shils, E. (1985), 'On the Eve: a prospect in retrospect', in M. Bulmer (ed.), *Essays on the History of British Sociological Research*, Cambridge, Cambridge University Press.

Shipman, M. (ed.) (1976), *The Organization and Impact of Social Research*, London, Routledge & Kegan Paul.

Shipman, M. (1981), *The Limitations of Social Research*, 2nd edn, London, Longmans.

Sieber, S. (1973), 'The integration of fieldwork and survey methods', *American Journal of Sociology*, 78, pp. 1335–59.

Silverman, D. (1985), *Qualitative Methodology and Sociology*, Aldershot, Gower.

Sinclair, I. and Clarke, R.V.G. (1981), 'Cross-institutional designs', in E.M. Goldberg and N. Connelly (eds), *Evaluative Research in Social Care*, London, Heinemann.

Smith, J., Smith, F.M. and Bealer, R.C. (1960), 'Client structure and the research process', in Adams and Preiss (eds) (1960), *q.v.*

Solomon, R.C. (1976), *The Passions: The Myth and Nature of Human Emotion*, New York, Anchor Press/Doubleday.

Spindler, G. (ed.) (1970), *Being an Anthropologist: Fieldwork in Eleven Cultures*, New York, Holt, Rinehart & Winston.

Spindler, G. (ed.) (1982), *Doing the Ethnography of Schooling: Educational Anthropology in Action*, New York, Holt, Rinehart & Winston.

Starbuck, W.H. (1981), 'A trip to view the elephants and rattlesnakes in the Garden of Aston', in Van de Ven and Joyce (eds) (1981), *q.v.*

Stephenson, J.B. and Greer, L.S. (1981), 'Ethnographers in their own cultures: two Appalachian cases', *Human Organization*, 40, pp. 123–30.

Stewart, A. Prandy, K. and Blackburn, R.M. (1980), *Social Stratification and Occupations*, London, Macmillan.

Stewart, R. (1976), *Contrasts in Management*, Maidenhead, Berks, McGraw-Hill.

Stinchcombe, A.L. (1959), 'Bureaucratic and craft administration of production', *Administrative Science Quarterly*, 4, pp. 168–87.

Strauss, G. (1976), 'Organization development', in R. Dubin (ed.), *Handbook of Work Organization and Society*, New York, Rand McNally.

Thompson, P. (1979), *The Voice of the Past*, Oxford, Oxford University Press.

Turnbull, P. and Cunningham, M. (1981), *International Marketing and Purchasing*, London, Macmillan.

Turner, B.A. (1971), *Exploring the Industrial Subculture*, London, Macmillan.

Turner, B.A. (1978), *Man-made Disasters*, London, Wykeham Press.

Turner, B.A. (1981), 'Some practical aspects of qualitative data analysis: one way of organising some of the cognitive processes associated with the generation of grounded theory', *Quality and Quantity*, 15, pp. 225–47.

Turner, B.A. (1983a), 'The use of grounded theory for the qualitative analysis of organisational behaviour', *Journal of Management Studies*, 20, pp. 333–48.

Turner, B.A. (1983b), 'The use of fuzzy logic for the social prediction of building failures', paper presented to the 6th EGOS Colloquium, Florence.

Turner, B.A. (1986), 'Sociological aspects of organisational symbolism', *Organisation Studies*, 7, pp. 101–15.

Useem, M. (1984), *The Inner Circle: Large Corporations and the Rise of Business Political Activity in the US and the UK*, New York, Oxford University Press.

Van de Ven, A.H. and Joyce, W.F. (eds) (1981), *Perspectives on Organization Design and Behaviour*, New York and Chichester, Wiley.

Van Maanen, J. (1979), 'Reclaiming qualitative methods for organizational research: a preface', *Administrative Science Quarterly*, 24, pp. 520–6.

Van Maanen, J. and Kolb, D. (1985), 'The professional apprentice: observations on fieldwork roles in two organizational settings', in *Research in the Sociology of Organizations, Volume 4*, Greenwich, Conn., JAI Press.

Vaught, C. and Smith, D.L. (1980), 'Incorporation and mechanical solidarity in an underground coal mine', *Sociology of Work and Occupations*, 7, pp. 131–58.

Vidich, A.J., Bensman, J. and Stein, M.R. (eds) (1964), *Reflections on Community Studies*, New York, Harper & Row.

Wallraff, G. (1977), *The Undesirable Journalist*, London, Pluto Press.

Warwick, D.P. (1982), 'Types of harm in social research', in T.L. Beauchamp *et al.* (eds), *Ethical Issues in Social Science Research*, Baltimore, Johns Hopkins University Press.

Warwick, D.P. (1983), 'On methodological integration in social research', in Bulmer and Warwick (eds) (1983), *q.v.*

Watson, J.D. (1970), *The Double Helix: A Personal Account of the Discovery of the Structure of DNA*, Harmondsworth, Penguin.

Wax, R.H. (1971), *Doing Fieldwork: Warnings and Advice*, Chicago, University of Chicago Press.

Webb, E.J., Campbell, D. T., Schwartz, R.D. and Sechrest, L. (1966), *Unobtrusive Measures: Nonreactive Research in the Social Sciences*, Chicago, Rand McNally.

Weiner, M. (1981), *English Culture and the Decline of the Industrial Spirit*, Cambridge, Cambridge University Press.

Weinshall, T.D. (1977), *Culture and Management*, Harmondsworth, Penguin.

Weiss, R.S. (1968), 'Issues in holistic research', in Becker *et al.* (eds) (1968), *q.v.*

Westwood, S. (1985), *All the Live Long Day*, London, Pluto Press.

Whyte, W.F. (1943), *Street Corner Society: The Social Structure of an Italian Slum*, Chicago, University of Chicago Press.

Whyte, W.F. (1955), *Street Corner Society: The Social Structure of an Italian Slum*, 2nd edn, Chicago, University of Chicago Press.

Willis, P. (1977), *Learning to Labour*, Farnborough, Hants, Saxon House.

Wilson, D.C. (1982), 'Electricity and resistance: a case study of innovation and politics', *Organization Studies*, 3, pp. 119–40.

Wilson, D.C., Butler, R.J., Cray, D., Hickson, D.J. and Mallory, G.R. (1982), 'The limits of trade union power in organizational decision making', *British Journal of Industrial Relations*, 20, pp. 322–41.

Woodward, J. (1965), *Industrial Organisation: Theory and Practice*, Oxford, Oxford University Press.

Yin, R.K. (1984), *Case Study Research*, Beverly Hills, Calif., Sage.

Zimmer, R. (1981), 'Observer participation and consulting: research in urban food cooperatives', in Messerschmidt (ed.) (1981), *q.v.*

AUTHOR INDEX

SUBJECT INDEX